THE NEW Working Woman's Guide
TO RETIREMENT PLANNING

THE NEW Working Woman's Guide
TO RETIREMENT PLANNING

*Saving and Investing Now
for a Secure Future*

Martha Priddy Patterson

University of Pennsylvania Press
Philadelphia

Copyright © 2000 Martha Priddy Patterson
Copyright material by Martha Priddy Patterson published 1993 by NYIF, a division
of Prentice-Hall, Inc.

Printed in the United States of America on acid-free paper
10 9 8 7 6 5 4 3 2 1

Published by
University of Pennsylvania Press
Philadelphia, Pennsylvania 19104-4011

Library of Congress Cataloging-in-Publication Data
Patterson, Martha Priddy.
    The new working woman's guide to retirement planning : saving and
investing now for a secure future / Martha Priddy Patterson. — 2nd ed.
        p.   cm.
    Rev. ed. of: The working woman's guide to retirement planning.
c1993.
    Includes bibliographical references and index.
    ISBN 0-8122-1703-9 (alk. paper)
    1. Women—United States—Finance, Personal.   2. Retirement income—
United States.   3. Women—Pensions—United States.   I. Patterson,
Martha Priddy.   Working woman's guide to retirement planning.
II. Title.
HG179.P294   1999
332.024′042—dc21   99-36954
                                                                CIP

To Bonnie Priddy Spaugh, who gave me the best assets any woman can have, a sense of humor and a dedication to self-sufficiency. And to Laurence I. Barrett, who gave me a triumph of hope over experience. And to the dozens of women who told me this book changed their lives.

Contents

Part IV. Life Phases and Retirement

Preface

Women can achieve economic security in retirement only if they start planning for it while they are in the work force. Your first day on the job isn't too early to start. You must understand how retirement plans—your employer's and your own retirement savings—work legally and financially. Too many women end their final years in poverty; only 21 percent of working women over 40 receive or expect to receive a retirement benefit. That translates to only about 10 percent of all women who expect their own retirement benefit. And women who do receive a retirement benefit usually get less than half the benefit received by their male colleagues. These facts reflect different, and usually more complex, problems that women encounter in establishing secure benefits for their retirement years.

Even small variations in the work pattern—those typical of women's careers—can have a very large impact on retirement income. For instance, a woman who takes seven years away from the job, during a career spanning forty years, may get half the retirement benefits received by someone earning the same salary who stayed in the work force for the full forty years. This dramatic loss, totally out of proportion to the time spent off the payroll, is *not* the worst-case scenario. Many women work for years for various employers who provide retirement benefits, but these women don't stay long enough with one enterprise to earn an irrevocable right to the benefits. They retire after a lifetime of work with no employer-provided retirement plan at all. Many more women than men work for firms that do not provide any retirement benefits. These facts aren't going to change soon—if ever. And future changes in retirement-benefit policy aren't much help if you are 45 or 50 now and have already spent many years in the work force.

As a woman employed by companies of varied types, I've dealt with retirement-planning issues as an individual. As an attorney who specializes in employee-benefits law, I've studied the subject from professional perspectives as well. Every day I saw a need for a guide to help women understand and plan for their retirement, and there was nothing available to help them do that. From all my employers over a quarter of a century, I have vested in only two retirement plans—one of which will pay me $4,000 a year twenty-two years from now and one to which I have contributed 90 percent of the value. Half of my employers provided no retirement benefits at all. Shortly after I began to specialize in benefits law, it became clear to me that if I was going to have a financially secure retirement, I would have to be the primary contributor to it—not my employer, and certainly not the Social Security system.

Research and personal observation of other women convinced me that my experience was typical. The need for this book became painfully evident to me after I had watched a female colleague deliver an hour-long lecture on litigation strategy without notes to an audience that hung on her every word. Later, as we were talking, she mentioned that her employer had a 401(k) plan to which she contributed. But, she inquired, was her contribution with pretax dollars or after-tax dollars? The big advantage of 401(k) plans that every employer stresses is the fact the savings are made with pretax dollars, and the earnings on those savings are not taxed until the money is withdrawn. In terms of retirement planning, this lawyer's question was like asking whether the tennis ball should go over the net.

Clearly, smart, hardworking women are not paying attention to their financial retirement future. Others don't know where to begin because the law and retirement benefit plans seem so complex. The following chapters eliminate some of the confusion and provide a planning map. The need for the book continues. Fortunately, things have gotten better since the first edition was published. Women are gaining equal pension coverage with men and women's wages are ever so slowly increasing. But the need for retirement saving and planning, for both women and men, has never been greater. For the past half century the boomers have been the consumers. When the baby boomers begin retiring shortly after 2010, if they don't have sufficient incomes or they are afraid to spend what they have, the economy will go into the tank. And we know the Social Security system needs fixing. We just don't know how to do it, short of cutting benefits or raising taxes.

Remember, for retirement planning, the future is now.

PART ONE
UNDERSTANDING THE BASICS

Why Retirement Planning Is Different for Women

Alice, now 60, has been in the nursing profession all her life. She would like to retire within the next few years, certainly by the time she is 65. Over the years she was out of the profession only three years, one year for the birth of each of her two children and a year to care for her dying mother and settle the estate, returning each time to a different work setting. But when Alice does retire, she can expect her retirement benefits from her more than thirty years of work to be at least 10 percent less than those of a male nurse who followed her exact same career pattern. She *earned* that much less than her male colleagues over her career and has only recently caught up in pay, and her retirement benefits will be based primarily on earnings over her career. (If Alice were an assembly-line worker, she would have earned about 26 percent less than her male colleagues in the 1990s and even less in earlier years.)[1] Additionally, her retirement benefits will be less than half of what they would have been had she not taken those three years out of the work force and if she had stayed with one employer over the years. But she can expect to live at least five years longer than her male coworker.

Why are retirement savings and financial planning different for women than for men? After all, money is money whether you are male or female. Or so you thought. But Alice's wage and career pattern experience shows us why saving for retirement income and security is different—and more difficult—for women.

Some Retirement Planning Issues Common to Men and Women

Of course, in many other ways retirement saving is not different for the two sexes. Starting early and keeping up a steady pattern of investment is equally important for women and men. Court cases and federal laws of the 1970s and 1980s have equalized most retirement plans for the sexes. There is little, if any, inherent gender preference in employer retirement plans or individual retirement savings plans. Most plans allocate benefits equitably. For example, by law plans can no longer reduce annual pension payments to individual women on the grounds that women in general tend to live longer than men. Additionally, women are staying with one employer for longer periods and their wages are getting closer to men's. Still, it will be years before past employment inequities are corrected and women begin to receive parity in benefits.

As the case of Alice has shown us, retirement savings planning is substantially different for women—in part because of several easily documented statistical facts and in part because of several social pressures that are less easily documented, but familiar to most women.

This book acknowledges those facts and pressures, but it is about solutions, not about the problems. There are two basic solutions. First, begin your retirement savings from the day you walk on the job—or begin today. Second, plan to depend more heavily on your own savings for retirement security rather than relying on employer-provided plans and Social Security retirement benefits as your male colleagues are better able to do.

In the next chapter four women at different stages of their lives—Alice, Susan, Bonnie, and Jennifer—will serve as case studies on how retirement benefits grow, or disappear. Alice, as we know, is a 60-year-old nurse; Susan is a mid-level manager age 50; Bonnie is a lawyer of 40; Jennifer is a secretary of 30. Each has a relatively typical career pattern for women their ages. We will see how retirement benefits for Alice, Susan, Bonnie, and Jennifer compare with the retirement benefits they would have earned from their employer had they followed a single-job career more similar to men's career patterns. The differences in their retirement benefits when compared with single-job career benefits are startling.

Reasons Women Must Save and Plan More for Retirement

Here are the plain, documented facts.

1. Women live longer than men.
2. Women earn less money than men.
3. Women change jobs more frequently.
4. Women leave and rejoin the work force more frequently.
5. Women tend to work in jobs less likely to have employer-provided retirement benefits.
6. Women in the work force before the enactment of the Equal Pay Act of 1963, the Civil Rights Act of 1964, and the Employee Retirement Income Security Act (ERISA) in 1974 were adversely affected by laws restricting jobs, overtime, and hours.
7. Women who are eligible for retirement benefits receive significantly lower benefits than men.

8. Women generally don't have a role model for retirement planning, are less likely to have calculated retirement needs, are less likely to have saved for retirement, and tend to invest too conservatively when they do save for retirement.

Social pressures make women's retirement planning more difficult, too. People can argue about social pressures, but most women believe the social factors affecting retirement security are equally as valid as the documented statistics.

9. Women are more likely than men to leave the job market to provide care for a family member.
10. Women are most often the "trailing spouse" who gives up a job and benefits when a family must move because a spouse has been relocated.

Some of these social facts may be changing. According to the Department of Labor, women's work patterns are getting more like men's. And men have been known to stay home with the children while their life partners continue working. But on balance, things aren't changing that rapidly.

Frankly, telling a 50-year-old woman that the women's wage gap is closing (which is true, but too little and too late in her case) does not give her the money she lost from this wage gap over the previous thirty years of her working life. Nor does it give back the years when she was "protected" from working overtime or in hazardous—and high-paying—jobs. Her retirement benefits earned to date and the personal savings for retirement she was or wasn't able to make both reflect that wage gap. And so will her Social Security benefits when she reaches age 65.

Leaving aside the social pressures, just look at the facts.

Women Live Longer Than Men

In 1996, a 40-year-old woman could expect to live another forty-one years; a 40-year-old man could expect only another thirty-six years. A 20-year-old woman can expect to live another sixty years; her male colleague only another fifty-four years.[2]

The longer you live, the more money you need. Clearly, a woman will need to build up a bigger retirement nest egg to see her through a financially secure retirement. Moreover, a married woman may also see her own retirement savings greatly eroded to pay for her husband's medical expenses prior to his death.

Women Earn Less Money Than Men

You are constantly being told the wage gap is closing, and any gaps that do exist result from a woman's shorter time in the work force, lower level of education, and so on. The good news is that facts from the U.S. Bureau of the Census suggest

Table 1.1
Average Earnings of Full-time Workers, 1995 and 1996

	Males		Females		Female Wage (as a Percentage of Male Wage)	
	1995	1996	1995	1996	1995	1996
All	$40,400	$42,100	$26,500	$28,400	66	67
25–34	32,300	33,100	25,100	26,100	78	79
35–44	44,500	45,800	28,800	30,900	65	67
45–54	49,600	51,700	28,800	31,200	58	60
55–64	45,800	49,900	27,000	27,600	59	55
65+	45,000	42,000	23,300	35,200	52	84

Source: U.S. Bureau of the Census, *Statistical Abstract of the United States: 1997* (117th ed.; Washington, D.C.: The Bureau, 1997), table 734, and *Statistical Abstract 1998,* table 754.

the gap really is closing. The bad news is that the gap is closing far too slowly. And education and age do not seem to help as much as they should to reduce women workers' wage inequalities.

In 1955 women annually earned 63.9 percent of male's wages. In 1989 women who worked year-round, full-time earned 68 percent of wages earned by men.[3] More recently, the U.S. Census Bureau has reported, "Women who were full-time, year-round workers earned 74 cents in 1997 for every dollar earned by men—A significant improvement over the low of 57 cents they received in 1973."[4] So as women flooded into the work force in the 1970s, they actually drove their wages down as compared to those of their male colleagues. In the eight years between 1989 and 1997, women increased their wages as compared to men by 6 cents—less than a penny a year.

The picture doesn't get better with increased education or age, as the following data for full-time, year-round workers indicate. In 1996 all males with a bachelor's degree or more schooling earned a mean income of $63,100; females earned $41,300 (65 percent of male wages). Male high school graduates earned $32,500; female high school graduates earned $21,900 (67 percent of male wages).[5] When divided into age brackets, the wage gap, while improving for women, remained consistent generally. The exception was among workers age 55 to 64 and over 65. From 1995 to 1996 among those age 65 and over, women reported a very large increase in wages, while men reported a decline in wages. During the same period, among those age 55 to 64, the ratio of women's earnings actually declined.

While there appears to be good news recently, the wage gap remains a triple hit on women's retirement planning and it has a geometric effect.

First, there is the obvious fact that if you make less money, you have less discretionary income and a more difficult time saving for anything, but especially for something so seemingly far away as retirement. A women who saves just $500 less per year for retirement over a thirty-year career will reduce her personal retirement savings lump sum by $39,500. And that lump sum could have meant an extra $3,100 each year during her retirement.

A less obvious but perhaps more important effect is the fact that almost every employer-provided retirement benefit, as well as Social Security, is based primarily on your salary while you were working.

Finally, the lower a worker's earnings, the less likely she is to have an employer-provided retirement plan. Twenty-two percent of women working full-time earn between $10,000 and $15,000 annually, and of that number, only 31 percent are covered by an employer-provided retirement plan. Among the 3 percent of women working full-time who earn between $50,000 and $75,000, 80 percent are covered by a plan.[6]

A low salary while you are working guarantees a low retirement benefit later.

Women Change Jobs More Frequently Than Men

Women over 25 stay with an employer only 4.7 years as compared to 5.3 years for men of that age, according to 1996 data from the U.S. Department of Labor.[7] Frequent job changes have several bad effects on retirement planning. First, most retirement plans require that you work for the employer for a minimum period before you "vest" in retirement benefits, that is, have a nonforfeitable right to the retirement benefits you are earning. By law, this period is usually five years, although vesting can occur gradually beginning after three years on the job and extending over seven years. Prior to 1989, the vesting period could be as long as ten years. So while the sixth-tenths of a year difference in job tenures between men and women might seem trivial, it is critical. Obviously, with an average service period of only 4.7 years, a woman might work continuously throughout her life, always with an employer who offered a retirement plan, but she might retire with no retirement benefit because she never vested in a single employer's plan.

Second, most employers require that you work for a minimum amount of time (by law this period can't be longer than a year in most cases) before you are eligible even to participate in the retirement plan. So each time you change jobs, you may have a period during which you earn no employer retirement benefits, even if you go directly from one employer who offers a retirement plan to the next employer who also offers a retirement plan. So if you have seven jobs during your career, you could have seven years during which you did not earn a retirement benefit.

Women Take Time Out of the Work Force

For whatever reason—care-giving to children or elderly parents, seeking work as a trailing spouse, or losing jobs—women are out of the work force more than men. In 1997, only 60 percent of females were working, compared to 75 percent of males. But the gap is projected to narrow, so that by the year 2006, 61 percent of females and 74 percent of males will be working.[8]

Obviously, when you are not on the payroll, you are not earning a salary to use for savings. But the losses don't stop with just your salary. You are also missing seniority leading to promotions and pay increases. From a retirement savings perspective, you also are not earning credits for retirement benefits from either an employer or from the Social Security system.

Women are also more likely to work part-time. In working part-time one earns less money, of course. But employers who offer retirement plans are not required to cover employees who work less than 1,000 hours per year (approximately twenty hours per week). Consequently, part-time workers rarely earn retirement benefits.

Women Are More Likely to Work in Jobs Without Retirement Benefits

Among workers and retirees over 40 years old, 36 percent of men expect to receive or are receiving an employer-provided retirement benefit, as compared with 28 percent of women.[9] Women who have been in the work force for twenty years or more are not as likely to have been offered a retirement benefit as their male counterparts. Women are also heavily concentrated in occupations that have lower pension coverage. For example, women make up 59 percent of the 14 million service workers in the U.S. Only 23 percent of those service workers are offered retirement benefits. By contrast, women comprise only 44 percent of the 18 million members of the "executive/managerial" occupation, which offers retirement benefits to 55 percent of its workers. On the good news side, the "professional specialty" (lawyers, architects, actuaries, among others) occupation has the highest retirement plan coverage rate—60 percent—and women represent 53 percent of that occupation.[10]

Pension coverage for women is improving. Comparing men and women in 1983, age 25–46, working full-time and at their current job for at least one year, 73 percent of men were likely to be offered a retirement benefit plan, as compared to 66 percent of women.[11] In 1990, 57 percent of men and 53 percent of women were offered retirement plans. But in that same group, only 39 percent of women actually earned the rights to future benefits, as compared with 47 percent of men.[12] In 1997, among full-time workers, 50 percent of women and 49 percent of men were covered by retirement plans.[13]

But there are two big problems here. First, while pension coverage is increasing for women, it is decreasing for men, which means cumulatively that employer-provided retirement plan coverage is decreasing. It seems that just as women are achieving the status in the work place to acquire certain important benefits, like retirement plans, those benefits are disappearing from the work place.

Second, there may be a gap between *coverage* (whether an employer has a retirement plan) and *participation* (whether an employee is actually earning retirement benefits). That gap may be attributed to a number of factors. For example, women may not be eligible to participate in the plan and earn benefits because they have not worked for the employer long enough or do not work enough hours each year to meet the threshold requirements to participate. Or, if the plan requires the employee to contribute to the plan in order to participate, women may not contribute. By failing to contribute, women deny themselves the value of the employer's contribution.

Women Lost Wages Through Legally Sanctioned Pay Discrimination

A woman who is 65 today entered the job market in the late 1950s. At that time it was entirely legal to pay a woman less for the same work performed by the man sitting next to her. And employers did. In fact, some union contracts required it.

Many states "protected" women through laws limiting the total number of hours they could work each week and the hours of the day they could work. Certain hazardous jobs or job classifications were barred to women completely— by law. These jobs frequently were high-paying given the relatively small amount of education or training required. Certain professions required a woman to quit her job or at least take a leave of absence if she became pregnant.

Women did not have the legal right to equal wages until the enactment of the Equal Pay Act of 1963, and reforms were not immediate. Women in their thirties reading this book may be shocked by these facts. While it is good to remember the strides women have made, it is important to be realistic, and that requires acknowledging facts. Many retired women today live in poverty, and many women close to retirement today are not financially prepared for it. In part, their poverty and their lack of financial preparation stem from the legally sanctioned discrimination in wages and job opportunities they faced prior to the equal pay and civil rights laws.

Women Receive Lower Retirement Benefits Than Men

Even when women participate in retirement plans and are eligible to receive benefits, they receive less than men on average. The most recent data on pension trends comes from a September 1994 Current Population Survey as compiled and analyzed by the Department of Labor in *Retirement Benefits of American Workers*.[14] The numbers in Table 1.2 speak for themselves. Women first receiving a retirement benefit in 1994 averaged 84 percent of the years of service men had, earned only 66 percent of the wages men earned, and were a year older than the men retiring. But they received less than half—46 percent—of what their male colleagues received in pension benefits. This is the same 46 percent received by women retiring in 1989. By contrast, a woman retiring in 1978 received on average a benefit that was 51 percent of what her male colleagues received.

Table 1.2
Pension Benefits for Men and Women
Earnings, Years of Service, and Payments

	1989		1994	
	Men	*Women*	*Men*	*Women*
Years of Service				
Average	26 years	22 years	25 years	21 years
Median	26 years	20 years	26 years	20 years
Annual Earnings				
Average	$33,100	$19,900	$46,153	$30,626
Median	28,200	18,200	39,000	26,000
Retirement Age				
Average	61 years	63 years	60 years	61 years
Median	62 years	62 years	61 years	62 years
Annual Pension				
Average	$9,460	$4,330	$14,564	$6,748
Median	$7,020	$2,570	$9,600	$4,800
Percentage of Final Wage Replaced				
Average	29%	23%	36%	23%
Median	23%	17%	30%	20%

Source: Data from U.S. Department of Labor, *Retirement Benefits of American Workers* (1995), table D6.

The numbers in Table 1.2 reflect only the women who are actually receiving retirement benefits, based on the woman's own earnings. If the averages included the many women who do not receive retirement benefits at all, they would be much lower. Nor do the averages reflect the lower retirement benefits received by the worker's survivor after the worker dies. Some of the reasons for this gap will be illustrated when we look at the experiences of Alice, Susan, Bonnie, and Jennifer in the next chapter.

These data also show that the relationship between work and entitlement to retirement benefits is *not* one to one. It is critical to remember that the relationships magnify the effect of lower wages and less time in the workplace at retirement. A dollar less in salary is not just a dollar less now. It may mean two dollars less in future retirement benefits as well.

Women Aren't Preparing for Retirement

Women's lack of role models for retirement planning was listed as the tenth reason for the differences in retirement planning needs in the first edition of this book. I listed it last, as part of the nonquantifiable "social pressures," because I didn't have the data to support what I knew from experience was true. Now I have the evidence, from the 1998 Women's Retirement Confidence Survey and from analyses done by U.S. Department of Labor pension statistical experts.

- In 1998, only 40 percent of women have calculated their retirement savings needs, compared to 49 percent of men. (The good news is that percentage has increased dramatically for both genders.)[15]
- Only 59 percent of women have saved for retirement, compared to 68 percent of men. Only 39 percent of those female savers are very confident they are saving wisely.[16]
- Over half of women view Social Security or employer-funded retirement—two sources over which they have little or no control—as their most important source of retirement income.[17]
- Although studies conflict on this evidence,[18] women may tend to invest their pension assets more conservatively than men, even when they have comparable incomes, ages, and marital status.

These latest data all suggest that women are not catching up on the retirement benefit track.

Don't Rely on Your Spouse's Retirement Income

The planning discussions of this book do not take into account the fact that many women plan retirement as an economic unit with their spouses or domestic partners. None of the examples, advice, or worksheets here includes any mention of the spouse's or partner's potential retirement income. Spouses and partners are not included in the planning because the data show that most women will have no spouse or partner during most of their retirement.[19] Even if we begin retirement with a spouse or partner, we are likely to spend most of our retirement alone.

Husbands are wonderful, but they tend to disappear. Loyal, dedicated ones die or they get sick and look to their wives for support, emotionally and financially. Others of the breed decide they want to be fully married to their jobs or to another person.

Much of this book tends to be based on worst-case scenarios, and that extends to the possibility you may not retire with a financially secure spouse or domestic partner. If you do, congratulations. You can spend the extra retirement income you have as a couple, vacationing in the south of France or Georgia, buying the racy sports car you always wanted, or endowing your favorite charity. This is not to say you should not consult with your husband or partner and coordinate your investment strategies and retirement planning. You definitely should. Certainly, as you near retirement, you should agree on life style and location. But plan financially as though you will be your own independent economic unit. The statistics say that you will be, at least for some of your life. Besides, there has never been a single documented case of a woman's feeling herself to be a less of a person because she was financially secure in her own right. Have you ever heard a spouse complain, "I love you, honey, but you have too much money"?

Conclusion: Women Must Plan for Retirement in Different Ways

For all these reasons, women must use different planning techniques in establishing financial security for retirement. You are never too young to start saving. Your own savings will be much more important for you than for your male colleagues because the statistics tell you several undeniable facts: your benefits will be less than a comparable male worker's of the same age and you will live longer than he will. Fortunately, women are accustomed to working harder for financial security. What may surprise you is the large difference a few years out of the work force at the wrong time can make on employer-provided retirement benefits and the positive difference early and steady savings, even on a small basis, can make for financial security at retirement. The next chapters detail these differences and offer some solutions.

Solutions to Implement Today

Start an automatic savings plan. Use payroll deduction, debits to your checking account, or any other mechanism that makes it automatic.

Find out if your employer offers a retirement plan and whether you are in it.

Fill out and mail the Social Security "Request for Earnings and Benefit Estimate Statement" on page 122 to determine how much you might receive from Social Security under current laws.

2

Retirement Benefit Growth
Alice, Susan, Bonnie, and Jennifer

What are the retirement planning obstacles that you as a woman have to overcome? Specifics show us better than theory. Four examples—Alice, Susan, Bonnie, and Jennifer, each with career patterns common to many women—will illustrate exactly how women can be robbed of huge amounts of employer-provided retirement income because of time out of the work force and job changes. Your solutions are

- to maximize employer-provided retirement plans when they are offered,
- to set up your own retirement plan when you don't have access to an employer plan, and
- to rely on your own personal saving, preferably beginning the first day you start working.

Alice, Susan, Bonnie, and Jennifer offer examples of how even a few years out of the work place, combined with changing employers, can result in the loss of *more than half* the employer-provided benefits one would receive after a career with a single employer. These dramatic losses result primarily from

- failure to vest in benefits,
- the effects of inflation on benefits earned early in one's career, and
- cashing out and spending benefits before retirement.

These factors may inflict more damage on the purchasing power of employer-provided benefits than do losses from the actual time out of the work force. We will also see how the ability to move benefits from employer to employer—called benefit "portability"—affected our sample population and how it may affect you.

Note that the dollar figures we will discuss from these scenarios are constant 1999 dollars. So, for example, when we say Bonnie will have an annual employer-provided benefit of $35,000 when she retires some twenty-five years from now, the actual dollar figure will be higher. She will have the equivalent buying power at that time of $35,000 in today's dollar value.[1] Our examples compare the benefits Alice, Susan, Bonnie, and Jennifer accumulate over their careers with a person who held one job over the same career span, earning the same salary with the same types of employer-provided retirement plans.

Alice: A Nurse at Sixty

Alice, now 60, began her nursing career at age 21. She is just now beginning to think seriously about retirement. In financial terms, however, she is not sure that she can manage it. Her own savings are small and she would be relying primarily on any employer pensions due her and on Social Security.

Alice's Nursing Career Path

Alice has worked full-time for six employers over her thirty-nine-year career, and she now earns $36,750. She served eight years at her first job with a large hospital, then took a year off for her first child. She went back to work in the emergency room at a smaller hospital, working full-time for four years, and then took another year off for her second child. After that for seven years she worked in a hospital nearer her home so she could be close to the children. She was offered a supervisory position at a different hospital and accepted that job, which she held for eight years. She then took a year off to care for her mother, who was terminally ill, and to help settle her mother's estate. She then joined a clinic specializing in children's care for six years. Two years ago she moved to her current job as supervisor of a neighborhood clinic. She plans to stay in this job until she retires.

What Alice Has in Pensions

If Alice retires at 65, she will receive an annual pension of less than $4,650. She would have received a pension of $12,700 if she had stayed with one employer over her career or had received credit for all her years of service. Her pension is only about one-third of what it would have been had she stayed with one employer and still taken three years off over her thirty-nine-year career.

What Happened to Alice's Benefits?

Alice's dramatically lower pension results from lack of "vesting" in her various employer's benefits. Over the years, as she left her various jobs, she left behind valuable retirement benefits because she had not stayed with her employer long enough to vest—that is, to have the right to take accumulated pension money with

Table 2.1
Lump-Sum Value of Alice's Pension Benefits
Lost by Lack of Vesting
(1999 Dollars)

	Value of Benefits When Alice Left Employer	Value of Benefits When Alice Is 65
First Job	$1,229	$15,500
Second Job	977	9,200
Third Job	3,261	17,200
Fourth Job	7,512	22,200
Total Benefits Lost	**$12,979**	**$64,100**

her or receive payments when she did eventually retire. During much of her career, the law allowed employers to require ten years or more of service before an employee vested in retirement benefits. Because of family duties or other job opportunities, Alice never stayed with any of her employers for ten years or more.

The lump-sum value of the benefits Alice left behind in each job tells the tale.

Alice usually worked at her jobs for several years. If the five-year vesting required by today's law had been in effect during her career, she would have been entitled to *all* of these lump sums except the $977 from her second position, where she worked for only four years. Five-year vesting did protect her in her fifth job. She earned the right to an annual pension of $1,670, worth a lump-sum value of $10,700 when she left the job, and her estimated total expected annual pensions of $4,650 includes $1,670 a year from the fifth job.

Could Alice Have Protected Herself?

Could Alice have protected herself in some way against these losses? Possibly, but only with her own diligence and demands. For example, in three of her jobs, she left after more than seven years. In the first job, if she had delayed child-bearing for two years, or taken the year off after the baby was two, she would have vested. But babies don't observe timetables, and most prospective parents don't plan families around pension-vesting.

When Alice changed employers in order to get a promotion, she could have attempted to negotiate a bonus from the new employer as compensation for lost retirement benefits. Such a special payment would lack the automatic tax-deferred status of regular pension benefits. However, she could have then invested the extra money in a tax-free instrument such as an annuity or municipal bond fund. The earnings on that investment would then have grown on a tax-favored basis, much as employer-provided retirement contributions do.

The most certain way to have protected herself would have been through her own saving. Diverting just 5 percent of her income to a tax-free investment would have given her $2,660 when she left her first job. By retirement at age 65, this amount would have grown to approximately $14,700, assuming a 5 percent rate of return. She could have done the same in each of her jobs and had her own retirement account of approximately $112,000 at age 65, by saving just 5 percent of her earnings and investing them at 7½ percent in a tax-deferred account.

What Should Alice Do Now?

At age 60 there is little Alice can do to change her bleak retirement future dramatically. Working full-time a few more years, perhaps even past age 65, is a necessity. Part-time work after retirement may be another option. Nursing is a physically demanding job, and Alice may want to find some other kind of part-time work. What follows will provide Alice with some detailed advice, but it won't be as helpful as it would have been when she was 30 or 40 or even 50.

Investigate Her Exact Amount of Social Security

First, Alice should contact the Social Security Administration to be sure that agency has an accurate wage history for her. The Social Security Administration also will send her a "Personal Earnings and Benefit Estimate Statement," showing what her expected Social Security benefits would be if she retired at 62 and if she retired at age 65.

Second, she should look at her current employer's summary plan description (SPD) to determine at what age she can retire early under the plan and what the reductions for early retirement before age 65 might be. If she retires now, she would receive an annual income from her current job's pension plan of only $1,077, which with her income from the prior job's pension would give her an annual income of only $2,747. This is clearly not enough to live on, especially considering that she will not be eligible for Social Security until age 62. If she stays another five years, her annual pension for this job will be $2,960, more than twice its current value. The dramatic increase in the worth of Alice's pension illustrates the value and the build-up of defined benefit pension plans (retirement plans that pay a sum certain annually at retirement based on years of service and wages) for older workers during their final years of service.

Nevertheless, even retiring at age 65, Alice will by no means have a financially secure retirement from her pension alone. At that time her two pensions will represent just 12 percent of her previous income. With the addition of Social Security, her retirement income will be just 42 percent of her final earnings.

Even with optimistic estimates that retirees need only 70 percent of prior income (which are not realistic, as we will discuss in Chapter 11), Alice will need additional income. Certainly, she does not have the income to retire now, even if her employer's retirement plan would allow retirement at 60 (and many plans don't begin paying benefits until age 62). Without savings of her own, Alice will be strapped, and her financial condition will only get worse over time because her pension income is not going to grow with inflation. Her Social Security payments will increase with inflation—at least under current law.

Consider a Lump-Sum Payment Form

To protect against inflation, Alice could consider taking one or both of her pensions in a lump sum at retirement, rather than taking the normal form of benefit, which is a monthly amount paid as long as she lives. She could then reinvest the lump sum. The lump-sum value of her pension when she is 65 will be $14,129 from her former job and $25,062 from her current job (compared with a lump-sum value of $107,400 for a one-job career with the same defined benefit pension plan). These sums could be rolled directly into an IRA without paying taxes on the money until it was taken out. Investments could be purchased which might give her a greater annual return than she would receive under the pension. But such a move would require very sound financial advice. (Chapter 16 will discuss in detail using the lump-sum payment form to protect against inflation.)

Redouble Savings Efforts

Third, Alice should begin—or hopefully redouble—her savings efforts now. She should look for investments that will protect against inflation. If she has her own home, she might consider trading down to a smaller, less expensive residence. If Alice chooses this option, she has time over the next five years to observe the housing market and sell at her convenience. Money remaining after the purchase of a smaller place should be invested for retirement income. Alternatively, she might consider renting part or all of her home if that could be profitable.

Look for Forgotten Benefits

Fourth, Alice should contact all her former employers and inquire about any potential retirement benefits. This is a long shot, but benefits plans do change, sometimes retroactively and for the better. Memories can become confused or perhaps Alice overlooked a benefit. After all, when she left these employers, pinning down her future retirement benefits was not a high priority, even though, with hindsight, it should have been. Clearly, if the employer does not know where she is today, it cannot deliver the good news that she has a retirement benefit waiting. Her investment in the search is a little time and a postage stamp or a phone call. Or she can start with the web site set up by the Pension Benefit Guaranty Corporation, the government agency that guarantees many defined benefit pension plans. That site (*http://search.pbgc.gov*) lists hundreds of people who are due pension benefits but have not claimed them. Annual benefits of even a few hundred dollars can pay the phone bill for a year.

Work After "Retirement"

Finally, Alice should think about a part-time job after retirement. After age 65 Alice can earn up to $15,500 in 1999 without having her Social Security benefits reduced. At age 70 she may earn as much as she wishes without any Social Security reduction. Any pension benefits she receives are not included in this limit. At any age she may have to pay tax on a portion of her Social Security benefits if she has income of more than $25,000 per year, which does include pension payments. (Couples pay tax on part of their Social Security benefits if they have income of more than $32,000.)

If Alice feels nursing will be too rigorous after age 65, she should begin thinking now about other possible job opportunities. Are there less strenuous jobs at the clinic? Are there paying jobs at the museum where she volunteers? Five years before retirement is not too early to begin thinking about possibilities, even if it is too soon to begin sending out resumes.

Of course her best retirement financial move would be to work more years for her current employer. Because she likely will receive a larger salary each year and because the pension plan is based on the last five years of work and on the number of years worked, she will be increasing two important variables in her ultimate pension benefit formula. Additionally, if she postpones receiving Social Security benefits past age 65, when she does retire, Alice will receive a higher Social Security benefit for the rest of her life.

Susan: A Middle Manager at Fifty

Susan began working when she was 20 and has never stopped. Over her thirty-year career she has had five jobs, and she plans to stay with her management job at a small auto parts manufacturer until she retires. Susan likes her job and doesn't plan to retire until she is 65. But when she does retire, she would like to travel, like her brother, who retired last year after thirty years with the same company Susan works for. She currently earns $25,200.

Susan's Managerial Career Path

Susan worked as a secretary at her first job for four years. Her employer did not have a retirement plan and at age 20 she never gave retirement a thought. She then moved to another firm, which promised some marketing training. Susan worked there for five years. Her employer had a defined benefit retirement plan, but she did not vest in it. Susan then took a job with a large appliance manufacturing company in marketing and moved into management. That company also had a defined benefit plan. Susan stayed with the company ten years and vested in her benefit. She moved to a new position with a start-up company, but was laid off as part of a downsizing after five years because the company was not growing. At that point she went to work for her current employer, which has a defined contribution plan.

What Susan Has in Retirement Benefits

When Susan retires at age 65 she can expect an income from all her employers' retirement plans of about $4,700 a year (in 1999 dollars). Of this, $570 will be from her defined benefit pension plan earned with the appliance manufacturer, where she spent ten years, and $4,130 will come from her current employer's plan. These amounts will represent about 16 percent of her final earnings. Compare this with the $8,300 she would have received annually from a single-job career covered by a defined benefit plan. Or compare her $4,700 with the $10,600 annually she would receive from a single-job career defined contribution plan (a plan that pays a lump sum at retirement equal to the employer's annual contributions for each year worked). Under these plans she could have received 29 percent or 37 percent, respectively, of her final earnings.

When Susan retires at age 65, she will have worked full-time continuously for 45 years. She will have about half of the retirement benefits a one-job career would have given her under plans similar to those of her employers. What happened to Susan's retirement benefits?

What Happened to Susan's Retirement Benefits?

Lack of a Retirement Plan in the Early Years Lost Thousands of Dollars

Susan's first job had no retirement benefits, but at 20 she didn't care. While that may be reasonable for a 20-year-old, let's look at what Susan missed in her early twenties by comparing her with a friend, Linda. Linda earned the same salary as Susan, but Linda worked in a company with a defined contribution plan devoting 5 percent of salary each year to her account. Contributions vested immediately. Linda was entitled to a lump-sum benefit of $4,000 in today's dollars after working four years. Or she could have opted for an annual benefit of $1,200 for life when she retired at 65, even if she never worked another day in her life. Not too shabby for earnings from age 20 to 24. Linda's situation is a simple illustration of how seemingly meaningless amounts of money saved early in life really grow.

Losses from Lack of Vesting

When Susan left her second job after five years she had earned a lump-sum value in the pension plan of $450, which she left behind. The benefit was not vested because in those years the law permitted plans to require ten-year vesting. That sum would have paid her $150 annually at 65 if she had vested in it. Granted, this is not enough to live on, but it is enough to buy a new coat every year or pay a month's utility bills.

Fortunately, Susan stayed for ten years at her third job, which had a defined benefit plan linked with Social Security. Because she stayed ten years and laws were enacted in those years to require a minimum ten-year cliff vesting or graduated vesting over fifteen years, she had the right to a benefit when she left. Susan had earned a benefit with a lump-sum value of $2,900 in today's dollars, which will pay her $570 annually for as long as she lives when she retires. If Susan could have taken that amount on termination and rolled it into an IRA, when she retired the amount would be worth about $7,300, assuming a 7 percent rate of return, or about $12,000, assuming 9 percent.

Her next job also offered a defined benefit plan, but she did not vest in the benefit she accrued. Susan was there for only five years, and the law did not require five-year vesting at that time. In that case she left a lump sum of about $1,600 in today's dollars, which would have paid $387 annually when she retired. If she could have taken the lump-sum amount and rolled it into an IRA at 9 percent she would have about $7,600 at retirement, growing to about $9,800 if she left it untouched until she was 68.

Compare that $7,600 amount to the $9,200 lump-sum value of Susan's current benefit under her employer's defined contribution plan. Again we see that small amounts casually left behind at an earlier employer really could grow to be significant at retirement.

Preretirement Inflation Erodes Benefits

Susan's annual income from her appliance manufacturing pension is suffering from what is known as "preretirement/retirement inflation." The $570 annual amount is based on the salary she was earning when she left more than a decade ago. The benefit will not be increased to reflect inflation since then or any other increases in Susan's wages. Because the last decade has not been one of high inflation, this erosion is not terribly dramatic, but it is there. If the years before Susan's retirement are high inflation years, the buying power of the pension she earned in earlier jobs may be reduced significantly.

Susan's Good Luck: No Waiting Periods

Susan actually was lucky. She could have lost even more benefits because each time she changed jobs her new employer was entitled to keep her out of the plan for one year. While that first year counts for vesting purposes, by law, the first year of work does not have to count for benefit calculation purposes. Under some plans your first year will not be included in calculating "credited service," a concept used especially in defined benefit plans formulas. If your employer has a defined contribution plan, chances are you will not receive a contribution for that first year. You may even be barred from contributing your own money to the plan in your first year at work. If you have six jobs, you may automatically lose six years of benefits simply because of these six one-year waiting periods.

How Could Susan Have Protected Herself?

Susan could have protected herself by being less casual about benefits in her first two jobs. After she had been in the work force for eight years she had no retirement benefits. At a minimum she could have been saving for retirement on her own during those eight years. By contrast, her friend Linda by that time had a retirement benefit with a lump-sum value of $8,500, which would pay her $2,700 a year at retirement even if Linda earned no further benefits. Compare this to the annual $4,700 Susan will have after working forty-five years.

Moral of the story: the early years count. The earlier you start, the easier it is to accumulate a significant pool of retirement capital. If Susan had "paid herself" 5 percent of her after-tax income, just for those early years, and invested it in tax-free investments or in an annuity, she would have an extra income of $2,700 a year at retirement. If she had done this throughout her career, she could retire with an annual income of $10,600 from her own personal retirement plan earnings in addition to the employer pensions she has.

When she was part of the layoff at her fourth job, she might have tried to negotiate taking the $1,600 lump-sum value of her benefits. True, this is only a possibility. But it never hurts to ask; $1,600 is a small sum to a company, and even a company in economic difficulties feels guilty about letting good employees go. As we saw, that $1,600 would have grown over the twenty-two years to about $9,000, a very tidy sum for Susan.

What Should Susan Do Now?

Susan is much more fortunate than Alice. Susan has begun to look at retirement income needs ten years before Alice did. A lot of savings can accrue in the fifteen years between now and Susan's retirement. Unlike her brother, who retired from the same company with an annual benefit for life worth 37 percent of his prior earnings, Susan will have only 16 percent from her employer's pension, assuming she retires at 65. Social Security will provide another 40 percent or so, giving her 56 percent of income at retirement. She doesn't think that's enough, and she is probably correct, as we will see when we run projections for her in Chapter 11. Susan can practice her own savings program for the next fifteen years to catch up.

Save in the Employer's Plan

Susan's employer has a defined contribution plan, which means that the company is also likely to permit her to contribute her own money to the plan. This is usually a 401(k) plan (Chapter 7 will give more details on 401(k) plans) that takes money from her pay on a pretax basis. No tax is due on her contributions or the earnings in the plan until she begins to withdraw money from the plan at retirement.

Use an Individual Retirement Account

Susan also can contribute up to $2,000 each year to an individual retirement account (IRA). She can choose between using a traditional IRA—in which she would take a deduction for the $2,000 and pay tax on all the distributions from the IRA after she retires—and using a Roth IRA. In a Roth IRA, she would not deduct the contribution to the IRA, but all withdrawals from the Roth IRA after she retired—both the original contribution and the earnings—would not be taxed. (Chapter 9 will discuss IRAs in detail.)

A $2,000 annual contribution to an IRA over the next fifteen years will provide her with an account of $46,550 if it earns 6 percent annually and $54,300 if it earns 8 percent. She might consider mutual funds with high income, where returns of 14 percent are not unusual, in which case she would have an IRA worth $87,000 at retirement. And, if she used a Roth IRA, none of that money would be taxable when it is taken out of the account after retirement.

Bonnie: A Lawyer of Forty

Bonnie did not enter the work force until she was 24 and out of law school. Since then she has had five jobs and taken off a year to be with her baby. She hopes to remain with her current employer, a Fortune 500 company engaged in food-processing, until she retires. But given the corporate world of mergers, acquisitions, downsizing, right-sizing, and management upheavals, she realizes this may be difficult. She hopes to retire at 62. As assistant general counsel, Bonnie earns $85,000.

Bonnie's Legal Career Path

In her first year after law school, Bonnie clerked for a judge; then she worked for a local public interest group for two years. From there she moved to a law firm, where she worked for four years. At that point she took a year off to spend with her family and decided to go to work in a corporate law office for a retail operation, hoping for mere fifty-hour weeks rather than the sixty-hour weeks at the law firm. After five years—and only fifty-hour weeks—with the corporation, Bonnie was offered the assistant general counselship with the food-processing corporation's law office. She gave her employers a chance to meet the offer and, when they didn't, Bonnie took the offer with the new corporation. Bonnie has worked for fourteen years and she plans to work another twenty-two years.

Bonnie's Present Retirement Benefits

In her first three jobs Bonnie received no retirement benefits. The clerkship and the public interest group had no retirement plans. The law firm had a defined contribution plan, but Bonnie did not vest in the plan because she was there only four years and the law permitted the plan to vest benefits after ten years.

In her first corporate job, Bonnie participated in a defined benefit plan linked with Social Security. Before she left that job, the law was changed to require five-year vesting or seven-year graduated vesting. The corporation adopted five-year vesting. With five years of service, Bonnie just qualified for a benefit under the plan before she moved to her current job. From that five years with the retail operation, she will be entitled to an annual pension of about $1,680 or a lump sum of about $15,200 at age 62. Without the change in the law in the late 1980s, she would not have been eligible to receive this amount.

At her job now, Bonnie also has a defined benefit plan linked with Social Security. If she follows her plan and remains with her employer, at age 62 Bonnie will be entitled to a total annual pension from both corporate employers of $34,700 in 1999 dollars, or 33 percent of her final earnings. A one-job career under the same plan would provide $41,300 annually, or 40 percent of final earnings.

What Bonnie's Experience Shows

The Value of Defined Benefit Plans Later in a Career

Bonnie's experience illustrates the advantage of having a defined benefit plan later in life. If Bonnie had held just one job throughout her career, but had only a defined contribution plan, she would receive only $27,500 annually, representing just 27 percent of her final earnings. The actual experiences of Bonnie, with a defined benefit plan, and of Susan, who had a defined contribution plan late in her career, show why it is impossible to say categorically that defined benefit plans are better than defined contribution plans or vice versa. It depends, at least in part, on the time in your career when you participate in the plan.

All things being equal, you are better off with a defined contribution plan early in life, while the employer's annual contributions have years to grow. You are better off with a defined benefit plan later in your career, when the employer must fund your benefit rapidly over the shorter time before you retire. But as we know, all things are never equal.

Even with the advantage of a defined benefit plan later in Bonnie's career, 34 percent of income is not sufficient to face retirement at age 62. Bonnie can expect to live another twenty years, during which inflation will reduce the buying power of that fixed percentage. With Social Security, Bonnie will have approximately 58 percent of earnings at retirement, still not enough to provide a secure retirement under most circumstances.

Effects of Pensions Linked to Social Security

Bonnie's situation also illustrates the value of pension plans "integrated" with Social Security for highly compensated employees. I will discuss this in detail in Chapter 7, but briefly, it works like this. Bonnie has always earned more than the Social Security wage base, which is the amount of wages subject to Social Security taxes and used ultimately to calculate Social Security benefits. (The 1999 Social Security wage base is $72,600; it is indexed for inflation each year.) That part of Bonnie's salary above the Social Security wage base will receive a proportionately higher retirement benefit under the integrated plan to compensate for the fact that Bonnie will not receive Social Security benefits for that higher wage.

By contrast, Susan's earnings never have been higher than the Social Security wage base. As a result, Susan receives a lower employer-provided retirement benefit under the retirement plan, which is integrated with Social Security, because she will receive proportionately larger Social Security benefits based on all her wages. If Susan had worked in one job all her career with an integrated defined benefit plan, she would receive only 29 percent of final earnings from her employer-provided retirement benefit, as compared to the 40 percent a one-job employee would receive at Bonnie's earning level under the same plan. But Susan will receive Social Security benefits equal to about 40 percent of her preretirement wages, while Bonnie will receive a Social Security benefit at normal retirement age of only about 24 percent of her preretirement earnings.

Theoretically, Social Security will balance out the difference in benefits under an integrated plan. But it may not, especially for women who do not work the maximum number of years for full Social Security payments.

What Should Bonnie Be Doing Now?

Bonnie's retirement planning outlook is much brighter than Alice's and Susan's for a number of reasons. First, and most obvious, she earns much more money. Her employer-provided retirement income will be based on those higher earnings, so retirement income will be higher. But she also has other advantages. Being younger than Alice and Susan, Bonnie has been helped for more years by changes in the law that allowed her to vest in her benefits in a shorter period of time. Those changes came after Alice and Susan were well into their careers and the changes were not retroactive. Bonnie could set up IRAs earlier in her career; IRAs weren't available to Alice and Susan until later in their careers. Finally and most important, Bonnie is starting retirement financial planning earlier.

Don't Coast

Things look fairly good for Bonnie. Indeed, some retirement or financial planners might tell her that she is close to having all the retirement assets she will need, with 58 percent of preretirement income due to come from employer-provided pensions and Social Security. They would be wrong. Those planners are assuming Bonnie's employer does not change the current retirement plan. Many employers do terminate plans or change the plans to reduce future benefits. Such planners are making three basic assumptions that you should never make:

- A person will want to stay with her current employer until retirement.
- The employer won't change the plan to reduce benefits in the future.
- Social Security will still pay the same wage replacements for highly paid workers when the person retires.

These assumptions are risky at best.

Personal Savings Can Buy the Freedom to Choose

Bonnie is not entirely set for retirement, but she has time to build her own personal savings, the most important part of any retirement financial planning. Bonnie already realizes that, much as she might like to stay with her company for the next twenty-two years, it may not be possible. What if her husband were transferred to a higher-paid job than hers in another city and she really wanted to follow? Or what if her company is merged with another and suddenly she is "redundant"? What if she were offered a really powerful government job or a judgeship? All of these are plausible possibilities. Some are even quite pleasant options. Bonnie wants to be prepared to meet each of them and still have a financially sound retirement.

For Bonnie, as for most women, her own retirement savings will be the key to creating the security she needs to avoid being chained to her current employer if opportunity or disaster knocks at her door.

Jennifer: A Secretary of Thirty

Jennifer entered the job market after graduation from college at age 21. She has held three jobs, has taken a year off, and has been in her present job for four years. She currently earns $21,000.

Jennifer's Unknown Career Path

Jennifer's career path is still to be mapped and traveled. So far she has had a difficult start. With a bachelor's degree in psychology, the entry-level jobs she found allowing her to use her training paid less than secretarial work. Lacking the money to go on for a master's and doctorate, Jennifer took a job as a secretary. The job was hellish and boring. It did offer a defined benefit plan, but, of course, after only one year on the job she did not vest in any benefits. After a year she took an interesting-sounding job as secretary to the president of a small exporting company. Jennifer found the work varied and low-pressure, and she liked the fact that the company had a defined contribution plan. She could easily see benefits being added and growing each year in her account. She worked there for three years. By that time she had saved enough to go back to school. She did not vest in the benefits in her defined contribution plan because she had only been there three years and the plan had five-year cliff vesting.

Jennifer returned to full-time work after only a year off. Jennifer has been with her present employer for four years and she really doesn't think she will go back to school. She is wondering what her retirement benefits would look like if she just stayed in her present job for the next thirty-five years—an unheard-of proposition in today's work atmosphere, but an idea nevertheless.

What Jennifer's Retirement Benefits Might Be

If Jennifer stayed in her present job, which has a defined benefit plan integrated with Social Security, she would receive an annual benefit of $8,000 in today's dollars upon retirement at age 65. Her full Social Security benefits would not be available to her at age 65 because, starting with people born in 1962, the normal Social Security retirement age will be 67 (at least under current law). She could receive a reduced Social Security benefit at age 65. Or she could wait until 67 and receive her full benefit, which should replace approximately 42 percent of her final earnings, assuming no change in Social Security benefits over the next thirty-seven years—a highly unrealistic assumption.

Her $8,000 annual pension represents about 28 percent of her final earnings. This is the same amount she would earn if she had held one job her entire career because, like many retirement programs, Jennifer's plan grants benefits only for a maximum period of thirty years of service. Jennifer will have been in her job for thirty-eight years when she is 65, so under this defined benefit plan, eight years of her work will not be valued for benefits purposes other than to take account of her higher earnings in the last years of her career. By comparison, a defined contribution plan contributing 5 percent of earnings over every year of her working life would provide Jennifer with $10,400 annually, or about 36 percent of her final earnings.

Jennifer was right to appreciate the defined contribution plan at her second job. When she left that job, her unvested benefit had a lump-sum value of slightly over $3,000. If she had vested in that sum and rolled it into an IRA earning 8 percent for the next thirty-five years, it would have been worth over $22,800, or about $52,300 if the IRA had earned 10 percent. If she had vested in even this small amount and left the money in the plan, at age 65 she would be entitled to $915 annually in 1999 dollars. True, this sum represents only 3 percent of Jennifer's final earnings at retirement. But the amount itself could pay the car insurance for a year or support a modest vacation each year.

What Should Jennifer Be Doing Now?

Jennifer is the only one of our examples who is beginning to look at retirement planning early enough. She can make choices now that will drastically affect her retirement. Even very small amounts of money saved now can accumulate to give Jennifer a significant retirement income. Jennifer realizes that she can expect to have less than a third of her final earnings made up by an employer-provided benefit, under the best of circumstances—and that assumes she stays with her current employer another thirty-five years.

Jennifer needs to begin her own savings program now. Because she earns less than $25,000, a traditional IRA contribution will be tax deductible to her even though she has an employer-provided plan. If she places $2,000 a year in a deductible traditional IRA, she could save about $300 a year in federal taxes alone. After thirty years she will have accumulated $189,000, if her IRA investments return 7 percent; $226,600 if her IRA earns 8 percent; and with a 10 percent return, she would have almost $329,000. Her own savings could give her a lump sum three times bigger than the lump-sum value of her pension. Clearly, saving almost 10 percent of her current income may not be easy. But as her income increases from year to year, it will become very easy. Starting now on her own retirement savings will not only give Jennifer a more financially secure retirement; it will also provide the freedom to change jobs if better opportunities come along without jeopardizing her retirement future.

Lessons Learned the Easy Way: Applying the Case Studies to Your Retirement Planning

Believe it or not, in many ways the examples of Alice, Susan, Bonnie, and Jennifer are best-case scenarios. As you apply the lessons of their circumstances, remember several facts.

- Only 21 percent of working women over 40 expect to receive or are receiving any employer-provided retirement benefits.[2] Only 40 percent of all working women report that they are covered by an employer pension plan; 50 percent of full-time working women report pension coverage.[3] Most of the jobs discussed in our examples actually *had* retirement plans. Many working women today do not have employer-provided retirement benefits at all.

- The case studies' benefits plans are relatively generous. Our benefits estimates were based on the fact that each of these women held full-time jobs for most or all of their working lives. Many women today work part-time for several years while their children are growing, and even if the employers provide retirement benefits, workers with less than one thousand hours annually usually do not earn benefits.

- Alice, Susan, Bonnie, and Jennifer remained—or are planning to remain—with one employer late in their careers and those employers' plans account for most of the retirement benefits. If they had been unable to stay with their late-career employers for a substantial number of years owing to layoffs or the need to care for ailing parents or other family members, their benefits would be much reduced.

Spending Retirement Benefits Before Retirement

Another reason why this group provides a best-case scenario is their wisdom in never cashing out and spending any retirement benefits due them when they leave a job. Alice, Susan, Bonnie, and Jennifer are unusual in saving it all. Unfortunately, only 56 percent of women who receive a lump-sum pension plan payout save any portion of that lump, as compared to about 61 percent of men. Only 24 percent of women save all of the lump sum and 26 percent spend it all; in contrast, 30 percent of men save all of the lump-sum distribution and only 20 percent spend it all. The average lump sum a woman receives is just under $7,000, while men on average receive just under $14,000.[4] Invested at 8 percent, that $7,000 amount over twenty years can grow to about $36,700 and over thirty years it would grow to over $70,000.

If Alice had cashed out her one previously vested benefit before she moved to her current job, her retirement income would be only $3,000 per year as opposed to her projected benefit of $4,600. She would have reduced her retirement income by 36 percent. If Susan had cashed out her retirement benefits from an early employer, she would have lost about 12 percent of her final retirement income, or almost $600 a year. Alice and Susan dramatically show why you should *never* spend retirement benefits you receive when you leave a job before you actually retire.

The growth of defined contribution plans that also permit employees to invest their own pretax money may be encouraging employees to cash out and spend their money as they move from employer to employer. Frequently these retirement plans are erroneously explained as "savings" plans, leading young employees leaving their jobs to feel it is perfectly acceptable to spend the money. After all, they "saved" it, so now it's time to spend it. Nothing could be further from the truth. It is true, you have savings. But those are *retirement* savings that you must live on for the rest of your life after you stop working. If you spend the savings on a new car each time you leave an employer, chances are you will never retire. You won't have the money.

A 10 percent early withdrawal penalty on preretirement lump sums not saved, introduced in 1987, was designed to discourage early consumption of retirement benefits. In 1993 Congress once again attempted to stop the waste of valuable retirement assets by requiring employers to transfer departing employees' pension lump sums directly to an IRA or other retirement plan or to withhold 20 percent of the lump-sum amount. (Chapter 9 explains these rules in detail.) Data suggest that preretirement spending is highest among the very young. But even among those old enough to know better—50- to 64-year-olds—16 percent spend lump sums.[5] Workers are cheating themselves out of years of tax-deferred investment growth. Remember Susan and Linda: after four years on the job when Linda was in her twenties, she earned a yearly retirement benefit for life of over $1,600, while all Susan got was a handshake. The importance of early benefits earning is clear. Can you live on $1,600 in retirement? Of course not. But there's a good chance it will pay for your groceries for a few months each year. A woman receiving a preretirement lump sum of $1,600 and investing it for thirty years could pay herself a yearly benefit during her retirement of $7,100. Now that would make a difference in retirement.

How Pension Portability Enhances Retirement Benefits

Many people argue that retirement security could be guaranteed and the reliance and political demands on Social Security reduced if "pension portability"—the right to keep some form of the pension benefits earned with one employer with you when you change jobs—were enhanced. While pension portability is a complex issue, the stories of Alice and Susan and Bonnie and Jennifer have already shown you how lack of portability destroys retirement income. Because the entire U.S. population is predicted to change jobs more frequently in the future, the loss of pension benefits due to job shifts is increasingly important. But you don't need theories to see how important it is.

There are three types of pension portability—portability of benefits, portability of assets, and portability of service.

Portability of Benefits: Cashing in at Retirement

Portability of benefits simply means the employer will give you your benefit at retirement. All Employee Retirement Income Security Act (ERISA) plans now provide for this type of portability by requiring that you vest after a legally defined maximum number of years. But as Alice and Susan have demonstrated, early benefits are heavily eroded by inflation. It is true the benefit exists, but by the time you receive it, its purchasing power may have been severely diminished.

Portability of Assets: Rolling Over Benefits from One Employer to the Next

Portability of assets permits the benefit you have earned to go with you when you leave an employer, to be rolled over either into an IRA or into another employer's plan, if the new employer's plan accepts rollovers from other employer plans. Many retirement plans today permit portability of assets. As we have seen from the data on preretirement lump-sum distributions, the problem with portability of assets is that too many people fail to use it. They spend the money they should be saving for retirement.

A second and more subtle problem is investing the money wisely to receive an acceptable rate of return. Many retirement plans give an employee a modest rate of return if the money is left in the plan. You don't need to take high risks with your benefit or be an investment genius to earn more with your benefit outside these funds than you would earn if you left it in. Of course, if you have a plan that is paying you an above-average rate of return, simply leaving the money there is a wise decision.

Portability of Service: Receiving Benefits for All Years of Work

The Social Security system is the best illustration of *portability of service,* a fully portable pension plan. You receive credit for every year you have worked, no matter how many employers you have. You never lose your Social Security benefits earned, no matter how short a period you may stay with the employer, and the plan is always the same with each employer. Social Security gives you portability of service and it provides the best protection for retirement benefits. You receive credit for all the years you have worked and your benefits are based on your full career earnings, including those important last years, which usually provide the highest earnings and those least eroded by inflation. For example, if Alice had pensions with portability of service over her career, she would receive credit for forty years of service over a forty-three-year career (remember her three years off at various times). Depending on her plan's formula, those forty years then would be multiplied by career average earnings or final five years' earnings.

Certain union plans, usually called multiemployer plans, also provide for portability of service, meaning that benefits are calculated by using all years of service among all the different employers who contributed to the union plan. So if Alice had worked only for hospitals that contributed to a nurses' union plan, all forty years of her service would have been counted for benefits in the plan. But in the case of these plans, employee benefit calculations and employer contribution calculations are easier. The plan is run by one board of trustees. The plan, not the many employers, is responsible for the recordkeeping, and all the benefits are calculated under one formula.

Employer Fears About Portability of Service

Employers generally oppose the portability of service concept because it would be difficult and complex to implement when applied among many different employers and their individual retirement plans. The employer fears she will have to come up with all the funding to pay for benefits for those employees working for her when they reach retirement age. If the earlier employer is required to contribute, she has had no control over the employee's earnings in the later years and the earlier employer fears she will be contributing to a much more generous benefit than she had contemplated. Recordkeeping for hundreds of employers and tens of thousands of employees would be expensive and difficult. As a practical matter, employers' pension plans probably differ too greatly to be able to calculate benefits for a given employee under portability of service.

From time to time over the past three decades, suggestions have been made for a clearinghouse at the federal level to serve as holder of pension funds to permit portability of service. These proposals are dismissed as too expensive and too complicated for the government to run effectively. Others have criticized the idea of making the federal government responsible for the investment of the huge sums of money that would be generated by such a program.

Increased Portability Not Likely

Legal or legislative action to require widely increased portability of benefits does not seem likely. Congress may take a few steps to make portability of benefits a bit easier, such as simplifying the rules regarding the benefit distributions that can be accepted by employer plans or totally prohibiting cash-outs unless they go directly to the employee's retirement account. But a mandated universal system for service portability does not seem in the cards.

Still, as our examples show, preretirement consumption of employer-provided benefits is a big cause of the loss of retirement benefits. Under current law, you—and only you—can prevent this benefit loss. It's simple—all you have to do is roll the money into an IRA or leave it in the former employer's plan. Congress is much more likely to change the law to prevent recipients from spending the money before retirement than to pass laws requiring other forms of pension portability.

Conclusion: Recognize the Effect of Changing Jobs and Employment Gaps on Your Retirement Benefits

The experiences of Alice, Susan, Bonnie, and Jennifer show why taking a year away from work is not *just* losing you a year's pay. Depending on your employer plan's vesting provisions and whether you return to that employer, the year off may lose you significant retirement benefits. Their experiences also show us how a new job, even with an increase in pay, can cost retirement benefits. Equally important, "cashing out" retirement benefits early in your career can dramatically affect your retirement finances.

The one-job career job is now a rarity for both women and men, so you and your spouse or partner will face many of the same issues in changing jobs or taking time off. The important thing is to recognize the impact of a job shift on retirement income as well as on current career plans. Whenever possible, time job changes to maximize your retirement benefits. Either take your vested benefits with you and put them in an IRA or keep track of them, including keeping your former employer informed of your current whereabouts. You can't run your career based on retirement considerations alone, but you must at least realize the effect of job moves on your final retirement income.

3

Basics of Retirement Savings and Planning

The examples of Alice, Susan, Bonnie, and Jennifer have made clear that employer-provided plans are important, but they are not enough. You need a three-legged stool for retirement planning—your own personal savings, Social Security, and employer-provided retirement plans such as a pension or a 401(k) plan. Realize immediately that only one of these legs is under your direct control: your savings. This chapter briefly discusses the roles of each "leg" and explains a financial concept critical to retirement planning, indeed to all financial matters, the *time value of money*. We will work through some sample calculations to illustrate how to consider the time value of money in your own planning.

Social Security: It's Not Enough

Social Security will probably always be available during your lifetime—unless you are reading this book in 2050. But levels of Social Security for today's workers who will be the twenty-first century's retirees are questionable at best. Under the current system, Social Security will replace about 44 percent of your pay if you earn average wages. If your earnings are lower than average, Social Security will replace a greater percentage of your income, perhaps as much as 88 percent, but generally around 59 percent. If you have higher earnings, you can expect a smaller percentage of your earnings, closer to 25 percent of that portion of your salary that was subject to Social Security taxes.[1]

These levels of replacement are more generous than the original replacement ratios. But Social Security was never intended or designed to be the sole source of retirement income. It alone will not give you a secure retirement. Yet too many retirees refuse to recognize this fact until it is too late. Don't be one of them.

Table 3.1
Social Security Workers and Beneficiaries

Year	Covered Workers (in millions)	Recipients (in millions)	Workers per Recipient
1945	46.9	1.1	42.6
1950	48.3	2.9	16.6
1960	72.5	13.7	5.3
1970	93.1	22.6	4.1
1980	112.2	30.4	3.7
1985	120.1	32.8	3.7
1990[a]	132.8	35.4	3.8
2000[a]	144.6	39.0	3.7
2030[a]	152.0	68.2	2.2

[a]Projections. Under other alternatives forecast by the Board of Trustees using different assumptions, the numbers are different, with the "workers per recipient" ranging from a high of 2.5 to a low of 1.9 in 2030.
Source: 1990 Report of the Board of Trustees of the Federal Old-Age and Survivors Insurance Trust Funds (Washington, D.C.: U.S. GPO, 1990).

Common sense tells us that a system that used over forty-two working payers of Social Security taxes to support one Social Security recipient cannot continue to grant as generous a benefit as when only two to three workers are supporting and paying taxes for each recipient of benefits. There is a limit to the amount of tax they are willing to pay. By the year 2075, the Social Security Board of Trustees estimates only 1.8 workers for each Social Security recipient.[2] Table 3.1, comparing Social Security taxpayers to Social Security recipients, tells the story.

The financial stability of Social Security is much in debate. The trustees of the Old Age, Survivors and Disability Insurance Fund, better known as the Social Security Trust Fund, project that, shortly after the baby boomers begin to retire in 2010, the fund will begin to pay out more in benefits each year than it takes in through Social Security payroll taxes. At that time, withdrawals will begin to be made from the Social Security trust fund, which currently consists solely of U.S. Treasury bonds. Circa 2030, the Social Security trust fund will be depleted. But even after the trust fund is depleted, Social Security payroll taxes each month will generate enough revenue to pay approximately 75 percent of benefits promised at today's levels.[3]

Fixes for Social Security

The "fixes" for Social Security are basically some form of reducing benefits (or projected benefits) and/or increasing the taxes to fund those benefits. Some reformers argue for creating private accounts in which workers would invest the amount they currently pay in Social Security taxes. The "private account" solution has several problems. First, it puts all the burden of investment on the individual. Poor investment choices or pure bad luck could result in the retiree having a very low benefit from Social Security. Second, neither the federal government nor private industry is capable of economically administering more than 200 million "private accounts," many of which would have less than a few hundred dollars in them. Third, the survivor benefits for minor children and disability benefits, both benefits that represent substantial portions of the cost of Social Security, would still have to be financed out of general taxes. Or we would have to decide as a society that we won't provide benefits to the workers who become disabled or to deceased workers' minor children. Chapter 8 focuses on Social Security, and I will discuss some possible reforms in more detail there.

The next few years will see significant debates on how to preserve some level of Social Security. The sooner changes are made, the less drastic those changes need to be. Pay attention to the debate. Given women's lower earnings and past lack of coverage by employer-provided retirement plans, Social Security supplies a far greater percentage of elderly women's income than it does for men. Without Social Security, the rate of poverty among elderly women would have been 52 percent; among elderly widows, the poverty rate would have been over 60 percent.[4] Clearly, Social Security is more important for women than for men. But it is important for virtually every American.

There will probably always be some sort of Social Security system for those who have paid into it. This book assumes so, but almost as certainly, future Social Security payments will be proportionately smaller than the benefits received by today's retirees. You must factor that possibility into your own retirement planning, and, most important, into your own retirement savings.

Employer-Provided Retirement Income

Employer-provided benefits are an important source of retirement income. In fact, since 1990 benefits paid from employer-provided pensions have exceeded benefits paid to retirees by Social Security.[5] In 1995 approximately 28 percent of retirees over age 55 were receiving or had received an employer-provided retirement benefit, with the median annual benefit being about $4,900 from private employer pensions and just under $12,000 from public employer pensions.[6] In career planning, always look for jobs with retirement plans. If your employer offers a retirement plan, do everything you can to maximize your benefits under the plan. If you can contribute to the plan, contribute as much as you can afford.

As the case studies of Alice, Susan, Bonnie, and Jennifer showed, you cannot rely entirely on employer-provided plans to supply all the income you need for a secure retirement. First and most obviously, employer plans are effective only when you are employed. Because women are frequently out of the job market, they will have gaps in employer-provided plans.

Second, not all employers offer retirement plans. Among active workers, retirement benefit plan coverage percentages actually declined from a rate of coverage for all workers of 56 percent in 1979 to 52 percent in 1983. Fortunately, these coverage rates appear to be on the increase again with rates of 57 percent in both 1988 and 1993.[7] But not all employees eligible for a retirement plan actually participate in that plan. For example, in 1996, about 60 million workers, or about 42 percent of the working population, were actually counted as participating in those plans. But of that 42 percent, not all had vested benefits.[8]

Increased Women's Pension Coverage

The good news is that the percentage of women workers actually participating in employer plans apparently is increasing rapidly. While only 43 percent of women in 1993 were participating in a retirement plan, very near the 45 percent of men, preliminary data indicate 50 percent of women working full-time are now participating in employer retirement plans, compared to 49 percent of men.[9] But when both full-time and part-time workers are included, only 40 percent of all women workers are offered pensions, as compared with 44 percent of all male workers.[10]

Termination of Plans

A third problem is that employers may terminate their plans at any time. In most cases the employer must give employees prior notice of the intention to terminate the plan. Employees will have the right to keep any benefits they have earned to date, in most cases even if the employee has not yet vested in the benefit. But no new benefits will be earned. (Chapter 5 has more details on plan termination.) Alternatively, the employer can change the benefit plan, providing future benefits that are less generous than the previous plan.

At least two economic risks could apply pressures on employer-provided retirement benefits that could encourage employers to drop retirement plans. First, U.S. companies face increasing international competition from countries where benefits are provided by government, rather than employers, or where benefits are nonexistent. Continuation of generous employer-provided retirement plans is also threatened by the cost of employer-provided health care. In past decades, retirement plans were the most expensive benefit provided by the employer. In the 1990s, health care programs are more expensive than retirement plans. Employers have only so many dollars to spend on labor costs, including both salary and benefits. The more dollars employers spend for employees' health care, the fewer dollars remain for retirement plans—or salaries.

Personal Savings

Personal saving is the critical leg of the retirement security stool; for women, personal saving should be the major leg. This is the one part of the triad you can control. Personal savings are especially critical for women because women lose employer benefits as a result of lower wages and time out of the work force.

There are several "tax-favored" retirement savings opportunities available to individuals. These include IRAs, Keoghs, universal life insurance, and tax-deferred annuities, all of which will be discussed in detail in Chapter 9.

You must recognize *today* that Social Security and employer-provided retirement benefits are only parts of your retirement security. The important point is *to begin saving as soon as you start working*—in any sort of safe account. If you wanted $1 million at retirement and began saving at age 30, when you have about thirty-five years before you retire, an annual $5,820 would give you your million dollar nest egg at age 65. If you wait until you are 35 to start, you will need to save $8,830 annually to have that one million dollars. If you wait until you are 45, you will have to save a whopping $22,000 a year, and at age 50 you need to save $37,000 annually. Have you ever heard anyone say, "Gee, I'm sorry I started saving money so early"?

Making Money Work as Hard as You Do: The Time Value of Money

In order to recognize the importance of your own savings and to begin your own retirement saving program, it is vital to recognize the concept of the "time value of money." A hundred dollars saved today, rather than spent, if invested very modestly at 7 percent, is worth $140 in five years, $197 in ten years, $387 in twenty years, $543 in twenty-five years, and $761 in thirty years. Would you rather have another new dress today or $387 dollars twenty years from now? Granted, $387 is not going to make or break your retirement. But let's say you decide to pass up spending just $100 each year from the time you are 35 until you retire. You invest that $100 each year at 8 percent. When retired you will have accumulated more than $11,300, which could make a very nice difference in your retirement.

The Appendix contains four tables that are more empowering than twenty self-help treatises. These tables will help you determine the time value of money by providing you with various factors to use as multipliers in given situations. Some expensive calculators, most computer spreadsheet programs such as Excel or Lotus 1-2-3, and computer-generated retirement planning programs, which we will discuss in Chapter 11, can also do this for you. But you may not have a sophisticated calculator, a computer, or the programs handy. These tables are cheaper and, with an inexpensive hand-held calculator, almost as easy to use. And they are easier to learn to use than most computer or calculator programs.

In all the discussions below, the sums involved have not been reduced to reflect inflation. Consequently, the buying power of those amounts will not be as great as the same amount of money in today's dollars. Inflation is a critical element in retirement planning that Chapter 11 also will discuss in detail. For now, just remember that inflation effects can be calculated just like interest rates. If you want to know what a sum would be in today's dollars, treat the interest rate as an inflation rate in any of the examples below. The tables do not reflect the effect of taxes on your savings, so you must keep in mind that tax will be due on the amounts you are saving. Chapter 6 compares the impact of taxable, tax-deferred, and tax-exempt investments on your retirement saving. Let's see how the tables in the Appendix work for you.

Calculating the Future Value of Money

Table A.1 shows you how a given sum grows at different interest rates over different time periods. Simply multiply the factor under the applicable interest rate and next to the applicable period of years by the amount of money you are saving or investing (or spending for that matter) to determine what the sum would be worth after the period of years.

For example, you are thinking about spending a windfall of $2,500 on a painting you have always wanted, but you're also thinking about investing the sum in a corporate bond paying 9 percent for ten years. Look down the 9 percent column to the ten-year figure and you find a factor of 2.367. Multiply $2,500 by 2.367 and you find your investment would be worth $5,917.50 in ten years. Regardless of whether you decide to spend or invest, you can at least weigh more accurately whether you would rather have the painting now or almost $6,000 ten years from now.

Calculating the Contribution Needed Today to Reach a Future Goal

Use Table A.2 to see how much money you need and what rate of interest it must earn to accumulate a given sum over a period of time. For example, let's say you want a $500,000 nest egg at retirement. At age 35 you have thirty years until you retire and you believe you can invest the money at 9 percent. How much do you need to invest today to reach your $500,000 goal? Look at the present value table. The factor under 9 percent over thirty years is 0.075. Multiply $500,000 times 0.075 and you will find that $37,500 invested today will provide you with $500,000 at retirement.

Calculating the Future Value of Known Annual Payments

Few of us can set aside a lump sum like $37,500 all at once for retirement. We need to make annual or monthly payments. Table A.3 shows you the future value of specific annual payments over various periods of years at different interest rates. For example, suppose you intend to save $2,000 per year from age 35 until you retire at 65. You want to invest it in a mutual fund that you think can earn 10 percent per year. Looking down the 10 percent column and across the thirty-year row, you find a factor of 164.494. Multiply this by $2,000. You find you will have

$328,988 at age 65 if you contribute each year and the fund earns the expected 10 percent.

Calculating the Present Value of Future Promised Amounts

Appendix Table A.4 tells you how much you will need today to reach a given sum at various interest rates and periods of time. For example, your employer has offered to buy out the remaining four years of your employment contract beginning with payments of $30,000 a year for the next four years. You fear the company won't last that long and you want a lump sum now. Assuming you could invest the money at 7 percent after taxes, how much should you demand from your employer now to give you the equivalent of $30,000 per year for four years? Look at the 7 percent column; find the four-year row and multiply the factor, 3.387, by $30,000. You find that a payment of $101,610 now would be the equivalent of $30,000 each year for the next four years. Your boss thinks she's saving over $18,000 because she doesn't understand the time value of money, and you get the lump sum.

Other Uses for Time Value of Money Tables

The tables will also show you how important higher rates of return are over long periods of time. This will help you balance the advantages of higher rates of return with the risks of investment that usually come with those higher rates. For example, compare the difference in the multiplier factor over twenty years between 6 percent, which you might get in a certificate of deposit, and 12 percent, which you might get from a mutual fund. At 6 percent the factor is 3.207, while at 12 percent, it is 9.646. The sum of $1,000 invested for twenty years at 6 percent will give you $3,207, but at 12 percent it would provide $9,646.

The tables will also show you the eroding effect of inflation. For example, if inflation runs at 4 percent each year for ten years you will need $1,480 then to purchase $1,000 worth of goods in today's dollars.

Another handy rule to remember is the "Rule of 72." Unlike the useful tables, this rule you can keep in your head to remind yourself of the wonders of compound interest. Divide the interest rate on any investment you are considering into 72, and the result will tell you how many years will pass before your money doubles. For example, suppose you are considering investing $2,000 in an 8 percent bond. Divide 8 into 72 and you find your $2,000 will double to $4,000 in nine years. If you could find a 9 percent bond, your money could double in eight years.

Conclusion: Build Personal Savings to Be the Major Source of Retirement Income

Employer-provided retirement benefits and Social Security are obvious sources of retirement income. Chapters 7 and 8 will discuss these sources in detail. But begin to think of your own individual savings as a necessary and critical element in your retirement planning. Start saving now—whether you are 25 or 65. Even if it must be a small amount, begin now. As you spend or save cash, think of it in terms of the time value of money. Get in the habit of using the tables in the Appendix to calculate future and present values of money when you are weighing a spending or savings option. You will be surprised at how differently you may feel about spending and saving money when you know how much the sum in question could be worth after a few years at different investment rates. Chapter 9 spells out the various tax-favored retirement savings vehicles available for your individual savings, and Chapter 11 will help you determine how much you will need for retirement. Chapters 12 and 13 discuss savings and investment programs in more detail.

4

Basic Retirement Benefits Buzzwords

Retirement planning and benefits can be lathered with seemingly impossible jargon and buzzwords. Understanding some basic concepts and terms commonly used in discussing retirement plans is an important step in planning your retirement savings strategy. If you don't know the terms, you can't talk as easily with or listen as carefully to the human resources people where you work or with financial planners or sellers of retirement saving products. You cannot really begin your planning until you understand the retirement benefits your current or potential employer is offering and how those benefits will grow for you over the years. Familiarity with the buzzwords will make the retirement planning process less complicated.

This chapter presents some of the basic terminology. The concepts are discussed in the order of importance to you. We start with you—otherwise known as the *plan participant*—and describe how you earn benefits, what legal protections exist for retirement plans, who controls the plans, how your benefits are paid, and how various plans differ. Chapters 7 and 9 discuss the various employer-provided and individual plans in detail, including the advantages and disadvantages of each. Many of the rules described here generally apply to those plans offered by nongovernment or so-called "private" employers, covered by the Employee Retirement Income Security Act (ERISA). (The next chapter discusses ERISA in detail.) ERISA does not cover government plans and plans offered by churches and church-related organizations. But most of the terms discussed here apply to all types of retirement plans.

The Basic Terminology

Eligible Participant: Getting into the Retirement Benefits Game

You are the *participant* in an employer benefit plan. If your employer has a retirement plan, in most cases you become eligible to be a participant after you have worked for the company full-time for a year or when you reach age 21, whichever comes later. Companies may permit you to become a participant sooner. An employer may also delay making you a participant for as long as two years, but, if so, you must then immediately own the right to any plan benefits you earn when you do become a participant.

Full-time employment is defined as 1,000 hours per year. An employer may also permit you to be a participant if you work part-time. But, if you work more than 1,000 hours a year, the employer *must* allow you to participate in any plan, even though both you and the employer consider you to be working "part-time."

Plan Sponsor: The Keeper of the Keys

The *plan sponsor* of a retirement program is usually your employer. However, in some cases, usually involving multiemployer plans, the plan sponsor may be a union or a combination of unions with the trustees of the plan consisting of representatives from both the union and the employers contributing to the plan.

Summary Plan Description (SPD)

The *summary plan description,* usually called the SPD, outlines the basic provisions of your employer's plan. This will be the document you receive from your employer when you are eligible to be a participant in the plan. An SPD is supposed to be written in plain English, understandable by the ordinary employee. It is also supposed to describe and disclose all the provisions of the plan accurately and completely.

These two goals are almost mutually exclusive. As a consequence, employers fear the "plain English" summary plan description will leave something out or misstate an important point, such as the distinction between benefit "accrual" and "vesting." Omissions or misstatements could lead to lawsuits and unhappy retirees. So the employer errs on the side of protecting itself, and the "plain English" SPD can become as complicated as the original plan document. Some employers even give up entirely and simply state the plan document is the SPD. In general, the SPD will set out the provisions of your plan in relatively clear language.

Your plan SPD is the most useful document in understanding your employer-provided retirement benefit. The SPD may not be as simple as you would like, but get it and read it. It will tell you:

- how you earn benefits,
- when you will have a nonforfeitable right to benefits (that is, be "vested" in the benefits),
- how the benefits will be calculated, and
- whether you have to contribute money to receive an employer contribution.

The SPD will also tell you other facts to help you begin to use your employer's plan as part of your retirement planning.

Benefit Accrual and Vesting: First You Earn It, Then You Own It

With employer-provided benefits you usually begin to *accrue,* that is, earn benefits, as soon as you become a participant. But it may be years before you are "vested" in those benefits.

Benefits "accrue" as you earn them over the course of working. Generally, after a year with an employer, you have become a participant in the retirement plan the employer offers, and you begin to earn benefits in the retirement plan. That means you are being credited with such benefits. For certain purposes, you will generally be credited with the time you worked before you became a participant.

Although you may have accrued substantial benefits with an employer, your accruals will be subject to forfeiture if you do not continue working for the same employer for a fixed period of time. You will not own the benefits until you vest in them. *Vesting* means you have not only earned the benefits, but you are entitled to keep them if you leave the company or become disabled. If you die before you retire, your surviving beneficiaries can receive your benefits. This is frequently referred to as having a *nonforfeitable right* to the benefits you have accrued.

Under ERISA there are basically two maximum vesting periods your employer may choose—cliff vesting or graduated vesting. Under *cliff vesting plans,* you vest in 100 percent of your benefits earned to date and all future benefits after you have worked with the employer at least 1,000 hours a year for five years. If the plan sponsor uses *graduated vesting,* also called *graded vesting,* you may have a nonforfeitable right in a portion of your benefits each year over a period of seven years beginning with 20 percent after three years of service and increasing by 20 percent each succeeding year. The details of vesting are discussed in Chapter 5 on ERISA.

Years of Service: How to Keep Score

Your initial right to participate in the plan is keyed to completing a *year of service.* Future rights to benefits, such as counting for vesting and for determining the *credited service* used to calculate most defined benefit plan payments, will be based in part on years of service. Under retirement plan laws, a year of service is defined as any twelve-month period stipulated by the retirement plan. The twelve months could be a calendar year, a tax year, or what is referred to as the *plan year*. A plan year can be any twelve-month period stated in the retirement plan document.

Three Ways to Count Service

There are three ways to count years of service. The *general* or *standard hours method* simply counts actual hours worked. However, many employers do not, as a rule, count actual hours worked. Instead, they keep track of work on a weekly or daily basis. In calculating "service" for retirement plan purposes, these employers may use an *equivalency system* based on weeks, payroll periods, days, or shifts. These periods are assigned an hourly equivalent, higher than the actual hours likely to be worked during the period. For example, a day is equivalent to ten hours. Under the equivalency method, 870 hours worked will be the equivalent of 1,000 hours. If either of these methods is used, most plans require you to have worked 1,000 hours during the year to be credited with a year of service.

The third way to count years of service is simply counting the period of time since the date you started working for the employer. This *elapsed time* method does not count hours. Under this method, twelve months after you started working for your employer, you will have a year of service, regardless of how many hours you worked during that time.

You cannot earn more than one year of service during a twelve-month calendar period, regardless of the number of hours you work.

Breaks in Service for Vesting and Benefit Accrual

Breaks in service are periods in any year when you work less than 500 hours. A break in service can occur when you quit or are laid off. You may also have a "break in service" if you are assigned to a part-time job when you had been working full-time. You may take up to approximately six months for the birth or adoption of a child without that leave being counted as a break in service.

If you have a break in service and then return to your employer, your years of service with that employer before you left will be counted for vesting and benefit calculations, unless you were gone for longer than five years or for the number of years you had worked before you left, whichever is greater. For example, suppose you work for Acme full-time from 1985 to 1989, when you leave for another job. In 1992, Acme asks you to return and you agree. Your earlier four years of service will count for vesting and benefits calculations because it is greater than your three-year break in service.

ERISA: The Cop on the Beat and Your Legal Protection

ERISA is the acronym for a 1974 federal law, the Employee Retirement Income Security Act. ERISA controls all retirement benefits provided by most nongovernment employers, as well as most "welfare" benefits such as health and life insurance. ERISA does not cover plans provided by state and local governments, the federal government, or churches. ERISA is enforced by the Department of Labor (DOL), the Internal Revenue Service, and, in some cases, you, the participant.

Qualified Plan

You may hear employer retirement plans referred to as *qualified plans.* Qualified retirement plans receive preferential tax treatment under the Internal Revenue Code and under most state income tax provisions as well. To be qualified, the plan must meet stringent IRS statutes and rules, many of which are identical to the ERISA statute. Usually, an ERISA retirement plan is also a qualified plan and vice versa. Unfortunately, the DOL and the IRS each write their own rules interpreting the statutes that Congress has passed. The DOL and the IRS don't always agree on how the statutes should be interpreted. So, for example, what may be a "highly compensated" employee for IRS rules may not be for DOL purposes. These inconsistencies are lots of fun for the two agencies, but not much fun for plan participants or plan sponsors. Fortunately, it is usually the employer, rather than you, who is charged with the duty to resolve the rules.

Defined Benefit or Defined Contribution Plan: Tell Me Later, Tell Me Now

Retirement plans usually are classified as either defined benefit plans or defined contribution plans. A *defined benefit plan* literally specifies the payment you will receive at retirement. For example, the plan may state that when you retire you will receive an annual benefit of 1 percent of your annual compensation times the number of years you worked. The benefits will be paid on a monthly basis for the rest of your life. Under this plan, a thirty-year employee earning an average of $40,000 annually would be entitled to $12,000. Beginning at the plan's normal retirement age, she would receive $1,000 per month as long as she lived—whether she lived one month after retirement or forty years.

You have probably guessed that in a *defined contribution plan* it is the contribution made by your employer—or occasionally you—which is specified in the plan document. A defined contribution plan document may provide that each year your employer will contribute 2 percent of your compensation or the employer will match 50 percent of any amount you contribute (up to legally set maximums). For example, if you earned $40,000 this year, your employer's 2 percent contribution would be $800 for the year.

The terms "defined benefit" and "defined contribution" frequently will be used to delineate the type of plan your employer has and will affect how you do your own planning. Typically, a defined benefit plan is referred to as a *pension.* 401(k) plans and profit-sharing plans are common types of defined contribution plans.

Which Is Better?

A typical question from employees is, "Which plan is better?" The obvious answer: "The plan that pays the most money." In fact there is no definitive answer to the general question. It depends on several factors: the amount of money involved in each plan, your age when you ask the question, and how long you will stay with the employer.

In general the defined contribution plan is better for younger employees who have been with the employer a shorter time. The defined benefit plan is better for older workers with long service with the employer. In the case studies of Alice, Susan, Bonnie, and Jennifer, we saw the actual differences in retirement benefits generated by the two types of plans in various career patterns. Chapter 7 has more on the comparisons.

Plan Trust: The Protected Piggy Bank

The funds for the employer's promised retirement benefits from a qualified plan are held in the *plan trust*. As with any trust, there are guardians of the funds, called trustees. Under ERISA, the trust and its funds must be used "exclusively" for the benefit of the plan participants and their beneficiaries and to defray the reasonable expenses of the plan. The employer has no right to the funds in the trust and neither the employer nor its creditors may reach the money. Likewise, in most cases your creditors may not reach your share of the trust fund.

Pensions

Pensions are defined benefit retirement plans that ordinarily pay you on a monthly basis when you retire until you die. If you choose, the payment can also continue after you die for the life of your surviving spouse or other beneficiary you name.

401(k) Plan: Funding Your Own Retirement

401(k) plans are named after the section of the Internal Revenue Code that created these plans. These are employer-provided plans that allow you to save your own wages without paying federal (and in most cases state) income tax on the savings or the earnings on the savings until you retire or take the money out of the plan. (You will have to pay Social Security taxes on the money you contribute.) Frequently, employers also will contribute to your account by matching your contributions. This may be on a dollar-for-dollar basis or as a percentage of what you contribute. 401(k) plans also sometimes are referred to as CODAs (cash or deferred arrangements) by the IRS or benefits specialists.

If your employer has a 401(k) plan, it should be the first place to think of saving. It is the best retirement savings vehicle you can possibly have because of the pretax benefit, the tax-deferred earnings, and possible employer contributions.

Other Types of Employer-Provided Retirement Plans

There are many other types of employer-provided retirement plans, which will be discussed in detail in Chapter 7.

Multiemployer Plans

Multiemployer plans are any sort of benefit plan sponsored by unions and arising from the collective bargaining process. Unlike *single employer plans,* which are sponsored by only one employer, multiemployer plans depend on the contributions of several employers that hire members of the union conducting the collective bargaining. As a member of a multiemployer plan, you have *portability of service,* meaning your years of service with all the employers contributing to the plan are counted. Suppose Acme Co., Buzzbe Inc., and Cramco are all employers participating in the Widget Workers Local Union Retirement Plan. You work three years for Acme, two years for Buzzbe, and six years for Cramco. You will have eleven years of service under the same plan, the Widget Workers Local Plan. As you moved to a new employer who contributes to the plan, you are considered to take the service with you; hence you have a type of pension "portability."

Multiemployer plans differ somewhat from single employer plans, primarily in the areas of funding and employer contributions. The most important difference from an employee's point of view is that multiemployer plans may require ten years of service before the employee is 100 percent vested, as compared to five years of service for single employer plans. In this book we will talk about single employer plans primarily. Where these plans differ from multiemployer plans, the differences will usually be noted.

Keogh Plans

Keogh plans, named for their sponsor, Congressman Eugene Keogh, are also referred to as H.R. 10 plans, after the bill enacting them into law. Keogh plans are retirement plans for the self-employed. Even if you are employed and have a retirement plan through your employer, you may have a Keogh plan if you also earn income as a freelance worker or independent contractor. For example, you work for a printing company and have a retirement plan there. You also have a graphic design business at home. You may open a Keogh account and put up to 25 percent or $30,000 of your net earnings from the graphic arts business into the account on a pretax basis. When you retire, you will pay tax as you withdraw money from the plan. We will look at Keogh plans in detail in Chapter 9.

Pension Plan Integration: Accounting for Social Security

Retirement plans that take into account payments from Social Security—or other types of retirement plans—in some form when setting the benefits under the plan are called *integrated plans*. Employers are permitted to integrate pension plans in order to receive credit for the employer-paid portion of Social Security payroll taxes. Integrated plans usually permit the employer to contribute a lower amount to the plan for the wages that are subject to the Social Security taxes ($72,600 in 1999) and to contribute a higher amount for those wages in excess of the Social Security taxable wage base. There are strict limits on the amount of integration permitted.

A typical integrated defined benefit pension plan might base benefits on:

1% of pay up to the Social Security wage base times years of service, plus
1.25% of pay in excess of the Social Security wage base times years of service

So for Bonnie, earning $75,000, in 1999 the amount used to calculate the benefit accrued for that year would be:

$$(1\% \times \$72,600) + (1.25\% \times (\$75,000 - \$72,600)) = \$726 + \$30 = \$756$$

A typical defined contribution plan might have a formula such as:

2% of pay up to the Social Security wage base, plus
3% of pay above the Social Security wage base

Annuity or Lump-Sum Payments: How Do You Get Your Money?

Retirement benefits, life insurance policies, and certain other financial investment vehicles generally are paid in a lump sum or as an annuity. The *lump-sum option* is obvious. You get all the money or assets of the investment at once.

In contrast, an *annuity* provides payments periodically over the course of a stated period of years or over your lifetime, and in some cases the life of your beneficiary. A true "annuity" keeps paying as long as you are alive. This is generally the form of payment for employer-provided defined benefit pensions. Annuities may also be paid over a stated number of years such as fifteen or twenty years.

Joint and Survivor Annuity: You Can't Take It with You, but You Can Leave It for Your Beneficiary

By law most employer-provided retirement plans pay a married employee in the form of a *joint and survivor annuity,* unless you and your spouse agree otherwise. Under this type of payment, you receive the benefit from the retirement plan in monthly payments for as long as you live. When you die, your spouse continues receiving payments. The payment you receive when you retire is less than the payment you would have received if there were no survivor benefits. The benefit received by your surviving spouse is usually reduced again after you die. These annuity forms are discussed in more detail in Chapter 14.

Preretirement Survivor Annuity: A Cushion for Survivors

Also by law, if a vested employee dies before retirement, most employer-provided plans must pay a spouse a *survivor benefit* from the retirement plan. These payments must begin no later than the earliest date the employee could have retired if she had survived. Chapter 7 outlines more on preretirement annuities.

Pension Benefit Guaranty Corporation (PBGC)

ERISA created the *Pension Benefit Guaranty Corporation* (PBGC) to guarantee defined benefit retirement plans, that is, the true pension. PBGC is funded by insurance premiums paid each year by employers sponsoring pension plans. If a plan is terminated by a company without sufficient funds to cover all the benefits, the PBGC will pay a portion of those unfunded benefits. Chapter 5 discusses the role of PBGC in detail.

Fiduciaries

A *fiduciary,* by law, is any person who is charged with the duty to act at her discretion for another in the other's best interests, without consideration of the fiduciary's own interests. Guardians of minor children are fiduciaries to the child. Trustees are fiduciaries to the trust. Corporate boards of directors are fiduciaries to the corporation.

A *retirement plan fiduciary* is any person or entity with discretion or authority over the plan or its assets. Such a fiduciary must act for the exclusive benefit of the participants of the plan and with the care and diligence a prudent person in the same or similar circumstances with the same business goals would use. The employer is a fiduciary to the plan if the employer exercises discretionary control over the administration of the plan. The "named fiduciaries," usually chosen by the employer to act as the plan's trustees, are, of course, fiduciaries. Anyone deciding how the general plan assets are invested, choosing investment options for plan participants, or giving advice regarding plan assets is a fiduciary. The plan "administrator" who decides how the plan will be interpreted is a fiduciary.

Mere record keepers for plans, who are also sometimes casually referred to as "administrators," are not fiduciaries because they have no discretionary authority. If a plan participant is not dealt with legally, the plan fiduciary is the responsible party and is liable for suit.

Actuaries

Actuaries tell employers how much money to put in defined benefit pension plans to ensure that there is enough money to pay you when you retire. Actuaries are mathematicians who make financial projections based on assumptions regarding interest rates, risks, the life expectancies within a group of individuals, and so on. *Pension actuaries* make projections based on life expectancies, usually referred to as mortality rates, employee turnover, expected retirement ages, and rates of return on investments made by the pension plan. These calculations tell the plan sponsor how much money should be placed in the pension plan trust in order to have adequate funds to pay benefits as the plan beneficiaries retire. *Enrolled actuaries* certify to the IRS, the Pension Benefit Guaranty Corporation, and the Department of Labor that pension plans are funded in compliance with law.

Actuarial assumptions are the estimates and projections an actuary uses to reach the funding calculations. By law, such assumptions used in qualified plan calculations must be "reasonable" in the aggregate. If the actuaries' assumptions are not reasonably accurate, there may not be enough money in the plan to pay retirement benefits.

Nondiscrimination Rules: Retirement Plans Are Not Just for Executives

Nondiscrimination rules in qualified retirement plans are not concerned with race, sex, or religion. These rules forbid discrimination in plan benefits between "highly compensated employees" and those benefits given "nonhighly compensated employees," by prohibiting retirement plans from paying executives and owners disproportionately higher benefits than paid to other employees. For example, a defined contribution plan giving everyone 5 percent of compensation is not considered discriminatory, even though it's clear that executives will receive more in absolute dollars than the rank and file. It would not be permissible to give everyone earning less than $30,000 a contribution of 3 percent and all those above $30,000 a 10 percent contribution.

Nondiscrimination rules are also designed to ensure that most employees are, in fact, covered by the benefit plan, if the employer establishes a plan. Tax-qualified retirement plans cannot be set up to cover just the executives, for example. Companies may create special executive plans that do not receive preferential tax treatment.

Highly Compensated Employees

Who are these *highly compensated employees?* Basically, highly compensated employees are roughly those employees earning over $80,000 in 1999 or owning more than 5 percent of the company. If more than 20 percent of a company's employees earn more than $80,000, the employer can choose to treat only the top

20 percent of employees as highly compensated employees. As you've already guessed, "nonhighly paid employees" are the rest of us. The dollar limitation is adjusted for inflation each year.

Conclusion: Learn Those Retirement Buzzwords

Retirement buzzwords help you talk the talk so you can be sure those in control of your retirement plans walk the walk with your benefits. A grasp of the basic terms will give you the confidence to question your employer, accountant, or investment adviser and to begin the process of retirement planning.

Now that you have mastered these terms, take a look—hopefully not for the first time—at your employer's summary plan description for your retirement plan. It should be easier to read now that you know the difference between accruing and vesting, and a joint and survivor annuity as compared to a single annuity. As you discuss retirement savings, you can focus on the substance of the plan or investment vehicle and its underlying value without being distracted by the terminology.

The Employee Retirement Income Security Act (ERISA)

The Employee Retirement Income Security Act (ERISA) is the federal law enacted in 1974 that regulates and protects employees' rights to pension and health and welfare plans provided by employers who are not governments or churches. This chapter sketches the protections ERISA can—and cannot—provide for your employer's retirement plans.

Neither ERISA nor any other federal statute requires employers to provide such benefit programs. But once employers do undertake to provide benefits, ERISA outlines the rules the employers must follow. Indeed, when ERISA was enacted many pundits predicted the end of employee benefits, arguing that the employers would terminate the plans. The reasoning: no employer would want to be subject to such complex, expensive rules. Fortunately, the pundits were wrong. Since the enactment of ERISA the number of retirement plans has grown from just over 311,000 to more than 690,000.[1]

Background

Pre-ERISA Law

The federal government applied some rules to employee benefits and retirement plans prior to ERISA. Because most retirement plans receive favorable tax treatment, the Internal Revenue Service first set the rules for retirement plans. During World War II, pay increases were limited, but benefits were not restricted by the emergency regulations. Employers, desperate for workers, lured them with benefits rather than with higher wages. As early as 1942, Congress began to place some limits on tax-favored retirement plans. If the employer offered such a program, it had to comply with the rules. The plan had to be in writing and be permanent and the employees had to be told about it. The plan had to cover a broad cross section of employees, not just owners and executives. The plan could not provide disproportionate benefits for executives or owners.

ERISA's Beginnings

Congress remained concerned with pensions, from time to time imposing additional disclosure requirements. In 1963, when the Studebaker car company closed, leaving many of its vested employees with less than their earned pensions, pressure to regulate the pension and retirement plan area more carefully increased. Extensive hearings and debate occurred almost immediately. But the first comprehensive pension protection bill was not introduced until 1967, and it became law only after seven years of legislative wrangling.

As with many proposed laws, its opponents viewed it as the "end of civilization as we know it"—or at least the end of the private pension plan system. Its supporters envisioned it as less protection than they wanted, but more than they had. And lawyers and actuaries saw it as guaranteed income for themselves. Only the lawyers and actuaries were completely correct.

The Basics: Secure Funds and a Guaranteed Right to Them

ERISA provided two basic and far-reaching protections for employees. First, it required retirement plans to be funded adequately through a trust that could not be reached by either the employer or the employer's creditors. Second, it required that a plan have a stated vesting schedule, not to exceed fifteen years (now only five years), after which an employee received a nonforfeitable right to some benefits, whether she was fired or quit, the plan terminated, or the company went bankrupt.

The Enforcers: The IRS, the Department of Labor, and You

ERISA is enforced by both the IRS and the Department of Labor. Generally, the IRS enforces the issues involving funding, participant rights, benefits levels, and discrimination in benefits between executives and the rank and file. The DOL enforces the disclosure and fiduciary rules.

ERISA employs two enforcement mechanisms. First, to receive a tax deduction for benefit plan contributions and other breaks, the employer must comply with the tax code provisions of ERISA. Failure to comply can "disqualify the plan," resulting in all contributions being taxable and in all employees being taxed on the value of their vested, but not yet received, benefits in the plan. Second, failure to follow ERISA rules subjects the employer and/or the plan to fines, some as high as $1,100 a day.

You as a plan participant also have the right to enforce ERISA rules by going to federal court. Unlike many employment laws such as the civil rights laws, you do not need to go first to a federal or state agency to seek enforcement through the agency procedures. Before you go to court, you must first complete any appeals procedures outlined in the plan. Once in court, you will not be able to seek a jury trial in most cases. The only recovery available to you will be the benefits to which you were originally entitled. No punitive damages are allowed. Even reimbursement for your attorneys' fees and court costs will be at the discretion of the judge. Indeed, there is the possibility that you could be charged with the employer's attorney fees and cost, although this is highly unlikely.

ERISA Details

ERISA uses a number of methods to achieve retirement plan security for employees, ranging from disclosure and reporting to employees to heavy penalties. The rest of this chapter describes how ERISA provides retirement benefits security.

Who and What Is Covered?

ERISA applies to virtually every employer and union plan, except the federal government, state and local governments, and churches. ERISA applies to retirement plans and to *welfare plans*. Welfare plans cover medical and hospitalization benefits, benefits for sickness, disability, vacations, certain training programs, and so on. Welfare plans are generally only covered by the reporting and disclosure portions of the law. Welfare benefits generally are not covered by the vesting and funding requirements, and depending on the benefit, they may not be covered by participation or nondiscrimination requirements. The DOL takes the position that ERISA does not cover off-site dependent care programs. Most sick-leave programs are not considered to be covered by ERISA. In addition, unfunded retirement plans for executives are covered only by ERISA disclosure and reporting requirements.

The ERISA rules for multiemployer plans are somewhat different, the most notable difference being rules regarding employer withdrawal from the plan and plan terminations.

Who's Not Subject to ERISA

ERISA does not cover the operation of benefit plans, including retirement plans sponsored by the federal, state, and local governments or by churches. Because many institutions, such as hospitals and schools, are operated by churches, plans in these institutions may not be covered by ERISA. This book cannot attempt to address the rules for the literally hundreds of plans offered by these non-ERISA plans. Except where specifically noted, the book will discuss retirement plans as though those plans are covered by ERISA. While specific rules for government and church plans are different from ERISA rules, many of the basic concepts, such as vesting, counting years of service, and so on, are the same. Additionally, many non-ERISA plans closely track ERISA rules.

Disclosure of Plan Provisions and Funding

ERISA requires a number of reports and disclosures. These include a summary plan description, a formal plan document (including any amendments to that document), the summary annual report, an annual report filed with the IRS and the DOL (Form 5500), and, if requested by a plan participant, a statement of benefits.

The Summary Plan Description: A Plain English Guide

Each benefit plan must have a summary plan description, or SPD, which must spell out the provisions of any employer plan in "plain English." If a significant number of employees do not understand English, the SPD must be in Spanish or any other language a significant percentage of the employees can read or understand. The retirement plan SPD tells you:

- whether the plan is a defined contribution or defined benefit plan
- when you are eligible to be a participant
- how you accrue benefits
- when you vest in those benefits
- when they will be paid to you
- how benefits will be paid to you, that is, as a lump sum or annuity
- who the plan administrator is
- where and how to get more information about the plan
- whether you must contribute to the plan
- limits on the amount of money you can put in the plan
- your rights under ERISA to get information about the plan
- your rights to appeal any denial of benefits
- your right to contact the Department of Labor for help if you feel the plan is not being properly applied to you
- your right to go directly to court if you don't get the information you are entitled to or if your appeal under the plan is denied
- your duty to keep the plan administrator informed of your whereabouts.

Because the plan sponsor has so much information to cover in the SPD and because the plan sponsor bears a heavy legal responsibility to be sure the SPD is both accurate and thorough, the sponsor tends to err on the side of length and complexity. SPDs are rarely "summary" and they frequently lapse into pension jargon. Don't be put off. After Chapter 4 you know the buzzwords—or at least most of them.

Retirement plan concepts can be complex, especially when you are just beginning to learn them. Read the SPD carefully, as soon as possible. If you don't understand it, make an appointment with your employer's human resources person and ask questions. Keep asking until you get clear answers. This is your future you're asking about. If the human resources person doesn't know, ask her to find out.

The Plan Document

You have the right to see the actual plan document and any amendments, in addition to the SPD. In most cases, the document will be too filled with jargon to be understandable. However, you will definitely want a copy of the plan document if you are nearing retirement and have doubts about the proper calculation of your benefit. Be warned, however; you may have to hire an expert to help you interpret the document.

The plan document is the legally controlling document. A rare court has ruled that the SPD will control, but this is usually in cases where there has been a blatant attempt by the plan sponsor to hide or obscure information. For your purposes, if there is anything contradictory between the SPD and the plan document, rely on the plan document.

Summary Annual Report and Benefits Statement

You have the right to a summary annual report that should show the plan's assets (that is, the plan investments) and its liabilities (that is, the benefits promised and administrative expenses). Once a year you can ask for a summary of your benefits, which will tell you how much you have accrued to date and whether you are vested in those benefits. Realizing that employees have a right to ask for their benefits statement annually, many employers provide all employees with this information once a year at the same time.

When you receive your benefits statement, read it carefully. In order to estimate the benefit you may be entitled to, especially in the case of a defined benefit, the employer must make certain assumptions, such as how long you may continue to work and how much your salary will increase. Be sure you understand and take into account these assumptions. Think about whether they are likely to be correct. For example, the benefits statement may base its payment estimate on the assumption you will retire at age 65. If you know you want to retire at 60, recognize that your benefit from that plan is likely to be much lower than the benefits estimate shows, because you will have worked five years less than the employer assumed in the benefits statement.

Other Plan Information You Can Get

If the plan is changed in a significant way, the employer must notify you.

Once a year the plan must file a report used by the IRS and the DOL. This *Form 5500* annual report contains detailed actuarial and financial analysis, including an audit of the funds, as well as information on the number of participants. Form 5500 is not likely to provide you with any additional relevant information under ordinary circumstances.

As a plan participant, you have the right to all relevant documents about the plan. This obviously includes the items listed above such as the SPD, the plan document, and a summary annual report. It also includes the Form 5500s and other documents under which the plan is established and operated. The employer may charge a reasonable fee for such documents. ERISA imposes a fine of up to $110 per day for each day the employer refuses to provide the documents after a thirty-day waiting period.

ERISA's Rules for Participating in an Employer's Plan

Under ERISA you must be able to participate in a plan after your twenty-first birthday or one year on the job in which you worked at least 1,000 hours, whichever is later. An employer may keep you out of the plan for two years of full-time work, but in such cases, when you do become a participant in the plan, you must be immediately vested in any benefits you earn. If you work for a tax-exempt school or other educational institution, your employer can delay your participation in the plan until you are 26 and have worked one year.

If you join your employer when you are near retirement, you cannot be kept out of a plan just because you are older. Since 1988, the law has required that retirement contributions continue for employees working past age 65. However, a plan sponsor may limit the years of service it will count for an employee. For example, a plan may provide that after the employee has thirty years of credited service, no further service will be recognized for benefits calculations or no further contributions will be made to the employee's defined contribution plan.

Vesting Standards

You "vest" in retirement benefits when you have a nonforfeitable right to benefits accrued under the plan. *But you are always vested in any money you contribute to an employer's retirement plan.* If you contribute to a 401(k) plan or a savings plan, you may take that money with you when you leave.

ERISA requires that plans vest benefits earned by employees under one of two schedules. These are maximum time periods. Your plan may permit vesting with fewer years of service. But the plan cannot exceed these periods.

A plan may have a vesting schedule that gives you the right to 100 percent of your benefits after five years of service with the employer. This five-year/100

Table 5.1
ERISA Gradual Vesting Schedule

Years of Service	Percentage of Benefits Vested
1–2	0
3	20
4	40
5	60
6	80
7	100

percent vesting schedule is often called *cliff vesting*. Or a plan may have a gradual vesting as shown in Table 5.1. This schedule is frequently called *graduated vesting* or *graded vesting*.

Vesting also occurs automatically when you reach the plan's designated normal retirement age, if that age is 65 or younger, regardless of the number of years of service you have with the plan. If the plan's normal retirement age is greater than age 65 and if you joined the plan within five years of the plan's retirement age, you will be vested after five years of participation. For example, if the plan's retirement age is 67 and you joined the plan when you were 62, you will be fully vested when you turn 67, even if the plan has graduated vesting for everyone else. Vesting also occurs if the plan is terminated, regardless of your age.

Vesting is based on years of service—not years of participation in the plan. To calculate vesting, in most cases you begin counting from the date you started working for the employer. But an employer need not count years you worked before age 18 or years you worked before the plan was put into place.

Once you are 100 percent vested, you own all benefits as soon as they are earned. You don't have to wait for a period of years after earning each benefit before that benefit is vested.

Prior Law Vesting Schedules

Prior to 1989, vesting could be 100 percent after ten years or graduated over fifteen years. *Class year vesting* was also permitted. Under class year vesting you vested in a benefit five years after you earned it regardless of how long you had worked for the employer. Multiemployer plans could use ten-year vesting until 1999 and even later in some cases.

Because the five-year or three- to seven-year vesting schedule only began to apply for plan years beginning in 1989, many women now in the work force who have worked steadily, but changed jobs every five or six years, may never have vested in a pension. Remember the situations with Bonnie, Alice, Susan, and

Jennifer. Each of them lost benefits because they changed jobs before the vesting period for the employer plans was completed.

Fiduciary Duty of Those Managing the Plan

Each ERISA plan must have a named fiduciary charged with the responsibility and discretion of operating and managing the plan. Any other person who exercises discretionary authority or control over the plan or its assets is considered a *fiduciary*. ERISA fiduciaries must act "solely in the interest of the participants and beneficiaries" of the plan. A fiduciary is to carry out her duties only for the "exclusive purpose" of providing benefits and paying the "reasonable expenses" of administering the plan.

The fiduciary is also bound by the *prudent man rule* (okay, okay, it should be "prudent person"). The prudent person rule requires the fiduciary to operate the plan, including its investments, "with the care, skill, prudence and diligence" that would be used by one acting in similar circumstances with the same goals.

The importance of this from your point of view is that the administrators, investment managers, advisers, and others must make decisions based on your best interests, not those of the employer. While representatives from the company will usually be the trustees and administrators of the plan, in their dealings with the plan their considerations should be for the employees, not the employer. Needless to say, this requirement demands a strong lack of self-preservation on the part of those fiduciaries who are also employees of the plan sponsor. It also raises some difficult issues in the case of certain plans such as ESOPs and 401(k) plans, which can and do invest heavily in employer stock.

Fiduciaries and Other Parties in Interest Must Avoid Prohibited Transactions

Fiduciaries and other *parties in interest* such as the plan sponsor, corporate executives, company owners, and major stockholders are prohibited from doing business with the plan. These *prohibited transactions* cover almost any business dealings other than providing office space and support staff for the plan administration. For example, plans that own office buildings cannot rent those buildings to the company that sponsors the plan. In specific cases, plan sponsors can apply to the Department of Labor for an exemption to the prohibited transaction rule. If the DOL determines that the transaction would benefit the plan, it will grant an exemption.

Trust for Plan Assets

All plan assets must be held in an irrevocable trust managed by trustees or by the named fiduciary. The employer has no ownership right to the funds or the trust. Most important, the creditors of the employer cannot reach the trust funds.

The trust must be audited once a year, which in most cases provides all the incentive a good-faith plan sponsor requires to keep the plan funded up to legally required standards. Once the assets are in the trust, the employees can be relatively confident the funds will be there to pay benefits at retirement.

In a defined contribution plan, the employer knows exactly how much money must be placed in the plan trust each year because the contribution amount is literally "defined under the plan." As a result, defined contribution plan trusts are rarely short on funds to pay accrued benefits to the individual accounts under the plan.

In a defined benefit plan, the employer must engage a pension actuary to calculate the amount of money to be contributed to the plan each year. The IRS will not permit the employer to put too much money in the plan or too little. The amount of money an employer must contribute depends in part on the amount of income earned by the plan's investments. When the stock market is high and investments have done well, the plan may become overfunded without any action by the employer. If investments do poorly, the plan may become underfunded, even though the employer has made contributions at the expected rate each year. Employee turnover, age, salaries, and retirement decisions also affect plan funding status.

Underfunding generally does not become an issue unless the plan is terminated, either by the employer or by the Pension Benefit Guaranty Corporation, which insures the benefits. The section on plan terminations in the following pages will discuss the underfunding problem and cures.

How to Challenge a Denial of ERISA Benefits

ERISA gives you the right to challenge a denial of benefits in several ways. For purposes of this discussion, "denial" of benefits also includes paying benefits at a level you believe to be incorrect. First, by law, the plan itself must contain an appeals procedure. ERISA does not detail this procedure, so the employer has a great deal of discretion regarding the appeals system, but the employer must follow the appeals procedures contained in the plan. At a minimum, the plan's appeals procedure must be spelled out in the summary plan description. You must be told in writing that your benefits are being denied and that you have the right to appeal to the plan administrator or other named person or body within a specified, reasonable period. The denial of benefits must give the reasons for the denial in understandable language and offer a complete and fair review of the denial. You must be given at least sixty days to appeal the denial.

If you follow the plan's appeals procedure, but are not satisfied with the result, you can proceed to the Department of Labor for help or go directly to federal court. The DOL's Pension and Welfare Benefits Administration can provide limited guidance on benefits questions. You should at least start by contacting the local or regional office of the DOL Pension and Welfare Benefits Administration. You can find that office in the phone book or go to the DOL's Pension and Welfare

Benefits Internet site: *www.dol.gov/dol/pwba*. Once there click on the "Programs and Services" box and then on the "Office of Enforcement." You can also contact the national office directly by writing to U.S. Department of Labor, Pension and Welfare Benefits Administration, 200 Constitution Ave., N.W., Washington, D.C. 20210.

Unfortunately, finding an ERISA lawyer may not be easy. While there are thousands of them, they work mostly for employers and may not be willing to represent an individual. A lawyer who does not specialize in ERISA, even though she may be brilliant, will have great difficulty in advising you because ERISA is so complex. At a minimum you may wind up paying for the lawyer's time to master ERISA's intricacies—an expensive and time-consuming project. Should you need counsel, shop carefully and don't be reluctant to ask whether a lawyer has experience with ERISA cases on the employee's side.

Projects to help with ERISA benefits denials are growing. The Women's Institute for a Secure Retirement (WISER) is a valuable resource for assisting women in resolving pension issues with their employers. WISER, linking with the National Center on Women and Aging, has also recently begun a Program on Women's Education for Retirement designed to reach out to the average woman through a national series of consumer education programs. WISER can be reached at 202-393-1990 or through its Internet site: *www.wiser.heinz.org*. The Pension Rights Center, 918 Sixteenth St., N.W., Suite 704, Washington, D.C. 20006, also provides counseling and information and can refer you to ERISA attorneys who represent individuals.

ERISA's Rules on Retirement Plan Changes

Employers may change their plans under ERISA, but such changes must be prospective only, if the changes affect benefits. Any benefit that you have accrued and in which you vested cannot be reduced retroactively. For example, you have a plan that pays 1 percent of compensation for each year of service. You have worked for your company for fifteen years and the company changes the plan to pay 0.5 percent of compensation for each year of service. Assuming no other changes in the plan, when you retire ten years from now, your benefit must be calculated as follows:

15 years at 1% of compensation (under the old plan),
plus
10 years at 0.5% of compensation (under the new plan),
equals
20% of compensation as your retirement benefit

Even though the plan at your retirement date provides for 0.5 percent of compensation for each year of service, you remain entitled to the provisions of the earlier plan for the years when you accrued benefits under those provisions.

If Your Employer Terminates the Retirement Plan

Under ERISA, employers are free to terminate plans completely, but employees must retain all the benefits earned to the date of termination. If you are not vested and the employer terminates the retirement plan, you immediately vest in any benefits you have accrued to the date of termination. Depending on your years of service with the employer, the benefits accrued are not likely to be large, but they are at least a reward for work completed.

Let's look at an example. You have been with Midnight Banking for thirty years and you will soon retire. Your colleague, Sallie, has been there four years, and Judith is just completing her first year. The Midnight plan requires one year of service before participation and five years' service with 100 percent vesting. Midnight decides to terminate the pension plan. You are entitled to your full thirty years of service–accrued benefits. Although Sallie has accrued four years of service and benefits, she is not yet vested under the rules of the plan. But because the plan is terminated, Sallie is vested in her three years of accrued benefits (she could not participate in her first year). Judith will not receive any benefits under the plan termination, because she has not yet become a participant or accrued any benefits in the plan.

At the termination of the plan, the plan sponsor may distribute the lump-sum present value of the benefit earned to date or may purchase an annuity to pay the benefit when the employee reaches the retirement age specified under the old terminated plan.

In the event there are plan assets remaining after all accrued benefits are paid out, those assets may be returned to the employer, if, for at least the previous five years, the plan document contained language expressly permitting such reversions. The employer will pay a heavy reversion tax and regular income tax on these reverted assets. Some employers, recognizing this penalty, have distributed the excess assets to the plan participants or transferred the assets to new retirement plans for their employees. Some lawmakers have suggested that all assets from terminated pension plans should be given to plan participants and that the employer should have no reversion rights. Others fear this draconian treatment of excess assets will encourage employers to underfund plans or to avoid setting up plans at all.

Employee Expectations May Be Dashed by Plan Terminations

This debate skirts the real issue: employees usually have relied on the promise that there will be a retirement payment under the existing plan when they reach retirement age. When you join a firm with a pension or a defined contribution plan, you expect a certain amount of money from that plan when you retire. You make your personal retirement savings plans, and sometimes even your career plans, based on this promise.

Let's say you joined Acme at age 35, planning to stay there until you retire at age 60. In part your decision was based on the fact that Acme had a pension plan and you realized that in twenty-five years you will have accrued a substantial monthly retirement check. If the plan is terminated after you have been with Acme for fifteen years, the amount you will receive from your accrued benefits is far less than what you expected. You will miss the contributions for the next ten years, which under a defined benefit plan would have been the years of greatest accumulations for you. You will also miss the retirement benefits that would have been based in part on the larger salary you can reasonably expect in the future. In effect, by terminating the plan, Acme has given you a substantial pay cut and you will need to scramble to revise your personal savings plan. True, Acme never promised you it would never change the plan, but you never expected to receive a substantial pay reduction after years of loyal service either.

Pension Benefit Guaranty Corporation: Insurance for Defined Benefit Plans

Even though ERISA protects plan assets with a trust, problems can arise in defined benefit plans, if the plan has not been fully funded. Given restrictive funding rules permitted by the IRS, a perfectly lawful plan may not contain sufficient assets at termination to pay all benefits. Defined benefit plans are based on numerous variable factors and ERISA permits funding at various levels. Additionally, for many years the IRS had the authority to grant defined benefit plans funding waivers for a year. As a result, some defined benefit plans are not adequately funded even though they have fully complied with ERISA and tax law funding rules. If an employer goes bankrupt or terminates the plan, there may not be adequate funds to pay all the promised benefits.

ERISA created the Pension Benefit Guaranty Corporation to cope with the underfunded plan termination problem. The PBGC is basically a government corporation, financed by premiums paid by plan sponsors. Each sponsor of a defined benefit plan pays a premium of approximately $19 per plan participant (the dollar amount is frequently adjusted). Underfunded plans pay an additional premium amount based on the amount of the underfunding.

PBGC's Role When Plans Terminate

PBGC oversees the terminations of defined benefit plans. A plan termination may be "voluntary," meaning the employer has decided to terminate the plan. In such cases, if the plan does not have enough assets to meet all benefit liabilities under the plan, the employer must come up with enough money to meet the obligations. This is referred to as a *standard termination.* If the employer wishes to terminate the plan, but cannot fulfill the plan's liabilities, he must prove that continuing the plan will cause the business to collapse. These *distress terminations* are unusual and are rarely granted except in cases of bankruptcies. The PBGC itself may terminate a plan without the employer's request, or even consent, if the PBGC finds the plan's liabilities are unlikely to be fulfilled either by plan assets or by the employer.

If a plan sponsor defaults on the plan and the plan is terminated, the PBGC will pay basic benefits up to a certain level for plan participants. Retirees currently receiving benefits will be paid up to a maximum amount based on the average wage earnings in the United States. Currently the maximum benefit PBGC will pay is just over $3,000 a month. For participants who are still working, the PBGC will guarantee benefits they had accrued at the time the plan terminated.

The PBGC will not provide the benefit the worker would have earned if the plan had continued and she continued working until retirement. Additionally, the PBGC will not pay benefits fully that are based on increases from new plan provisions that were granted within five years of the plan termination or benefit increases granted while the plan was not in compliance with the law.

Different rules apply for multiemployer plans. Because several employers are involved in such plans, the PBGC will become responsible for the plan only if the plan becomes insolvent. Employers who stop participating in the plan remain liable to contribute to the plan for a number of years. Consequently, the financial health of the plan is not tied to the fate of one employer. If the PBGC does pay benefits for the plan, the payment limits are much lower than those for single employer plans. The maximum multiemployer benefit that PBGC will pay is $600 per month for a thirty-year participant. And PBGC will not pay for any benefit increases granted in the last five years.

Even after the PBGC takes responsibility to pay plan benefits, the plan sponsors remain liable to the PBGC for the amounts owed the plan. However, in cases of bankruptcy, the courts usually rule PBGC is an unsecured creditor and, as such, unlikely to collect the debt. PBGC is actively working to improve its status as a priority creditor in bankruptcy cases, but to date has been unsuccessful with either the Congress or the courts.

What to Do If Your Employer Terminates the Plan

Unfortunately, if your employer decides to terminate your benefit plan, you have few options. You will receive a notice of the termination. If the plan is a defined benefit plan guaranteed by the PBGC, you must receive a benefits statement showing your accrued benefit and the facts used to calculate that benefit, such as your age, date of hire, earnings, and so on. Be sure to double-check these facts and inform the plan administrator immediately if your records disagree with any of the data.

If your plan is a defined contribution plan, you may receive only a notice that the plan is being terminated, and later a check for your accrued benefit. If you don't get a benefit statement, ask for one immediately. Be sure those records match your records of your benefits.

You may be given the choice of receiving your benefit in a lump sum or as an annuity held by an insurance company. Even if the plan has been previously guaranteed by the PBGC, that agency will not guarantee the annuity. In the early 1990s, retirement plan annuities issued by some insurance companies have reduced payments because of the financial difficulties of these issuing companies. But most annuities have been safe and paid benefits regularly. Ask the plan administrator who will be paying the annuities and try to research that company.

Or take the money as a lump sum. You can then transfer the money into an IRA and invest the money any way you wish. (IRAs can accept transferred amounts over $2,000 a year, if the amount comes from an employer-provided retirement plan.) If the terminating plan is a defined contribution plan invested in stocks or mutual funds, find out whether you can receive your account in these assets rather than receiving a check for the value of the assets after they have been sold. This may not be a good time to sell the assets in your defined contribution plan and, if you can receive the assets, you may be able to hold them until the price increases.

Arrange to have any money or other assets you receive transferred directly to an IRA or to another employer's plan, if you have access to one. If you don't get the money into an IRA or another employer's plan, the employer or the PBGC must withhold 20 percent of the amount for federal income taxes. Chapters 9 and 10 give you more details on the importance of getting all retirement plan distributions into a rollover IRA as soon as possible.

Your Strategy Plan for ERISA

- Get up-to-date copies of all employers' summary plan descriptions. Do this for both current and former employers.
- Arrange a meeting with your employer's retirement plan benefits specialist to discuss areas of the SPD or other forms you don't understand.
- Begin a file folder for all materials on employer plans to keep with your financial records.
- Read each plan SPD, and on the front cover note dates relevant to you, such as your date of hire, date of vesting, date of your leaving the employer, if it is a previous employer.
- Do a rough calculation of your benefits under your employer's plans. We will use those calculations in later chapters to determine the savings you need for retirement.

How Taxes Affect Retirement Planning and Retirement Income

Most of the retirement planning devices we've mentioned have one thing in common: they defer the payment of income taxes on savings and on the earnings of those savings until the money is withdrawn from the plans or accounts during retirement. Table 6.1 illustrates why this is so important. The premium derived from tax-deferred savings, as compared with currently taxed savings, is dramatic: if you saved $2,000 a year for thirty years, you will have $92,117 more if you put it in a tax-deferred account.

Pretax dollars are those you have not paid taxes on, such as your gross salary quoted you by your boss. After-tax dollars are what you have left after you have paid your taxes, such as your take-home pay.

Of course funds sheltered during your working years will be taxed eventually as you withdraw them from the tax-deferred retirement plan. But until that point, you have the advantage of using the money that would have been paid immediately in income taxes to earn additional income instead. The Congressional Budget Office calculates that $1,000 using tax-deferred dollars saved under a tax-favored plan, such as a 401(k) or a tax-deductible IRA paying 8 percent, provides a 37 percent greater rate of return after fifteen years, if you are in the 28 percent bracket. It provides an 18 percent greater rate of return if you are in the 15 percent bracket.[1] This comparison assumes that you pay taxes on the account after you retire and stay in the same tax bracket when you retire. If your tax bracket is lower after retirement, you save even more.

Saving After-Tax Dollars

Even if your original contributions to a retirement plan consist of after-tax dollars—as in an employer's thrift plan, a nondeductible IRA, or a Roth IRA—you

Table 6.1
Balances in Tax-Deferred Versus Taxed Savings Accounts

Year	Tax-Deferred Account	After-Tax Savings Account
1	$ 2,000	$ 1,440
10	$ 31,875	$ 22,950
20	$114,550	$ 82,476
30	$328,988	$236,871

Note: Assumes a 10 percent rate of return and a 28 percent tax rate.

still realize significant benefits. The earnings on those nondeductible contributions are tax-deferred. That deferral improves the compounding factor over many years. In such cases the 28 percent taxpayer has an 11 percent greater return and the 15 percent taxpayer has a 6 percent greater return in a tax-deferred plan than in a savings plan that is taxed annually. These higher rates are calculated after all tax has been paid on the amounts. The figures also assume the tax bracket is not lower at retirement. If the tax bracket is reduced from 28 percent while working to 15 percent at retirement, the difference between taxable and tax-deferred savings could be as great as 62 percent.[2] With a Roth IRA, you *never* pay taxes on the earnings.

These savings calculations don't include the amounts you save on state taxes, which could be proportionately similar. Most, but not all, states also give favorable tax deferral treatment to all federally tax-deferred plans.

How Federal Budget and Tax Policy Affect Retirement Savings

One of the motivating factors for the growth of retirement plans in the 1940s was the ability to fund such plans with tax-deductible dollars and hence save corporate earnings from the very high tax rate of those days. Today, the tax deferral permitted to individuals and the tax deductions granted employers for the various retirement plans costs the federal government over $92 billion a year in tax revenues which would otherwise go into IRS coffers.[3] This is the single largest tax break, or "tax expenditure," as the IRS calls it, in the Internal Revenue Code. The retirement account tax break is bigger than the home mortgage deduction by $42 billion and is used by more people, some of whom may not even be aware of the fact they benefit from this tax break.

Looking at it another way, in the bad old days, when federal deficits ran more than $300 billion per year, eliminating the tax-favored treatment of private retirement plans would have reduced the deficit by about 20 percent per year. Fortunately, Congress never looked at it that way. But it is not surprising that congressional and IRS tax writers were constantly tinkering at the margins to shave a few million off the retirement plan tax breaks. With the beginning of apparent federal budget surpluses in 1998 (not to mention the impending retirement of baby boomers who desperately need more retirement saving rather than less), Congress stopped cutting back on retirement benefits and even made some favorable changes. But years of tinkering to raise tax revenues has meant not only a loss of the tax advantages, but also constant changes in an already devilishly complex law.

Whether the twenty-first century will find the U.S. budget still in surplus is unclear. But regardless of whether tax policies in coming years are more encouraging for retirement savings or less so, you should always exploit these tax savings to the hilt. For most U.S. taxpayers, these retirement saving advantages are their only tax break. Don't lose it. Congress usually has been sensitive to not changing the rules for money already saved for retirement, and in some cases, such as the Roth IRA, Congress has even permitted existing retirement savings to benefit from favorable changes. This sensitivity to the protection of money already saved only argues more vigorously for the wisdom of saving as much as possible now while retirement saving tax advantages remain on the books.

Tax-Deferred Versus Tax-Exempt Savings Vehicles

Most retirement savings plans defer the payment of taxes until payment begins at retirement. So retirement plan benefits are not tax exempt; they are merely tax deferred. You will not pay tax on the benefits until you begin to take the money out of the plan. This should not be until you retire around the age of 65. Even then, you may take employer money in a lump sum and roll it into a traditional IRA. In that case you can defer tax on the money further. But for most retirement benefits, you cannot defer paying taxes on the tax-deferred retirement money after age 70½. At that point, the IRS will treat all such monies as though they were being distributed to you over your remaining life expectancy or the life expectancy of you and the named beneficiary of the retirement accounts you may have.

If you do not begin taking money out of these accounts and paying taxes on the distributions, you will be hit with a 50 percent excise tax on the amount you should have taken, in addition to the income tax on such amounts. This will not be a problem for most of us, since we will have begun using our retirement savings well before age 70½. Our concern will be making the sum last through our life expectancy, not sheltering it from taxes.

Tax-Deferred Savings Vehicles

401(k) Plans

In general, the major portion of your contributions to retirement savings should first rely on tax-deferred savings vehicles such as IRAs and any 401(k) plans available to you, for two reasons. First, these retirement savings accounts usually enable you to earn more money than tax-exempt investments without paying taxes while the money is growing in the retirement plans. Second, buying other investments such as stocks and stock mutual funds for your 401(k) plan or IRA also permits you to diversify your investments beyond just tax-exempt bonds. Diversity of investments is an important rule for any investment strategy. Once you have fully funded all the tax-deferred retirement savings plans available to you, you can move on to tax-exempt and taxable savings vehicles in addition to these tax-favored accounts.

Traditional IRAs

Fortunately, no one who is earning income or married to a person earning income is denied access to a tax-deferred retirement savings plan. If your employer does not have a retirement plan, you can set up a tax-deductible traditional IRA on your own. That money and its earnings will not be taxed until you begin to withdraw it at retirement or if you become disabled. If you are self-employed, you may set up a Keogh or a "simplified employee pension" plan, which permits you to save tax-deductible amounts, again deferring tax on that amount and its earnings until retirement.

Annuities and Universal Life Insurance

Individual annuities and universal life insurance policies are another tax-deferred method of saving. Individual annuities, usually underwritten by insurance companies or banks, are basically pensions you purchase yourself. Generally, a fairly large initial investment of at least $2,000 or more is required. Depending on the annuity, you may make additional investments over a period of years. The earnings on the money invested is not taxed until you begin to receive payments from the annuity. Universal life insurance works much the same way. Usually it does not require a high initial investment, but it does require subsequent payments. Chapter 9 on individual retirement saving discusses these investments in detail.

Tax-Exempt Savings Vehicles
Roth IRAs

Beginning in 1998, the Roth IRA offered a new type of tax-exempt saving vehicle. In a Roth IRA, you put up to $2,000 per year of after-tax dollars into the account, but the money that account earns is *never* subject to tax. Consequently, once you reach age 59½ any money coming out of a Roth incurs no federal income tax liability. A few special rules apply to Roth IRAs. Chapter 9 will talk about Roth IRAs in more detail.

Tax-Exempt Bonds

Of course, a substantial part of your retirement savings could be in other currently tax-exempt investments, such as municipal bonds or municipal bond mutual funds. But this source of income is subject to the federal alternative minimum income tax and may be subject to state income taxes as well. These investments also return relatively low rates of interest, which make them unsuitable for long-term retirement savings. Tax-exempt investments should not be part of your traditional, non-Roth IRA because their income will become taxable once it is withdrawn from the IRA.

Beware Early Withdrawal Tax Penalties

The IRS does not give you these tax breaks without some strings. We have already been introduced to some of the rules surrounding tax-favored retirement plans. Another string, or noose if you prefer, is the early withdrawal penalty tax imposed on withdrawals from tax-favored plans, including IRAs, Keoghs, annuities, and 401(k) plans. If you withdraw money from these plans before age 59½, you generally pay an additional 10 percent penalty tax.

There are a few exceptions. If you die or become disabled, no penalty tax applies. If you begin receiving the money in a "life stream" over the number of remaining years you are expected to live there will be no penalty. You may also escape the penalty tax if the withdrawals come as a result of early retirement after age 55 or if they are used to pay deductible medical bills (with the restriction that such bills exceed 7½ percent of your income). These last two exceptions do not apply to IRAs.

These penalties are designed to enforce the purpose for the tax breaks in the first place: money in these accounts is to be saved for retirement. The accounts are not to be used as a tax-favored way to save for your luxury car or a trip along the Grand Canal—at least not until you are past age 59½.

Capital Gains Versus Tax-Deferred Savings

Investments that grow in value, such as a stock share that increases in price, have two important tax advantages over investments that generate annual income. First, for the first time in many years, the Internal Revenue Code offers a significantly lower rate for capital gains—that is, the amount of money you make when you sell an investment for more than you paid for it—than for income from investments (or wages). The top tax rate for such capital gains held more than one year is limited to 20 percent, regardless of your taxable income. Depending on your other income, the capital gains tax rate may be as low as 15 percent. Contrast the 20 percent capital gains tax rate with a 28 percent tax on earned income over approximately $26,000 for singles and $43,000 for marrieds or up to 39.6 percent for very high income brackets. Second, you can avoid paying taxes on capital gains for years, because you do not pay tax on capital gains until you sell the investment.

Given these two big advantages, tax professionals advise savers to buy investments that will grow in value, such as stocks, rather than investments that pay earnings each year, such as savings accounts. Tax advisers usually recommend that investments expected to grow through capital gains should not be held in a traditional IRA or 401(k) plan. All amounts paid from traditional IRAs or 401(k) plans, whether earnings or capital gains, are taxed at ordinary income rates rather than the lower capital gains tax rates. (The only exception to taxes are nondeductible contributions you originally made to the traditional IRA or 401(k) plan.)

This is good advice for those individuals who have funded their IRAs and 401(k) plans to the maximum and are now ready to save additional money. It is also good advice when it comes time to diversify your savings. Investments that earn income annually are better for your IRA or employer retirement plan. Investments that you expect to grow in value and provide you with an increase in your investment only when you sell it should be invested outside your individual investment accounts or employer-provided savings plans.

But beware: capital gains tax rates have gone up and down over time. Remember you are planning on investments that you hope to own for decades. Consider the capital gains tax rates once you have enough money to invest outside tax-favored retirement accounts, but bear in mind that those rates, like other tax laws, can change.

Pay the Tax Now to Avoid Higher Tax Later?

Today's tax rates generally are lower than they have been in decades. But already, the rates have crept up several points from the low rates enacted by the Tax Reform Act of 1986. Some tax advisers argue it is wiser to pay current tax on earnings and investments and avoid what are certain to be higher rates at retirement. This argument cannot be dismissed. However, the advantage of tax deferral over a number of years, such as you have in retirement savings plans that exist for decades, is still likely to outstrip the possible loss from higher taxes for most individuals unless the federal income tax rates become very high. Certainly, while we expect federal budget surpluses rather than deficits, tax rates are not likely to increase. Those surpluses could quickly turn to deficits and rates could go up again—sharply. But when and how much we don't know.

Avoiding tax-favored saving today or paying taxes before you have to simply doesn't make sense for most people. Even if tax rates do increase in the future, more tax brackets likely will be created and, as a retiree, you are likely to qualify for the lower brackets.

Conclusion: Maximize Tax-Favored Savings, but Save Even if It Isn't Tax-Favored

Unless you are already vested in a very generous retirement plan or you can begin saving the maximum Keogh amount each year early in your self-employed career, you probably will not be able to provide a secure retirement simply by using tax-favored retirement plans. Remember the Duchess of Windsor's dictate, "You can never be too rich or too thin." You should save beyond the amounts permitted to you under the employer, Keogh, and IRA tax-favored plans. You will want to make other investments, when you can afford it. Just be sure you use the tax-deferred retirement programs to their fullest before you start other retirement savings programs.

You have seen how valuable tax-preferred investments can be to savings growth. But never let tax considerations totally drive retirement or any other type of savings or investment plans. A bad tax-exempt investment or a bad tax-deferred investment is still a bad investment. True, not making money is the ultimate tax dodge, but it's a painful way to avoid the IRS.

Finally, even if tax rates are increased in the future, the amounts you saved on an after-tax basis won't be taxed again when you spend them at retirement.

PART TWO
SOURCES OF
RETIREMENT SAVINGS

Employer-Provided Retirement Plans

Alice, Susan, Bonnie, and Jennifer are among a minority of employees because each of them now works for an employer that provides a retirement plan. More than 690,000 private retirement plans cover over 85 million active and retired employees.[1] Still, only about 44 percent of the civilian work force participate in an employer-provided plan.[2]

Employer retirement plans contain over $6 trillion in assets to pay benefits, a significant sum in comparison with a gross domestic product of approximately $8 trillion.[3] Pension assets not only represent an important source of retirement security for Americans, but a powerful source of investment capital for national savings and growth. In fact, private employer-provided retirement plans pay more benefits to retirees than Social Security does.

As we have seen, these plans are heavily regulated by the federal government. This regulation helps protect the rights of employees, but it also means the laws affecting retirement plans are extremely complex. This chapter seeks to decode some of that complexity by explaining the basic outlines of some common employer retirement plans and listing the advantages and disadvantages of each.

Tax Breaks and Changing Laws

Between 2000 and 2003, these employer-provided retirement plans will enjoy tax breaks worth an estimated $78 billion a year, the largest single area of tax preferences in the federal budget.[4] The complexity of employer-provided benefit plans is increased by frequent changes in retirement plan laws. These changes in part are a function of the 1980s decade of unprecedented deficits. During that time Congress constantly needed new sources of revenue. In its search to raise revenues, Congress repeatedly trimmed the tax breaks given employee benefits. With billions at stake, Congress changed the benefits rules for the same reason Willie Sutton said he robbed banks. It's where the money is.

With the beginning of small federal budget surpluses in the late 1990s, Congress stopped shaving away retirement plans' tax advantages, and even added a few new ones. While these recent improvements still have not returned retirement plan rules to the generosity of the 1970s, these changes are good news for individuals. But they are even better news for the overall U.S. economy both in the short run and in the long run. In the short run, encouraging the growth of retirement savings means more domestic money is available to invest in U.S. companies. In the long run, it means retirees will have the funds to continue their working-life spending habits and thus help maintain the economy.

The material in this chapter is based on the law as it exists in 1999. Changes are possible at any time. You should be certain that you—and your employer—are operating under the most recent effective law. Usually, when Congress changes retirement plans laws, the effective dates are delayed one to three years to give employers time to amend their plans and inform employees about required changes. But some employers do not keep up with changes in a timely way. In their defense, unless one has access to the very expensive special service publications that report employee benefits law changes, it can be difficult to find the most recent law.

Be Sure You Have Your Plan's Up-to-Date Rules

You should look for dates on any summary plan descriptions (SPDs) you have. If your company's SPDs are more than five years old, they are likely out of date. Either the SPD has not been changed to reflect plan changes or (worse) the plan has not been changed to comply with the latest law. If you are concerned about a specific provision, ask the human resources department to confirm that the provision does, in fact, represent the latest version of the plan and the law. If you are still concerned, contact the local or regional office of the Department of Labor's Pension and Welfare Plan Administration and pose the question to that office.

How New Living Patterns Can Conflict with Old Retirement Plans

For many people the retirement benefits provided by their employers will be the largest segment of their retirement income. But as we saw from Alice's experiences, significant retirement benefits will only be available if you worked for one employer for several years or if you contributed heavily to the retirement plan with your own money. For example, data show that on average an employee with a defined benefit plan and ten years of service with her employer could expect her benefits to replace between 10 and 12 percent of wages; with twenty years of service, she could expect between 20 and 23 percent; and with thirty years of service between 29 and 35 percent.[5] Because women frequently change jobs or take time off the payroll, it is more difficult for them to receive the full benefit of employer retirement plans that require long, uninterrupted service.

Originally, retirement plans were designed to reward many years of continuous service. Many still operate that way. This goal may have been appropriate when employers sought to keep employees for decades and when one-earner families were common. Today, employers frequently want employees to move on after a few years. Two-earner families often need one of the earners—still usually the woman—to take time off the payroll to care for families or to relocate. As the experiences of Alice, Susan, Bonnie, and Jennifer have illustrated, these changes in the way we live make some retirement plans less effective for women than the employer may have intended.

Some employers are addressing their changed goals for retirement plans, recognizing that, since they no longer want workers tied to the company solely by the promise of a large pension, the companies should change their retirement plans. Other employers simply want to spend less money for benefits. Both of these desires are fueling a move to defined contribution plans and away from defined benefit plans. Private employer defined benefit plans have shrunk from a high of over 175,000 in 1983 to about 74,400 in 1994, while defined contribution plans have steadily grown from about 207,000 in 1975 to over 615,000 in 1994.[6] As we have seen, because defined contribution plans emphasize the need to begin saving early in your career, you need to begin retirement saving from the first day on the payroll.

Investigate Employer Plans Early, Not at Retirement

To achieve the maximum benefit from employer plans, you must understand how your employer's plans operate. Most employers give you the plans' summary plan descriptions (SPDs) as soon as you join the company. Most employees ignore them. Be the exception—read the SPD. Employers are eager for you to know about and understand your retirement benefits. Employers spend literally millions on these plans and they are happy to publicize them. Getting information won't be a problem.

But you have to do your part. Read and understand the materials the employer gives you. And to plan effectively for maximizing these benefits, you have to read and understand the provisions and act on them early in your career, not two weeks before you plan to quit or retire. This chapter will help by explaining the basic legal framework of some common types of employer retirement plans. Your employer's plans will probably have additional rules. In general, an employer's plan may be more generous than the law requires, but plans may not be more restrictive than outlined here.

Defined Benefit Plans and Defined Contribution Plans: The Basic Differences

You know employer-provided retirement plans come in two basic varieties: *defined benefit plans* and *defined contribution plans.* The first defines the benefit you will receive after you retire. For example, the defined benefit plan might pay you 1 percent of pay times years worked each year in retirement for as long as you live. Under a defined benefit plan, if you live longer than average, you beat the system, because you are guaranteed a payment as long as you live.

In contrast, a defined contribution plan specifies the amount the employer will deposit in a trust fund each year while you work in that firm. Such contributions are usually based on a percentage of your salary. For example, such plans might promise to contribute 5 percent of your pay each year you work for the company. At retirement you have a lump sum of money that you can spend or invest any way you want. If you invest well, you may be able to make the money last for your lifetime and leave some behind for your heirs. But if your investments don't prosper or you live a very long time, you may run out of money.

Which Type Is "Best"?

As we have already seen with the experiences of Alice and her friends, whether a defined benefit plan or a defined contribution plan is "best" depends on

- the specific formula of the plan;
- your age when you are accruing the benefits;
- whether the plan requires you to contribute; and
- how long you stay with the company.

Generally, defined benefit plans are thought to favor older workers who have been with the employer for a long time or who plan to work for the employer for a long time. This is because the money needed to supply defined benefits for a young employee with only a few years of service is very small. Only when a worker is near retirement and has served many years with the employer does the money needed for the benefit reach a significant sum.

By contrast, defined contribution plans are usually considered to be more favorable for young workers with few years on the job. There are several reasons for this. First, the size of the employer contribution is usually not dependent on the number of years worked or the employee's age. The same percentage contribution is made for a 30-year-old employee and for a 60-year-old employee.

Second, a contribution put into an account for a young employee has more years to earn investment income before that employee retires.

For example, assume that Alice, age 60, and Jennifer, age 30, both earn $24,000 a year and receive a contribution of 1 percent of pay this year. That $240 will earn interest for five years before Alice retires, giving her a mere $307 when she retires. But Jennifer's $240 will earn interest for thirty-five years before she retires and give her $1,324 at retirement. (This example assumes a modest 5 percent rate of interest; the differences would be even more dramatic if higher interest rates are used. See Table A.1 in the Appendix and work out your own examples.)

Defined contribution plans are usually more portable than defined benefit plans. Defined contribution plans' values can be easily calculated when an employee leaves. The sum can be transferred to another employer's plan, in some cases, or directly to an IRA. Once invested, the amount can grow. By contrast, many defined benefit pension plans do not permit cash-outs when an employee leaves. Because the payment is fixed as of the date the employee leaves the plan and is based on the employee's salary when she leaves, the benefit does not grow and can be eroded by inflation even before the employee receives the first retirement payment.

For example, if Alice vests in a defined benefit plan in a previous job, but the annual amount for that benefit is frozen for eight years before she retires, preretirement inflation will erode the value of that amount each year.

Even if the pension plan does permit cash-outs, the value of the benefit will be reduced by a "mortality" factor that takes into account the possibility that the employee might have died before collecting the pension. These reductions are not made in defined contribution plans.

Limits on the Amount Your Employer Can Provide

While it is rarely a problem for most women, there are IRS limits on the amount an employer can contribute annually for you under a defined contribution plan and on the amount of benefit you can ultimately receive under a defined benefit plan. These limits are sometimes called the "415 limits," a reference to their Internal Revenue Code section.

Contributions under all an employer's defined contribution plans for an employee in one year may not exceed the *lesser* of $30,000 (will be adjusted for inflation in the future) or 25 percent of the employee's compensation.

Once you retire, annual *benefits* under all defined benefit plans from one employer cannot exceed the *lesser* of 100 percent of employee's compensation or $90,000 adjusted annually for inflation (the 1999 inflation-adjusted dollar amount is $130,000). The benefit limit will be reduced further if you retire prior to Social Security retirement age or prior to having completed ten years of service or participation in the plan.

In calculating your benefits, the employer also cannot consider compensation earned in excess of a specified amount. In 1999, that amount was limited to $160,000. This amount is indexed each year for inflation. For example, if your employer's plan contributed 5 percent per year to your account and you earned $175,000 in 1999, the benefit your employer could contribute for you would be 5 percent of $160,000, not 5 percent of $175,000.

Defined Benefit/Pension Plans

Defined benefit plans are usually what you think of when you hear the word *pension,* so I will refer to defined benefit plans as pensions throughout this chapter. Pensions are the most complicated retirement benefit plan, both for you as an employee to understand and for the employer to fund and administer. As with all nongovernment employer-provided retirement plans, pension plans are regulated by the Internal Revenue Service and the Department of Labor, which are responsible for all ERISA-covered employee benefits. But most pension plans are also regulated by another quasi-government agency, the Pension Benefit Guaranty Corporation, the agency that partially insures the pension plan's assets to be sure there are adequate funds to pay your promised benefits when you retire.

Common Formulas for Pension Calculation

Most pension plans base their formula for retirement benefit payments on a percentage of your "compensation" times your "years of service" with the company. The formula used for the defined benefit plans discussed in the examples of Alice, Susan, Bonnie, and Jennifer was 1.25 percent of the final five years of pay per year of service with the company up to a maximum of thirty years. Under this formula, if you earn $25,000 a year after twenty years with the company, your payment per year would be:

1.25% $\times$ $25,000 $\times$ 20 years = $6,250 per year.

Such payments are usually made on a monthly basis, so you would receive $520.83 a month for life.

Other common formulas are a percentage of salary, for example, 50 percent of compensation, or a flat dollar amount per year of service, such as $2 times years of service per month. Flat dollar amounts are frequently seen in union-sponsored pension plans.

Different Definitions of "Compensation"

These formulas seem simple enough, but in actual operation several complex factors come into play. *Compensation* can be defined in many ways. For example, it could be the average of compensation over your career (so-called "career average plans"), your compensation over the last five years you worked, or your compensation over the highest five years of compensation you received (or over some other period of years).

There are other variations of these definitions, and they can have a big effect on your actual benefit. For example, a "career average" definition of compensation will produce a much lower benefit than a definition of compensation based on your highest five years of compensation. A definition based on the highest year of compensation, obviously, provides the largest benefit.

For example, assume you have worked for Acme for twenty years, currently make $25,000 annually, and will receive a retirement benefit of 1 percent of compensation times years of service. You are retiring this year. If the plan uses final year's compensation, your annual benefit will be $5,000. If the plan uses the average of the highest five years, the annual benefit would be $4,600 (assuming raises of $1,000 per year each of the past five years). If the plan is career average plan, your earliest years of compensation will be averaged in to determine the benefit. Assuming you started at $10,000 and received steady increases each year, your annual benefit would be far less than the benefit calculated under other models.

Your benefit will also be affected by the earnings included within the plan's definition of compensation. For example, depending on the plan, compensation may or may not include overtime, bonuses, commissions, matching contributions made by the employer to other retirement plans the employer sponsors, or amounts from your paycheck that are deducted before taxes to pay for your health insurance or other benefits.

If you have been working overtime or used bonuses to meet daily living expenses and your retirement plan does not take those earnings into account in calculating your pension benefits, you may have a more difficult time living on your pension than you anticipated. The plan's definition of compensation is a good example of information you should have and consider early in your career while you can still adjust your personal retirement savings plan accordingly.

For example, as a salesperson you receive a very modest base salary of $10,000, but you earn annual commissions of about $40,000. Your employer's plan will pay you an annual benefit of 2 percent of "compensation" and you have been with the firm for ten years. If only your salary is counted, your pension benefit if you retired today would be $2,000 annually. If your total compensation of salary and commissions are counted, your pension benefit would be $10,000 per year. In order to plan the amount of money you need to save for retirement, you need to know now whether your pension will be $2,000 or $10,000.

Defining Years of Service to Determine Pension Benefits

Years of employment or so-called years of service also have meanings. A single pension plan may even use different definitions of "years of service" for different purposes. For example, plans frequently require an employee to work for a year before she is eligible to participate in the plan. In such cases the first year of service may not be counted for benefit calculation purposes, but will be counted for vesting purposes.

Years of service for vesting purposes may not be the same as years of service for benefits calculation purposes. Recall that the concept of vesting determines when you have an irrevocable right to the benefits you have earned. By law you must either have such a right to all benefits earned to date after five years, the so-called cliff vesting, or earn a right to benefits gradually at the rate of 20 percent per year after your second year of service, until you become 100 percent vested in all benefits after seven years of service. Plans can provide for faster vesting. Prior to 1989, plans could delay vesting for up to ten years for cliff vesting and permit graduated vesting over fifteen years. Plans could also permit vesting under a "rule of 45" whereby vesting occurred gradually under a schedule based on your combined age and years of service.

Frequently, the years of service used to calculate the benefits are referred to as "credited years of service." As with vesting, the years in which you worked at least 1,000 hours are legally required to be counted. For example, when Jennifer works part-time and later moves to a full-time position with the same employer, her part-time years will not count as years of service if she did not work more than 1,000 hours a year during those part-time years.

The Difference Between Accruing Benefits and Vesting in Benefits

By law an employer may not prevent an employee from participating in the employer's retirement plan for more than one year after the employee begins full-time employment, or two years if the plan provides immediate 100 percent vesting of benefits. If the employer's plan only allows employees to *enter* the plan at certain times during the year, a waiting period before the plan entry date may be tacked on. Plans must permit employees to enter the plan at least twice a year.

For example, in February Jennifer goes to work at Acme, which has a pension plan and a 401(k) plan. Both plans require employees to work for one year before they can participate. The plans also provide that employees may enter the plan only on January 1 or July 1. Jennifer is eligible for the plan the following February, but she will not be able to contribute to the 401(k) plan or have her service counted for the pension plan until the next plan entry date, which is July 1. So Jennifer loses seventeen months of benefits because of the participation rules.

Once she begins to participate in the plan, she begins to accrue benefits. If the employer's pension plan gives 1 percent of pay per year of participation, on the July following the July she entered the plan, she will have *accrued*, or earned the right to, a future benefit of 1 percent of pay for the one year of participation. But if she leaves after that year, she will receive no benefit, because she did not vest in the benefit she accrued. Until she vests, the accrued benefit is simply a contingent promise of the employer to provide the benefit. Once the initial vesting period has elapsed, Jennifer will own all benefits as she accrues them. She does not have to wait after accruing the benefits to actually own them.

Receiving Benefits: Life Stream Versus Lump Sum

Pensions are designed to be paid in regular installments over the course of your lifetime after you retire. This is called the *annuity* form of payment as opposed to a *lump sum* form of payment. The concept is to provide you with an income for as long as you live. These payments are not adjusted for inflation in private plans, except in very rare cases. Even among large employers, only about 28 percent of plans offer an automatic, plan-required benefit increase, but about 78 percent of pensions provided by federal, state, and local governments frequently do provide for some inflation adjustment, usually referred to as a cost-of-living adjustment or COLA.[7] If you live for several years after you retire and/or inflation increases rapidly, the buying power of your monthly annuity payment is likely to erode significantly.

Some pension plans do permit retirees to receive the current value of their pension plan in a lump sum. This sum will be calculated based on the retiree's age at retirement and current interest rates. The lump-sum amount equals the total amount that the retiree would have received had she fulfilled her life expectancy according to established mortality tables, discounted for the amount that money will earn over the period until her expected death. The mortality factor represents a reduction based on the probability the retiree might have died earlier than her established mortality, but is now guaranteed to have the money regardless of the time of her death.

The law requires plans to use a single table for all employees, whether they are men or women. Most plans use a unisex mortality table, or a mortality table based on male life expectancy. These tables anticipate fewer years of life than a female mortality table, because women live longer than men. Because of this difference, a healthy retiring woman will almost always receive a lump sum lower in value than the amount she might ultimately receive by taking payments over her lifetime.

Choosing Payment Forms If You Are Married

Under ERISA plans, if you have a spouse, the pension payment form will automatically be paid as a joint and survivor annuity, unless you and your spouse request a different form of payment. In order to make up for the possibility that the payments will have to be paid over two lifetimes—yours and your spouse's—the monthly payment you receive will be reduced at the beginning of your retirement. Once you die, the payment to the survivor may also be reduced, depending on the provisions of the plan. Joint and survivor annuities are almost always a bad method of pension payment for a woman, because her husband is not likely to outlive her and the reduction in benefits during her lifetime will have been for naught.

If you die before you retire, your spouse may receive a payment at the time when you would have reached retirement age. This payment form is a "qualified preretirement survivor annuity." Chapter 14 discusses the payment forms in more detail.

How Your Employer Plan Ties in with Social Security

In a retirement plan—whether it is a defined benefit or a defined contribution plan—employers may take into account their contributions toward Social Security taxes on your salary by "integrating" the plan with Social Security. In more up-to-date legal language, the plan is said to recognize "permitted disparity" between wages earned that fall below the Social Security taxable wage base and wages earned above the Social Security taxable wage base. These adjustments for Social Security payments are more common in defined benefit pension plans than in defined contribution plans.

A Brief History of Pension Integration

Prior to the Tax Reform Act of 1986, such Social Security integration could dramatically reduce benefits. For low income workers, Social Security integration sometimes totally wiped out the pension benefit. For example, a pension plan might provide for 1.5 percent of compensation times years of service, minus an amount equal to one half of Social Security. For a woman who had an average compensation of $15,000 and worked for fifteen years the formula would be:

$15,000 × 1.5% × 15 years = $3,375
Full Social Security benefit = $7,650
Half Social Security benefit = $3,825

The half Social Security benefit, $3,875, exceeds the benefit calculated under the pension, thus no pension payment is due.

Workers who thought they would have a pension found at retirement that, in fact, the pension was nonexistent. Social Security replaced enough of their wages to satisfy the pension plan formula with no further payments from the pension plan. These reductions were permitted by law, so the employees and retirees had no right to claim fraud. The employee simply never read the fine print and calculated the complex formula for the benefits with Social Security. But retirees felt defrauded, regardless of the legality of such reductions.

After a series of congressional hearings in which tearful retirees described their disappointment and financial difficulties caused by the Social Security integration rules, Congress changed the rules effective in 1989. While plans can still recognize Social Security benefits in calculating benefits under the plan, the retirement plan benefit cannot be reduced to less than half what it would have been if there had been no recognition of Social Security.

There are other extremely complex rules surrounding the use of permitted disparity based on Social Security. The bottom line is that pension plans must always give some credit for wages earned at or below the Social Security wage base. For example, a permissible pension plan using Social Security integration or permitted disparity could have a formula such as:

1% of pay up to the Social Security wage base ($72,600 in 1999),
plus
1.5% of pay in excess of the Social Security wage base,
times
years of service.

If Joan's pay as defined by the plan were $75,000 and she had worked thirty years when she retired, her annual benefit would be:

1% of $72,600,
plus
1.5% of $2,400 [$75,000 − $72,600],
times
30 years,
equals
($726 + $36) × 30 = $22,860 per year

By contrast, if the plan did not take into account Social Security, by providing a lower benefit for wages at or below the Social Security wage base, she would receive 1½ percent of all pay and her annual benefit would be $33,750 per year. Of course the employer could also argue that, without taking into account his payments to Social Security, he could only afford to fund a plan that paid 1 percent of pay times years of service. In that case Joan's benefit would be only $22,500 per year.

Pension plans that take Social Security into account in calculating benefit payments will spell this out in the SPD. If you have a pension plan with your employer, be sure you read this section of the SPD carefully and remember to take into consideration the effects of this Social Security adjustment.

Additionally, while the laws have changed to limit the reductions that can be made for Social Security, the changes were not effective until 1989. For benefits earned before 1989, the old rules can apply and greater reductions can be made. A more typical illustration of Joan's case would show the calculation using the old rules for Joan's first twenty-six years of service and the new Social Security integration rules only for those benefits earned in the last four years. The SPD should explain any reductions made under the old rules. These rules are complicated and even pension experts frequently must read the plan provisions or SPDs several times to get the precise meaning. Don't be intimidated: if you don't understand this section of the SPD the first time you read it, read it a few more times. If you still have problems, ask your employer to explain it with an example based on your benefits earned to date.

Advantages of Defined Benefit Plans

Guaranteed Payments

Defined benefit pension plans guarantee a specific benefit payment as long as you live. You don't have to worry about how to invest the money or how to divide the money to ensure it lasts a lifetime. Indeed, as discussed earlier, if you are willing to receive a lower monthly payment, you can even be sure it lasts to cover the life of your husband or, in some plans, another beneficiary such as a dependent child.

No Investment Decisions Required

Unlike defined contribution plans, where the employee is frequently encouraged to contribute her own money, which in turn requires decisions on how much should be contributed and how it should be invested, with a defined benefit plan, the employee usually has no investment decisions. The plan trustees decide how to invest the money and the actuaries, guided by law and regulation, tell the employer how much money to contribute.

No Investment Risk for the Employee

The employer bears all the investment risk of the plan's trust fund. If the investments made by the trust don't earn as much money as projected, the employer has to supply more money to the trust to be sure the trust is fully funded to pay the promised benefits. By contrast, in a defined contribution plan, such as a profit-sharing plan or 401(k) plan, if the assets in the employee's account don't earn acceptable returns, the employee simply has a smaller account than she expected. The employer is not required to contribute any additional money.

Benefits Guaranteed by PBGC

The defined benefit plan payments are guaranteed by the Pension Benefit Guaranty Corporation. Even if there are insufficient funds in the plan trust, plan beneficiaries will receive all or most of their benefits. Some very large benefits may be reduced, if PBGC has to pay, but minimum benefits will always be available.

Disadvantages of Defined Benefit Plans

Low Benefits When You Are Young

By design, defined benefit pension plans provide the greatest advantage to older workers who stay with one employer for several years. Pension plans' benefits are heavily back loaded. This means the benefits build up very slowly for a younger employee with little service. This is not because old age and wile conspire to cheat youth and enthusiasm. It's simply a factor of the time value of money we discussed in Chapter 3.

This is how it works. The benefits are based in part on number of years of service. Obviously, the fewer years of service, the smaller the benefit. But the plan investment for the employee is also based on the amount of money needed today to provide benefits for the employee when she reaches retirement age, usually 65.

Assume Ruth has worked at Acme for fifteen years, since she was 20, and assume the pension plan formula is 1 percent of compensation times years of service. The benefit she has accrued after fifteen years of service at age 35 in today's dollars is the amount of money invested today at a reasonable rate of interest (spelled out in the pension plan document), which will provide her with 15 percent of her pay when she reaches age 65. When Ruth is 35, even though she has fifteen years of service, this amount of money is relatively small because she is only entitled to an amount that would pay her 15 percent of her salary thirty years from now. The amount of money needed to fund that obligation is small, because it has thirty years to grow with investments.

Assume Shirley is an employee with fifteen years of service and making the same amount of pay as Ruth, but Shirley is 60 today. Shirley's accrued benefit is much larger than Ruth's because the amount of money needed to provide Shirley's 15 percent of pay benefit at age 65 has only five years to grow.

This growth period between the time the money is contributed and the retirement date of the employee is also the reason why defined contribution plans favor younger workers. The money contributed to the defined contribution plan has more time to earn income before the employee retires. Pension plans reward long service and encourage loyalty to the employer. Both of these goals are admirable. But some argue the goals may not fit the reality of the twenty-first century.

Plan Termination May Erode Expectations

Another disadvantage of pension plans occurs when a plan, which an employee is counting on for her retirement, is terminated long before she is ready to retire. If the employer does terminate the plan, the employee is entitled to all benefits she has accrued to date. But as we have seen above, the accrued benefit for a young—or even middle-aged—employee may be quite small in relation to what she had expected if she had worked until actual retirement age.

No Adjustment for Inflation

Finally, pension plans are rarely indexed for inflation once the benefits are accrued or the payments begin. A few years of high inflation can substantially reduce the buying power of the monthly pension payment. Because women live longer than men, they face more years of inflation eroding the payment. If inflation is particularly high when an employee retires and has the choice to take annuity payments or a lump sum, she may attempt to avoid inflation's ravages by taking the lump sum and investing it. But if inflation jumps after she has retired, there is no way to change the benefit payments.

Defined Contribution Plans

Common Traits

Defined contribution plans come in many varieties, each with a number of options and alternatives. There are some elements common to all defined contribution plans. First and most obvious, the employer makes a contribution for each employee. The amount and timing of that contribution and the method for calculating it for each employee are spelled out in the plan document. Unlike defined benefit plans, the employer does not make a general contribution based on actuarial calculations of the work force as a whole. Defined contribution plans frequently permit the employees to contribute to the plan on their own account. Defined benefit plans, by contrast, rarely permit employee contributions. For recordkeeping purposes, each employee has her own "individual account," unlike a defined benefit plan. The amount in your individual account will depend not only on the employer's contributions but on any contributions you are permitted to make, as well as on the earnings of the contributions.

Investment Choices

Many defined contribution plans give you some options for how the money in your account is invested. With these options, you become responsible, to a degree, for the growth of your retirement account. Remember that, unlike defined benefit plans, the Pension Benefit Guaranty Corporation does not guarantee any of the funds in defined contribution plans—an important distinction from PBGC's role in protecting defined benefit assets.

Where investment options are available, the plans usually offer four or more different investment choices. The employee is given the option to invest portions of her defined contribution individual account in these different choices. The investment choices range from "guaranteed income contracts," which provide a fixed rate of return for a given period, to bond or stock funds. The latter funds may be mutual funds that are also available on the open market or they may be funds set up and managed by the trustees of the plan. These are usually a mixture of growth funds, income funds, and fixed-rate funds. One of the investment choices is commonly the employer's stock, if the stock is commonly traded.

As with most investments, the higher the rates of return, the higher the risk of loss resulting from market fluctuation. Investments that are safer are likely to have lower rates of return. The major exceptions to this rule that the lower the rate of return, the lower the risk to your investment—in my opinion—are the so-called *guaranteed income contracts* or *fixed income contracts*. Note that your investment in these contracts is in *no way* guaranteed by anyone other than the company sponsoring the contract. The only thing that is "guaranteed" is the rate of interest, and that guarantee is usually only for one year. The assets in the contract are dedicated to repaying the investment in the contract, but those assets may or may not hold their value.

Yet these contracts offer a substantially lower rate of return than other funds offered in many defined contribution plan investment elections, and thousands of employees invest in GICs, as they are called in the trade, believing that their investment money is as safe as in a certificate of deposit. Nothing could be further from the truth. Investing in GICs may offer the worst of both worlds—a low rate of return and potentially higher risk. After all, if you invest your defined contribution assets in a mutual fund, the value will go up and down, it is true, but to lose your total investment, every company the fund has invested in has to go bankrupt. With an individual GIC investment, only one company, the GIC sponsor, has to go bankrupt for you to lose all your retirement plan investment.

Employees, even sophisticated employees, make a retirement planning mistake by investing their accounts in the lowest-paying funds because these funds tend to be the most conservative and safe investments among the options. As a result, the account's growth is dramatically reduced over the years. For example, if you invested $4,000 per year for twenty-five years in your 401(k) plan in the conservative GIC account paying 4 percent, at the end of that time you would have $166,584. But if you invested it in a mutual fund that returned 6 percent, you would have $219,460. A fund paying you 9 percent would provide a lump sum of $338,800 and one averaging 14 percent would give you $716,000. Clearly, in a defined contribution plan, allowing you to choose your investments, your life style in retirement will depend to some extent on the risks you're willing to assume during your working years with your retirement savings.

Extremely conservative investments with low rates of return are an especially poor investment for young employees. Young employees have a great deal of time to accrue investment earnings. Even if a young employee's investment has a low return or drops in value for a year or two, the younger employee has plenty of time to wait before she needs the money. As an employee nears retirement, it may make sense to move to more conservative investments to preserve the retirement nest egg, asset value, but for younger employees conservative investments cheat them of growth in their money.

Receiving Benefits: Payment in a Lump Sum

Defined contribution plans usually pay the retirement benefit to you in a lump sum when you retire or leave the employer. You are responsible for investing and spending the lump sum to give you an income for the rest of your life. Some defined contribution plans allow you to receive an annuity form of payment— that is, in regular payments over the course of years. Such annuities may or may not guarantee payment for a lifetime.

Advantages of Defined Contribution Plans

- The contributions for younger, less senior employees (a common status for women because they change jobs frequently) are proportionately larger than they would be under a defined benefit plan.
- Defined contribution plans frequently permit you to add your own money to the plan, thus offering you a tax-deferred place to hold your retirement savings.
- You may have a choice of specific investments.
- Defined contribution plans are more portable, meaning that these plans are more likely to let you take a lump sum when you leave your employer. You can then invest the lump sum in ways to protect its value from the ravages of inflation.

Disadvantages of Defined Contribution Plans

- You bear the risk of investment of the plan's assets. If the investments in the plan don't do well, you will simply have less money than you had planned on for retirement. The employer will not provide more money to the plan just because the investments don't earn as much as originally expected.
- The plan's funds are not guaranteed by the Pension Benefit Guaranty Corporation.
- The employer may be placing too much of the burden of retirement saving on you by providing a very small employer contribution or no contribution at all.

Types of Defined Contribution Plans

Let's look at some of the different defined contribution plans and their unique advantages and disadvantages: profit-sharing plans, money purchase pension plans, thrift plans (also called savings plans), 401(k) plans, stock bonus plans, employee stock ownership plans (ESOPs), hybrid plans (target and cash balance plans), and simplified employee pensions (SEPs).

Profit-Sharing Plans

Profit-sharing plans are really misnamed in some respects. The employer does not need to have profits in order to make contributions to the profit-sharing plan. Nor is the employer required to contribute to the profit-sharing plan because the company makes a profit in a given year.

Profit-sharing plans, when used as retirement programs, simply permit—but do not require—an employer to make a contribution to your retirement account when business is good. A profit-sharing scheme gives the employer the discretion to fund the defined contribution retirement plan from year to year.

Not all profit-sharing plans are used as retirement plans. There are three basic types of profit-sharing plans: the current or cash profit-sharing plan, the combination profit-sharing plan, and the deferred profit-sharing plan.

CURRENT OR CASH PROFIT-SHARING PLAN

In this type, the employer gives a profit share in cash to the employee. This money is immediately taxable to the employee. Current or cash plans are not used as retirement plans, although the smart retirement planner will use this usually unexpected sum to fund an IRA.

COMBINATION PROFIT-SHARING PLAN

Here the employer declares the profit share, but the employee gets to decide whether to take the money in cash, pay taxes on the money, and use it as she wishes, or to defer the profit-share money into the retirement savings plan set up by the employer. If she elects to put the money in the profit-sharing retirement plan, she pays no tax on the money—or on its earnings—until she withdraws the money from the plan.

DEFERRED PROFIT-SHARING PLAN

In this plan, the employer permits the profit-sharing contribution to be used only for deferrals into the retirement plan. The profit share is set aside in each employee's account. The employee pays no tax on this account until she retires or otherwise takes the money out of the account. Earnings on this money accumulate in the profit-sharing account and are not taxed until the employee receives the money from her account.

PROFIT-SHARING FORMULAS

Usually the contribution the employee receives is based on her compensation. For example, a profit-sharing formula may be based on the ratio of an employee's salary as compared to the total payroll. That percentage of the profit-sharing contribution will be deposited in the employee's account. For example, if Alice earns $30,000 and the employer's total payroll is $1 million, Alice will receive 3 percent of the profit-sharing contribution. If the employer's total profit-sharing contribution is $100,000, Alice will receive $3,000 in her profit-sharing account for that year.

Some profit-sharing plans base contributions on a simple percentage of compensation—for example, 5 percent. Profit-sharing contributions can also be based on a formula that combines compensation, age, and/or years of service. For example: employees over age 21 with one to five years of service might receive 2 percent of pay, employees over age 30 with five to ten years of service receive 4 percent of pay, employees over age 40 with ten to fifteen years of service receive 6 percent, and employees over age 45 with over fifteen years receive 10 percent of pay. Such plans are referred to as age- and service-weighted profit-sharing plans. Such plans are becoming popular, especially in smaller companies, because they enable an older, higher paid worker to receive more benefits than she would under an ordinary profit-sharing plan, while also enabling the plan to satisfy certain IRS nondiscrimination rules.

Profit-sharing contributions may be made in cash or the employer's stock. If the employer's stock is used, the plan also may be referred to as a stock bonus plan or employee stock ownership plan, also called an ESOP (pronounced "e-sop," like Aesop's fables—you'll see why later). ESOPs and stock bonus plans are discussed in detail later in the chapter.

ADVANTAGES OF PROFIT-SHARING PLANS

- Like most defined contribution plans, profit-sharing plans may give younger, less senior employees proportionately larger benefits than they would receive under a defined benefit plan.
- The account balance in a profit-sharing plan is easy to understand and easy to calculate.
- Profit-sharing plans, like most defined contribution plans, are more likely than defined benefit plans to permit lump-sum cash-outs, if the employee terminates prior to retirement age. Consequently, the plan usually offers more portability of benefits.

DISADVANTAGES OF PROFIT-SHARING PLANS

- The employer has the discretion each year to fund the plan and may not want to make contributions every year.

Money Purchase Pension Plans

Money purchase pension plans require the employer to contribute an amount each year based on a percentage of your salary. There is no discretion to eliminate a contribution in any year. (Of course, as with any employer-provided plan, the employer still has the right to terminate the plan entirely.)

Money purchase plans are commonly integrated with Social Security. If the plan is integrated, the contribution percentage for salary below the Social Security wage base will be lower than the contribution for salary above the wage base. A money purchase pension plan might be integrated with a formula such as:

3% of compensation up to the amount of the Social Security taxable wage base for the year in which the contribution is being made,
plus
5% of any compensation earned above the amount of the Social Security taxable wage base.

These yearly contributions, plus earnings, provide your "pension" at retirement. Unlike other defined contribution plans, the payout for these plans is frequently in an annuity form.

ADVANTAGES AND DISADVANTAGES OF MONEY PURCHASE PLANS

Money purchase plans share most of the advantages and disadvantages common to defined contribution plans. But with money purchase plans, the employer's annual contribution is not optional. The employer must contribute to the plan each year, unless the plan is terminated. This lack of discretion is an advantage for the employee and a disadvantage for the employer.

Thrift or Savings Plans

Thrift or savings plans basically require the employee to fund at least part of her own retirement. A thrift plan may consist of only the employee's contributions and the earnings on those contributions. Or, if the employer does make contributions to the thrift plan, the employee generally must contribute to the plan in order to receive those employer contributions. Frequently, the employer contributions are in the form of a matching contribution.

As with profit-sharing plans, each employee has a separate account to track her contributions and the contributions of the employer, if any, and the earnings and losses on those contributions. Thrift plans, too, may permit the employee to choose among a number of different investment funds. The employee is always vested in her own money saved in the thrift plan and in earnings on that money, so she is entitled to her account when she leaves the employer for any reason.

TAX TREATMENT OF THRIFT PLANS

An employee generally contributes to the thrift plan with money on which she has already paid taxes. If you contribute on an after-tax basis, you obviously will not receive a tax break on the amount you contributed during your working years. When you retire, you will pay no tax on your contributions as they are withdrawn, because you have already paid tax on that amount. You will pay tax on the employer's contribution and the earnings on all contributions, because that money has not been taxed before.

Thrift plans may also be designed to allow employees to contribute with their salary before the money has been taxed. If you contribute on this pretax basis, the thrift plan is called a 401(k) plan after the section of the Internal Revenue Code that permits such pretax contributions. These 401(k) plans have almost completely replaced after-tax thrift plans. Because 401(k) plans are covered by such complex rules, they deserve separate discussion.

401(k) Plans: Cash or Deferred Arrangements

401(k) plans are thrift plans in which you contribute dollars before federal taxes are paid or withheld on that amount; that is, contributions are on a pretax basis. Such plans are also known as cash or deferred arrangements—CODAs for short—because you may take the money as part of your ordinary salary in cash or you can "defer" that part of your salary into the 401(k) retirement plan. Another name for 401(k) plans is "salary reduction plans" because you "reduce" your take-home salary by the amount you contribute to the 401(k).

IMMEDIATE TAX SAVINGS

The money you contribute to your 401(k) plan will not be subject to withholding for federal income tax, and in most states there will also be no withholding for state taxes. The money will be subject to FICA taxes for Social Security and Medicare and to unemployment taxes. The benefit of this pretax savings is clear from the following example. Let's say Alice decides she can save another $100 from each of her biweekly paychecks. Alice earns just under $37,000, so she generally pays a 15 percent federal tax rate and a 2 percent state income tax rate. She could use a savings account or she could use her employer's 401(k) plan, as shown in Table 7.1.

As Table 7.1 shows, Alice can save almost $450 more each year using the 401(k) account than she could using an employer's after-tax thrift plan or a regular savings account. That extra $450 per year in the 401(k) plan for ten years will give her over $6,500.

Even at the lowest federal tax brackets, for every dollar earned, you have only 85 cents to save through ordinary savings plans. The first 15 cents must be paid in federal taxes. In a 401(k) plan, you only need a dollar to save a dollar. As with other defined contribution plans, you do not pay taxes on any employer contributions to the 401(k) plan or on any earnings on your account until you retire.

Table 7.1
Savings Account Versus 401(k) Plan

	After-Tax Savings Account	401(k) Account
Amount to Be Saved per Year	$2,600	$2,600
Less Federal Tax (15%)	390	0
Less State Tax (2%)	52	0
Actual Amount Available to Save	$2,158	$2,600

POPULARITY

Popular with employees and employers, 401(k) plans have grown phenomenally over the last decade even though they are governed by extremely complex tax rules. The number of 401(k) plans increased from 1,703 in 1983 to 174,945 in 1994, and the growth continues.[8]

Employers like 401(k) plans because they can be inexpensive and employees appreciate them. The employee is essentially funding her own retirement plan. Additionally, the 401(k) plan forces the employee to think about the need for retirement savings and requires her to take some responsibility for her retirement security. Unlike a pension plan, where the employee has no idea how much the employer is contributing for her each year, if the employer contributes to the 401(k) on her behalf, the employee knows exactly how much was contributed. Human nature as it is, most people appreciate a definite and known contribution to the 401(k) plan more than the vague build-up of pension rights that are difficult to see in terms of precise dollars until actual retirement.

Employees like 401(k) plans because the plans are usually paid as a lump sum when workers leave the employer, are easily understood, and provide both significant immediate tax breaks for current salary and long-term tax shelter for the earnings on the salary saved in the 401(k). And, when you move to a new employer, the 401(k) account can easily go with you in most cases. You can transfer the 401(k) money to the new employer's plan, if the new employer accepts transfers, or you can put the money into an IRA.

Because your account will consist primarily of your own money and earnings on that money, which is always fully vested, the issue of vesting is less important than with a defined benefit plan. In a 401(k) plan, vesting rules affect only the amounts, if any, the employer contributes. Additionally, because the 401(k) plan benefit consists of your individual account, which is easily and obviously calculated, you know the value of your retirement benefit. By contrast, pension plans use a number of factors including years of service, age of the employee, and number of years to retirement to calculate the current value of benefits. The average mortal cannot calculate the current cash value of her pension plan without an actuary.

BASIC IRS RULES FOR 401(K) PLANS

Limits on Contributions

Several limits apply to the amount you and your employer can contribute to the plan each year. The *lowest of these limits* always applies.

- You and your employer may not contribute more than 25 percent of your pay to a 401(k) in any one year.
- You and your employer may not contribute more than $30,000 to the 401(k) and any other defined contribution plans the employer may have.
- You may not contribute more than $10,000 to the 401(k) in 1999. This $10,000 limit is indexed annually for inflation. This $10,000 limit does not include any amount the employer may contribute.

For example, assume Ruth, who earns $85,000 annually, elected in December 1998 to contribute 11 percent of her salary on a pretax basis in 1999. Her $9,350 contribution meets both the percentage limit and the 1999 dollar limit of $10,000. But in February she gets a raise to $95,000. Her 11 percent elected contribution, even with the lower contribution for the month of January, would exceed the $10,000 limit. She must notify her employer to reduce the amount of her contribution so she will be within the limits.

Even though most employers will automatically make adjustments to prevent an employee from overcontributing, Ruth should not rely totally on her employer to prevent excess contribution. If the employer does not stop the excess contribution, Ruth could face tax problems. If the employer doesn't notify her in time, Ruth may have to file an amended federal tax return and perhaps an amended state return as well. If the mistake is not corrected within a year after the overcontribution, the money in the 401(k) account may be frozen. Ruth will have to pay taxes on the contribution and its earnings twice—once in the year the overcontribution is discovered and again when she withdraws that money at retirement. The inconvenience of overcontributing is simply too great to rely completely on your employer.

Some 401(k) plans also allow you to contribute after-tax money, which is not subject to the $10,000 limits, but is subject to the 25 percent of compensation and $30,000 limits. Although you don't get an immediate tax break for these contributions, the earnings on them are not taxed until you withdraw the money.

Withdrawals Before Retirement Age

Congress designed and intended 401(k) plans to be retirement plans, not savings accounts—regardless of how your employer may try to sell the plan to you as a savings account. By law, your employer's 401(k) plan generally cannot distribute money to you unless you "separate from service" with that employer. Once you separate from service with the employer sponsoring the 401(k) plan, you can delay paying taxes and any early withdrawal penalties on the money from your 401(k), if you put your money into an IRA or another employer's plan within sixty days of receiving it. Even when you separate from service, plans are not required to distribute your 401(k) holdings to you until you reach retirement age. In fact most plans do distribute the money to you once you leave the employer, if you choose to receive it.

If you don't put your 401(k) plan distributions into an IRA or another employer's plan, in addition to the income tax you will pay on your 401(k) distributions, you will pay an additional 10 percent penalty for early withdrawal of the money unless you have received your 401(k) account because you have retired, reached at least 59½ years old, become disabled, or died. The only exceptions to the 10 percent penalty are

- payments made in equal annual amounts over your expected lifetime;
- payments for tax deductible medical expenses, if such expenses exceed 7½ percent of your income; and
- payments for health insurance premiums, if you are unemployed and have received more than twelve consecutive weeks of unemployment benefits.

Even in these cases you will still pay income tax on the amounts distributed to you.

Hardship Withdrawals

Plans may be designed to permit 401(k) plan withdrawals before separation of service, if you experience a hardship. Plans are not required to permit hardship distributions, but many plans do. Even if your plan permits such distributions, you still will pay income tax on the amount you withdraw and the 10 percent early withdrawal penalty tax (unless you meet one of the penalty exceptions listed previously).

Technically, the IRS will permit the 401(k) plan administrator to determine what constitutes hardship. But if a plan makes the wrong decision in even one case, it can lose its tax-exempt status. As a result, few 401(k) plans permit hardship withdrawals except in cases that the IRS has stated will be "deemed to constitute an immediate and heavy financial need." The general rule is that such a need will be deemed to exist only if the money is needed because you:

- are about to be evicted or your mortgage is about to be foreclosed,
- must have the money to make tuition payments for yourself or a child (this does not include dorm or living expenses),

- have or will incur substantial medical expenses, or
- will use the money for the purchase of a principal residence.

As noted above, if the withdrawal is for medical expenses, you may be exempt from the 10 percent penalty for only the amount of those expenses exceeding 7½ percent of your income.

If your plan relies on these *deemed hardship* rules, you will be further punished for the withdrawal. The law will not permit you to continue or begin contributing to the plan again for at least twelve months after you made the deemed hardship withdrawal. You will have lost the opportunity to contribute twelve months of retirement savings, as well as earnings on those savings and any employer match you might have received, in addition to losing the withdrawn amount and paying taxes and penalty on the money.

If the plan sets its own standards for hardship, you may avoid the prohibition against contributing for twelve months. However, you should be prepared to prove to your employer your precise financial position, including the fact you have sought other loans and been refused.

In addition to these limits, you must show that you have no other resources available to you. You may withdraw no more than the amount needed to meet the hardship expenses and pay the taxes and penalties due on the withdrawal.

Loans on 401(k)s: The Good News

Because the hardship withdrawal rules are so strict, many employers permit loans from the 401(k) plan. Under the law, you may borrow against the amount you have contributed to your 401(k) plan. These loans must be at market interest rates and cannot extend for more than five years except for a mortgage. Loans may not exceed $50,000 or half of the amount in your account, whichever is less. The good news is that many 401(k) plans will credit your account with the interest you paid on the loan. So you literally borrow the money from yourself and you reap the interest.

The Bad News: You May Be Cheating Yourself Out of Retirement Savings

The bad news is the amount you are paying yourself in interest on the loan will probably be far lower than the amount you would have earned had you left the money in the plan and invested it in something else. For example, Lisa takes a loan from her 401(k) of $30,000 payable over five years at a 6 percent interest rate. But when that $30,000 was in the plan, it was earning 12 percent. Had she left the money in the plan, she would have earned $22,860 on her $30,000 during that time. And that $22,860 will continue to earn tax-deferred dollars until she retires, increasing her account even more. By contrast Lisa will pay herself only about

$6,500 in interest over the course of the loan. By taking the loan, Lisa has cheated herself of over $16,000 in retirement savings.

Special 401(k) Nondiscrimination Rules

As with all qualified retirement plans, 401(k) plans may not discriminate among employees by limiting the plan to only highly paid employees or by giving other preferences to highly paid employees. In addition to the rules on vesting, participation, and contribution and benefit amounts, 401(k) plans are subject to very detailed and complex rules regarding how much highly compensated employees—generally those earning over $80,000 per year—may contribute on average as compared with other employees' contributions. These rules require the employer to test the plan each year to be sure the contributions comply with the rules.

Since compliance with 401(k) nondiscrimination rules is the employer's responsibility, why do you as an employee care? Because, if you are a highly compensated employee, the amount of money you can contribute to your 401(k) account may be reduced below the annual $10,000 limit if your employer's lower-paid employees did not, on average, put a large enough percentage of their money into the 401(k). Another reason for concern is that many of the same problems associated with overcontributing in excess of the dollar limit apply to contributions exceeding the nondiscrimination limits.

If you are not highly compensated, you also care, because the employer will be taking steps to encourage you to increase your contributions, such as providing matching contributions. In rare cases, the employer may even give the lower-paid employees additional nonmatching contributions designed to increase the percentage of salary saved by the lower-paid.

Because highly paid employees are likely to have more discretionary income to save than other employees, more highly paid employees are likely to participate and set aside a higher percentage of salary. On average the participation rate among nonhighly paid employees is 59 percent, while 81 percent of highly compensated employees participate.[9] These limiting rules can dramatically lower the amount you may contribute to the 401(k) plan, if you fall into the definition of "highly compensated." For example, according to *Forbes* magazine, the 401(k) contribution averages for lower-paid employees at a major hotel chain were so low one year that the highly compensated employees were permitted to contribute less than $2,000 that year. If you are relying on a 401(k) plan to be your primary employer-provided retirement plan, this kind of limitation could dramatically reduce your retirement security if it continued year after year.

Obviously, these rules place a high premium on significant contributions by all employees. The rules encourage employers to provide matching contributions. If contributions by lower-paid employees are too low to pass the IRS-required tests, some employers may also contribute directly to the 401(k) accounts of lower-paid employees to raise the averages and enable the plan to satisfy the tests. More commonly, employers simply distribute the higher-paid employees' "excess" contributions back to them.

401(k) Nondiscrimination "Safe Harbors"

Alternatively, beginning in 1999, 401(k) plans may use certain "safe harbors" to avoid these rules. The employer may avoid this nondiscrimination testing and additional limits on highly compensated employees in one of two ways. First, the employer may choose to contribute 3 percent of compensation for all employees eligible for the plan, regardless of whether these employees actually contribute to the plan. Or the employer may grant a matching contribution of 100 percent on the first 3 percent of compensation the employee contributes and a match of 50 percent on the next 2 percent of compensation contributed. The amounts the employer contributes using safe harbors, just like the amounts you contribute, must vest immediately.

Taxes on 401(k) Savings at Retirement

When you withdraw money from a 401(k) plan at retirement, you pay federal income tax on any money that hasn't been taxed before. In most cases this means you will pay tax on all money as you withdraw it. But, if your 401(k) allowed you to contribute after-tax dollars to the plan and you did so, you will not pay taxes on any after-tax contributions you made. It is your responsibility to keep track of the amount of after-tax money you have contributed and to properly calculate the tax.

ADVANTAGES OF 401(K) PLANS

Greater Control over the Retirement Plan

401(k) plans enable you to have some control over your employer-provided retirement plan. The more money you contribute, the more you will have for retirement. And in plans where the employer also matches your contributions, you can, in effect, give yourself a raise by contributing to the 401(k). For example, if your employer gives a 50 percent matching contribution and you contribute $20 per week to the 401(k), at the end of the year, you will have savings of $1,560—$1,040 from you and $520 from your employer. Better yet, you don't pay federal income tax on that $1,560 until you retire.

Ability to Control Contributions to Your Retirement Plan

The ability to control contributions to your retirement plan can be especially valuable if you plan to be off the payroll in the future to start your own business or to care for your family. You have the ability to save heavily during those years with the employer to make up partially for those years in which an employer will not be contributing toward your retirement.

Deferred Taxes on Savings

The tax advantages make it easier to save. Because you are using pretax dollars, you can save more. You are paying lower federal income taxes.

Automatic Savings

The 401(k) savings are automatically taken from your paycheck. Savings discipline is enforced, so it is easier to save. If you never see the money, you have no chance to spend it.

Flexibility to Borrow or Withdraw for Hardships

Most 401(k) plans allow you to borrow against your contributions in the plan or allow you to withdraw your money in cases of severe hardship. While a 401(k) plan should never be thought of as a savings account, this ability to borrow or withdraw money does give you a hedge against significant financial disaster.

More Investment Choices

You will probably have several types of investments to choose among for your 401(k) plan, unlike a pension plan, whose investments are solely in the control of the pension plan trustees. Investment control and decisions can be an advantage or a disadvantage, depending on your investment savvy—and luck. Young employees should choose the more aggressive investment options, which will have a higher rate of return and earn more money. Employees nearing retirement should shift into more conservative investment choices, which will have a lower rate of return in some cases, but will also be less subject to ups and downs in the stock market or the economy.

DISADVANTAGES OF 401(K) PLANS

Difficult to Save Enough

No matter how disciplined you may be, you may not be able to save and earn enough in your 401(k) to last a lifetime. While 401(k) plans do have some enforced discipline in savings, you can change your contribution level from time to time. When financial crises arise, you may reduce your contribution level, robbing yourself of retirement security in the long run. Or you simply may not have enough discretionary income to save as much as you need for a woman's long retirement.

Bearing the Investment Risk

Your 401(k) account will bear the risk of investment because it will grow only if you invest it wisely. If the investments give a poor rate of return, the employer is not obligated to increase contributions, if any, to the 401(k) plan. Yet you will be limited to those investment choices the employer's plan provides for you. The fewer investment choices your 401(k) provides, the greater the potential disadvantage of lack of investment diversification. This lack of diversification can become a severe problem if the only investment option is the employer's stock or if the employer's contribution must be invested only in the company stock because you will have too many eggs in one basket.

Lack of Options

Another disadvantage of a 401(k) plan arises if the employer terminates an existing pension plan and replaces it with a 401(k) plan as the company's sole retirement plan. Many pension rights advocates argue that 401(k) plans are simply a trick by employers to force the employee to fund her own retirement plan. Employers would answer these arguments by saying a 401(k) plan is better than no plan at all, a premise difficult to refute.

401(k) PLANS ON BALANCE

Clearly, if you could choose whether your employer would have a pension plan or a 401(k) plan, the pension plan will almost always be better from the older employee's point of view because the employer pays for all of it in nearly all cases. But few of us get such choices. Unless you are in a position to influence the employer's decision—that is, if you are considering whether to take the job, if you are part of a collective bargaining team, or if you are the director of human resources tasked with choosing a new retirement plan for the employees—you don't need to be concerned about these philosophical arguments.

If the 401(k) plan is there, use it. Contribute as much as you can, from the minute you can. In many cases the employer will have both a pension and a 401(k) plan. If the employer doesn't have a pension plan, using the 401(k) plan doesn't prevent you from urging the employer to adopt one.

Stock Bonus Plans

Stock bonus retirement plans receive the employer's contributions in shares of the employer's stock rather than cash that is then invested in other assets. Unlike a defined benefit, which is prohibited from holding more than 10 percent of its assets in stock of the employer, the stock bonus plan will have all or most of its assets held in the employer's stock. These stock contributions may be part of a profit-sharing plan or combined with a 401(k) plan.

By using stock rather than cash to contribute to the retirement plan, an employer gives his employees partial ownership of the company and a built-in incentive to make the company profitable and sound. If the employer can use unissued treasury stock, rather than stock purchased on the open market, the employer also saves a great deal of money. The employer is diluting the ownership of the company by issuing the stock to the retirement plan, but the advantages can far outweigh the disadvantages to the employer.

Frequently, stock bonus plans are referred to as employee stock ownership plans—ESOPs. But true ESOPs, as defined by law, are different from ordinary stock bonus plans and deserve special discussion. With a stock bonus plan or an ESOP both your job and your retirement security may rise and fall with the price of company stock and the market.

Employee Stock Ownership Plans (ESOPs)

ESOPs are unique among employer retirement plans because only ESOPs can borrow money from the plan sponsor or permit the plan sponsor to guarantee a loan to the ESOP. Although this power to borrow does not seem extraordinary on its face, investment bankers have proved differently.

ESOPS AND HIGH FINANCE

This power to borrow, coupled with some significant tax breaks provided by Congress, has made ESOPs a big favorite as a financing tool for companies. Almost without regard for the role of ESOPs as retirement plans, money from ESOP loans has been used occasionally by shaky companies to generate cash flow, to take companies private, and to make or resist takeover bids.

Of the literally thousands of ESOPs, only a relative handful have been abused. But when ESOPs are introduced as a retirement plan, especially if they replace an existing pension plan, you should be aware of the other factors that might be driving the employer to create an ESOP. The ESOP may have been created for business purposes totally unrelated to the employees' retirement security or welfare. The retirement benefit impact of the ESOP may not have been the primary focus.

To the extent ESOPs give you ownership in the company, you and your fortune can grow with the company. But don't start packing up to move into the management suite immediately. Standing alone, ESOPs do not give you, the employee, management power and authority. If the company is to be truly employee-owned, management must share its rights and duties. Additionally, company fortunes don't always prosper even with good management and the best employee productivity and support. With the thrill of ownership can come the agony of watching stock prices plunge in spite of your long hours and hard work.

LEVERAGED ESOPS

When an ESOP borrows money it is called a *leveraged ESOP*. You probably won't find this term in your employee benefits manuals or in the summary plan descriptions of the ESOP, but it does have significance in the rights you may have. In a leveraged ESOP, the employer sets up an ESOP plan and contributes stock to the plan or sells stock to the ESOP. That stock is placed in a "suspense account," which means it has not been distributed to any employee's account, but is being held for eventual distribution among employees.

The ESOP or the employer borrows money from a lender to finance the ESOP's purchase of the stock. The loan is secured by the shares of stock in the ESOP's suspense account. Each year as the employer contributes to the ESOP, those contributions are used to pay the original loan. This payment frees an equal proportion of stock in the suspense account (not an equal dollar amount of stock) for distribution to employees. That stock is then distributed to the accounts of employees.

As with most employee retirement plans, the amount of stock contributed to your account can be based on several different factors. Frequently, the amount contributed to you will be based on salary. Some ESOPs do base contributions on a flat rate to each employee or on a formula that takes into account years with the company.

With a leveraged ESOP the amount of stock issued to your account also is based on the loan payment and the number of the stock shares released as a consequence when the loan is paid, not the value of the shares when the shares are distributed into your account. If the value of the shares goes up, you can receive greatly increased contributions, even contributions in excess of certain IRS limits on annual contributions. But if the value of the stock goes down, the loan still has to be paid at full value. This can work against you. Under those IRS contribution limits, you will be treated as receiving a proportionate share of the amount used to pay the loan. You will be receiving contributions of stock worth very little and at the same time may be limited on amounts you could receive in other employee plans or even amounts you could contribute to the employer's 401(k) plan.

VOTING RIGHTS ON ESOP STOCK

Employees must be permitted to exercise the voting rights of the ESOP stock held in their accounts. If the stock is not publicly traded, these rights can be limited to voting on major issues such as dissolving, selling, or merging the company. Stock shares in the suspense account that have not been distributed to individual employees' accounts must be voted by the plan trustees for the best interests of the ESOP participants, not the employer.

DIVERSIFYING YOUR ESOP AS YOU NEAR RETIREMENT

By law the ESOP must permit you to diversify your ESOP stock acquired after 1986 after you have been in the ESOP for ten years or reach age 55, whichever date comes later. The law recognizes that the risk of overinvestment in the employer's stock is too great as you near retirement. The ESOP either must permit you to make other investments within the ESOP or must give you cash. After you reach the ten-year and age 55 threshold, you have the right to move up to 25 percent of your ESOP holdings each year for five years and up to 50 percent in the fifth year. This ability to diversify gives you some protection against overinvestment in your employer's stock.

GETTING YOUR STOCK—OR YOUR CASH—WHEN YOU LEAVE

You can elect to receive your ESOP benefits in stock or cash, except in rare cases where state law prohibits the ownership of the stock outside the corporation. If the stock is not freely traded on an open market, the employer must give you a "put option." This means the employer must buy the stock from you at fair market value over a period as long as five years or longer, if you own substantial amounts of the stock.

The stock distributions must begin within one year after the close of the plan year in which you retire, become disabled, or die. If you leave for any other reason—you quit, are fired, or are laid off permanently—the employer can delay your benefit payout for up to five years after the end of the plan year in which you left. Once you are entitled to begin receiving your ESOP account, regardless of whether you retired or quit, the employer may distribute it to you over five years, but the distributions must be in at least annual installments. If you own more than $735,000 of stock, the five-year payout period can be extended. This $735,000 threshold is effective for 1999 and will be increased for inflation in coming years.

For example, Joyce has $50,000 in her ESOP account. The ESOP plan year runs from July 1 through June 30. Joyce will retire on August 1, 2000. The ESOP stock distribution does not begin until June 30, 2002. This is almost two years after Joyce retires, but it is still within the one-year limit after the close of the plan year when she retired. She is entitled to receive one-fifth of her stock, or $10,000, in 2002. The plan must give Joyce one-fifth of her account each year after that for the next four years. She will not receive her final benefit from the account until 2006.

You should bear these potential delays in mind and consult with your employer about when payments can be expected. Most employers do not use the full time permitted by law, but most do need some time to do the paperwork involved. Don't plan on receiving the full account as soon as you leave.

ESOP ADVANTAGES

If the employer's stock does well, the ESOP has several advantages.

- The employer can start a benefit plan with relatively little money. This seed of stock can grow to be a far more generous retirement benefit plan than the employer could have afforded if she had made a cash contribution.

- As an employee, you own a piece of the company and may see a direct result of your effort.
- An ESOP permits a young, growing company to share that growth with its employees.
- As a stockholder you also have a voice, small though it may be, in the operation of the company.
- In some cases, particularly in enterprises owned by one person or one family, an ESOP may be the only way to carry on the business and keep the worker employed when the family wants to sell out or the owner wants to retire.
- In other cases, the capital provided by the ESOP loan may provide the financing necessary for the company to regain or improve its financial health and prevent the collapse of the company and loss of jobs.

ESOP DISADVANTAGES

Greater Investment Risk

If the stock does poorly, the retirement plan can become worthless. Many retirement planning experts urge diversification and argue that a retirement program that consists solely of an ESOP is inherently bad retirement planning. The heavy investment in the employer's stock simply makes the plan too vulnerable to stock price declines affected by factors that may have no real relation to the value of the company.

Greater Risk of Losing Both Your Job and Your Retirement Security

When the company does undergo bad financial times, the employees may suffer a double hit. The company may decide on layoffs or forced early retirement just when the stock is so low that the employee hasn't enough to live on. By law the retiring employee can take the stock of most companies and hold it until the price of the stock goes up. But if the ESOP is the only retirement plan, the retirees may not have any choice but to sell the stock to help meet daily living expenses.

Less Control over the Retirement Investment

The value of the stock may be influenced by factors far beyond your control as an employee. If management has used the money from the ESOP loan to go on a takeover buying binge, the interest needed to pay the loan may severely strap even a successful, high-revenue company. Many a sound company has damaged itself and its stock with so much debt that even the highest revenues cannot pay the interest on the debt, pay dividends, and keep the payroll high. If your company is one of these, both your ESOP's worth and your job could disappear.

Hybrids: Target Benefit Plans and Cash Balance Plans

So-called target plans and cash balance plans combine elements of both defined benefit plans and defined contribution plans.

TARGET PLANS

In a target plan the employer determines the percentage of your salary she wants you to receive as an annual retirement payment for life after you retire. This calculation is based on actuarial assumptions about your life expectancy and likely earnings of the plan trust. Each year the employer contributes an amount to the target plan trust fund calculated to reach that "targeted" sum for you. Each employee has a separate account.

If the trust fund's investments earn more money than anticipated, you will retire with an amount that exceeds the target set for you when you entered the plan. If the invested funds do not earn as much income as anticipated, you will retire with less than the targeted amount. In other words, you bear the risk of investment performance in a target plan.

The important difference between ordinary pension plans and target plans is that your retirement benefit is not a fixed, guaranteed sum. Instead, the target benefit will vary depending upon the fund's investment performance. Unlike a defined benefit pension plan, the employer is not required to make additional contributions to the trust to make up for disappointing investment performance, nor does she reap the rewards of superior investment results. The fixed contribution burden gives the employer the advantage of knowing in advance the fixed cost of the contribution she must make to the retirement plan each year.

CASH BALANCE PLANS

Cash balance plans, while relatively new, are becoming increasingly popular. They are actually defined benefit plans masquerading as defined contribution plans. The plan itself defines future retirement benefits, not the contribution to be made each year. But the annual benefit earned by each participant is expressed as a lump-sum amount added to each participant's account. In reality the plan assets remain in a common trust fund. The accounts are a mere bookkeeping device and no individual accounts actually exist. Contributions for the participant usually are based on a flat dollar amount or on a percentage of compensation.

Each "account" earns interest at a rate stated in the plan or linked to an index stated in the plan, such as the rate on U.S. Treasury bills or notes. This rate is not dependent on the actual rate of return on plan assets. In cash balance plans, unlike target benefit plans, the plan, not the employee, bears the risk of investment. The participant is guaranteed the rate of return stated in the plan, regardless of whether the plan actually earns that rate of return. The employer must make up any shortfall with additional contributions to the plan.

Cash balance plans are insured by the Pension Benefit Guaranty Corporation. Such plans do not accept employee contributions as a general rule.

Benefits are usually available as a lump sum or an annuity. If the retiring employee chooses the annuity, the payments are based on the actuarial equivalent of the lump-sum value. Some cash balance plans also provide a minimum annuity that will be the greater of the employee's cash balance or a sum calculated on a traditional pension basis of years of service times a percentage of pay.

Simplified Employee Pensions (SEPS)

Simplified Employee Pensions (SEPs) are a relatively little-used form of employer-provided retirement benefit. These plans can be used by employers of any size; however, they were designed to appeal especially to small employers. They are essentially IRAs the employer sets up for you, but the contribution is not limited to the $2,000 IRA limit. Generally, SEP contributions will be limited to the lesser of $30,000 or 15 percent of compensation.

Like other employer retirement plans, SEP contributions are not taxed until you take the money out of the SEP account. Unlike other retirement plans, SEP contributions must be vested immediately. By law the employer cannot limit the timing of SEP withdrawals. So if you decide to take the money out of the SEP the day after the employer puts it in, you can. But you will pay both regular income tax plus a 10 percent penalty on the amount you withdraw (if you are younger than age 59½) and you will lose the tax deferral on the earnings the money would have made.

ADVANTAGES OF SEPS FOR EMPLOYERS

No "plan document" is required for an SEP other than a standardized Form 5305-SEP the IRS provides, which you and the employer sign. This form does not have to be filed with the IRS or the Department of Labor, and no annual reporting on Form 5500s is required. The employer need not contribute to an SEP each year, nor is there any requirement the contribution be based on the same formula each year. But when a contribution is made, it must be according to a written formula and must bear a uniform relationship to compensation. Some disparity in contributions is permitted for Social Security.

The employers usually leave the choice of investments to the employee, although by law the employers can choose the investment. Usually the investments are certificates of deposits, insurance annuities, or mutual funds. You tell your employer where you want the money invested and she forwards the money to the SEP fiduciary, usually a bank, insurance company, mutual fund family, or stockbroker.

SEPs have never become very popular with employers, primarily because of their strict participation rules. The employer must contribute for every employee who is over 21, worked for the employer for three of the past five years, and received compensation of $400 or more from the employer for the year the SEP covers. (The 1999 $400 threshold will be adjusted for inflation each year.)

Contributions must be made for employees satisfying these criteria even if the employee is not working for the employer at the time the contribution is made. Any period of service, even a day, counts as having worked for the employer. Thus part-time employees, including those working a few hours for a few weeks during a busy season, would have to receive a contribution. Every employee must agree to participate in the SEP. If one employee refuses to participate, no contributions can be made. This sounds rather draconian, but, fortunately, most people rarely refuse to accept money. Given these strict participation and contribution requirements, it is not surprising that SEPs have not been overwhelmingly popular.

ADVANTAGES OF SEPS FOR EMPLOYEES

The biggest advantage of SEPs is that you may be able to convince your employer to establish one if you don't have a retirement plan at work now. Because the SEP has virtually no reporting and recordkeeping requirements and because the employer has the right to decide each year whether and how much to contribute, she may be agreeable to establishing an SEP even though she has rejected requests for other benefit plans. After all, it would provide her with a retirement plan, too.

Another great advantage is the fact that the SEP contribution is immediately vested.

Finally, the fact that most employers permit the employee to choose the investment option can be a big advantage. You can choose an investment option that matches your other retirement financial planning objectives. If there is a mutual fund you have been tracking, but haven't had the money to invest in, the SEP contribution will be the perfect opportunity. If you still only feel comfortable with certificates of deposit, you may invest your SEP in them.

DISADVANTAGES OF SEPS

One disadvantage of SEPs is the employer's discretion not to contribute and the ability to change the levels of contribution each year. You never know whether you will have a retirement plan contribution, and if so how much you can count on. Depending on your discipline, the easy access to SEP money can also become a temptation. You essentially control the money and you can withdraw it from the SEP account at any time. Of course, the heavy taxes you face on the withdrawal can be an effective deterrent.

Plans Limited to Nonprofits: 403(b) Plans

Most nonprofit organizations, as well as educational institutions run by state or local governments, may sponsor so-called 403(b) plans, also referred to as tax-sheltered annuity (TSA) or tax-deferred annuity (TDA) plans. If you work for a nonprofit hospital, museum, college, or social charity or for a school system or university, you probably have access to a 403(b) plan. These plans are usually managed by an insurance company. The two largest 403(b) plan investment managers and providers are the Teachers' Investment Annuity Association—College Retirement Equity Fund (TIAA–CREF) and VALIC, a subsidiary of American General Financial Group.

General Government Rules for 403(b) Plans

403(b) plans, like 401(k) plans, are named for the section of the Internal Revenue Code that authorizes the plans. 403(b) plans actually predate 401(k) plans by more than thirty years. 403(b) plans became the primary way employees of nonprofits could add their own pretax earnings to employer-provided retirement plans. (From 1986 through 1996, nonprofits were prohibited from offering 401(k) plans.) In many ways 403(b) plans are similar to 401(k) plans. Frequently, the employee must contribute to the plan and these contributions are subject to a dollar cap. Beginning in 1997, some of the more restrictive 403(b) rules were removed and 403(b) plan rules became even more similar to 401(k) plans. Generally, employees may contribute up to $10,000 to 403(b) plans in 1999. However, several other 403(b) contribution limits apply and, as with 401(k) plans, the lowest limit controls.

403(b) plans may not be subject to ERISA protections for a number of reasons. First, many of the organizations, such as state and local governments, are not covered by ERISA. Second, there is a specific exclusion under ERISA rules for 403(b) plans if the employer has no contact with the plan other than simply deducting the amount you chose to contribute to a 403(b) annuity provider. Under this exception, the employer must permit a reasonable number of annuity providers to seek your business—and your contributions. But the employer can have no other involvement with the plan.

403(b) Plan Provider Rules

As with other retirement plans, the IRS and, if the plan is an ERISA-covered plan, the Department of Labor set general rules. And, as with other retirement plans, each 403(b) plan also may have additional rules, so long as those rules do not conflict with government rules. But 403(b) plans are different from most other retirement plans where the plan sponsor, usually the employer, runs the plan and the employer imposes only one set of rules. In 403(b) plans, the employer may permit any number of outside vendors that provide 403(b) annuity contracts (i.e., investments) to approach employees to sell the vendor's 403(b) investment products. All of these vendors will have different rules applying to their products.

If your employer permits several of 403(b) vendors to sell to employees, you may face literally dozens of different sets of rules, depending on the company or companies in which you chose to invest your 403(b) contributions. Read the rules for each company's contracts carefully before you decide to invest. Be sure you understand what the underlying investments of the contract are, when you can receive your money, what your payment options are, and when you must make a final election on those payment options.

Differences Between 403(b) and 401(k) Plans

Unlike a 401(k) plan, the amount the employee or the employer may contribute to a 403(b) plan each year may be reduced if the employer sponsors a defined benefit plan for the employee. Both employer and employee contributions to 403(b) plans must be immediately vested. 403(b) plan amounts cannot be rolled over into 401(k) plans, if you move from an employer offering a 403(b) to an employer offering a 401(k) plan, nor can amounts from 401(k) plans be rolled over into 403(b) plans. You may roll 403(b) plan amounts into an IRA.

Plans for Small Employers: SIMPLE IRAs and SIMPLE 401(k)s

Beginning in 1997, employers with one hundred or fewer employees could offer Savings Incentive Match Plans for Employees—SIMPLEs—in two different forms, the SIMPLE IRA and the SIMPLE 401(k). Unfortunately, SIMPLEs aren't simple. And small employers appear not to be flocking to them.

Certain rules apply to both types of SIMPLEs:

- An employer who offers a SIMPLE plan cannot offer any other type of retirement plan.
- An employee may defer up to $6,000 of compensation per year to a SIMPLE. This amount will be indexed for inflation.
- Employers must match the amount contributed by the employee, up to an amount equal to 3 percent of the employee's compensation. Alternatively, the employer can contribute 2 percent of compensation for each employee, regardless of whether the employee contributes to the plan.
- All contributions are vested immediately.

SIMPLE IRAs

In a SIMPLE IRA, the IRA trustee, not the employer, is responsible for annual filings with the IRS. Also, the employer may reduce her match to as low as 1 percent of compensation for any two out of five years. If an employee withdraws amounts from the SIMPLE IRA within two years of joining the plan, the amounts withdrawn will be subject to a 25 percent penalty, plus regular income tax. After the two-year period, withdrawals from a SIMPLE IRA are subject to the same tax rules that apply to ordinary IRA accounts. Generally, income tax will be due on withdrawals from SIMPLE IRAs, and, for most withdrawals prior to age 59½, a 10 percent early withdrawal penalty will apply.

SIMPLE 401(k) Plans

SIMPLE 401(k) plans are not subject to the complex nondiscrimination rules that afflict other 401(k) plans. But employees in a SIMPLE 401(k) plan are limited to a $6,000 annual contribution and an employer matching contribution of no more than 3 percent of the employee's compensation. By contrast, in a regular 401(k) plan the employee could contribute up to $10,000 annually (increased for inflation) and, depending on the plan's design, usually could receive a higher percentage of compensation from the employer in matching contributions.

But these disadvantages may not be significant if you haven't been offered a retirement plan in the past. If your employer offers a SIMPLE plan, by all means use it. It can be more generous than many other types of retirement plans, given the mandatory matching and immediate vesting.

Conclusion: Make the Most of Your Employer-Provided Retirement Plan

You now know the various retirement plans employers can provide. This chapter, coupled with the plan's SPD, gives you the tools to understand generally how the plan operates and what pitfalls and problems might arise with it. Before we move on to look at Social Security and your individual retirement savings, take these steps now to maximize your employer-provided benefits:

- Review all the employer SPDs you have collected.
- Try to determine your accrued benefit to date from each employer-provided plan.
- Contact your former and current employers and ask for their records on your accrued benefits.
- Compare your estimates of accrued benefits with those of your employer or former employers. If they are not the same, contact the employer in writing to find out why.
- Be sure the plan administrators of all retirement plans that will owe you benefits have your current address. Keep your address current with each of those plans. Without a current address, the plan cannot notify you of important information regarding your benefits.

Government-Supplied Retirement Benefits: Social Security and Medicare

Alice will have a monthly Social Security benefit of about $1,100 to bolster her retirement income when she retires in five years. As a 60-year-old worker earning almost $37,000 annually, Alice has enjoyed slightly above average earnings over her career. She can expect her Social Security benefits to equal about 35 percent of her earnings. Coupled with her expected employer-provided retirement benefit of 12 percent of final earnings, she will have less than half of her previous income for retirement. Unfortunately, an annual income of less than half of Alice's final earnings today is not likely to be sufficient for her to live on for the next twenty-five years or so without her own personal savings or assets. Nevertheless, Social Security and Medicare will provide significant—if not sufficient—benefits in retirement for all Americans. In fact, combined Medicare and Social Security benefits payments represent approximately 60 percent of the federal budget.

While this chapter focuses on Social Security *retirement benefits* and Medicare *health benefits,* recognize that Social Security provides valuable coverage every day to nearly all working people and their minor children in the United States. Social Security actually offers three types of basic benefits:

- *disability coverage,* which will provide you and your dependents with income should you become disabled during your working years,

- *survivor benefits* for your minor children, and possibly your spouse, should you die during your working years before your children reach age eighteen,
- *retirement benefits* payable when you reach retirement age; retirement benefits may be based on your personal earnings history or on your spouse's history, depending on which will give you the highest benefit.

Social Security provides 51 percent of the income of elderly unmarried women (including widows). Social Security is the only income received by one-quarter of elderly unmarried women.

This chapter discusses Social Security benefits as provided according to the law in 1999. But the Social Security trust fund is projected to begin paying out in benefits more than it takes in in payroll taxes some time around 2013 and by about 2030 the trust fund will be depleted. After that time the payroll taxes taken in will be sufficient to pay only about 75 percent of currently promised benefits. Clearly, the system has to change, and the changes can be less dramatic if we change sooner rather than later. Bear this in mind as you read this chapter and consider your possible benefits.

Let's look at what you can expect from Social Security retirement benefits and Medicare and how these benefits will be calculated under today's law.

Social Security: A Supplement, Not a Living

Your Social Security retirement benefit is based on your highest thirty-five years of earnings on which you paid Social Security taxes. If you did not work for at least thirty-five years or worked but your pay was not subject to Social Security taxes, those years will be averaged in as zeros.

Since 1935, when Social Security was first enacted, its administrators have warned that its payments to an individual are not sufficient for retirement security and should only be looked upon as a supplement to private sources of income. The average monthly benefit paid in 1999 for a worker who retired at 65 is $780; the average benefit for a couple is $1,310. The maximum benefit paid to a worker retiring in 1999 is $1,373.

Clearly, most people cannot live on $780 per month. Yet 70 percent or more of Social Security recipients rely on those Social Security benefits for 50 percent or more of their retirement income. At the end of the 1990s Social Security payments will provide 42 percent of preretirement earnings for those earning an average income. It will provide just under 60 percent of preretirement earnings to those who earned half of the average U.S. wage over their working lives. For those who had earnings at or over the maximum Social Security taxable wage base most of their working lives, Social Security benefits will provide about 25 percent of that portion of their pay that was subject to Social Security taxes.

Table 8.1
Ratios of Social Security Benefits to Final Pay

Year	Low Earnings (%)	Average Earnings (%)	Maximum Earnings (%)
1955	52	35	33
1960	49	33	30
1965	46	31	33
1970	48	34	29
1975	60	40	29
1980	63	47	30
1985	61	41	23
1990	58	43	24
1995	58	43	24
1997	59	44	25

Note: Average earnings are defined as the national average wage; low earnings are defined as 50 percent of the national average; and maximum earnings are those at the top of the Social Security wage base.

Estimated Social Security Monthly Benefits

By design Social Security replaces a greater percentage of income for lower-paid employees than for higher-paid employees. There are two reasons for this. First, lower-paid workers pay a higher percentage of their income in Social Security taxes than those workers whose pay exceeds the maximum taxable Social Security wage base. Additionally, one of the major goals of Social Security is to help support those whose lower income during working years made it more difficult for them to save individually for retirement.

Table 8.1 gives a history of the wage replacement ratios for Social Security. For example, 1980 was the peak year for workers with low or average earnings. Social Security paid 63 percent of final pay to workers who earned less than 50 percent of the national average wages and paid 47 percent of final pay to workers earning average wages. Since then, the percentage of wages replaced by Social Security benefits has declined.

A Brief History of Social Security

When first adopted, Social Security covered only employees in industry and commerce, about 60 percent of workers. Over the years it has expanded coverage to include the self-employed, many state and local government workers, federal workers hired after 1983, and employees of nonprofit organizations. Today approximately 95 percent of all employees are covered by Social Security.

Social Security was designed to be a self-supporting federal program, financed with payroll taxes and providing not just retirement income, but a host of other insurance programs for workers. In addition to retirement payments to workers and spouses, Social Security benefits include:

- disability benefits for workers and families,
- survivor benefits to families of workers,
- Medicare hospital insurance for retirees, their spouses, and disabled persons receiving Social Security (Medicare Part A), and
- supplemental medical insurance covering doctors, outpatient treatments, and other treatments for retirees, their spouses, and disabled persons receiving Social Security (Medicare Part B).

These benefits are financed by a payroll tax called the Federal Insurance Contribution Act (FICA) paid by you and your employer or the Self-Employed Contribution Act (SECA) tax, paid only by you if you are self-employed. The Social Security taxable wage base subject to these taxes has grown steadily over the years from the original $3,000 wage base to a 1999 wage base of $72,600 for the Old Age, Survivors and Disability Insurance (OASDI) portion. This wage base is adjusted annually based on the increases in average wages in the country. The Medicare hospitalization insurance (HI) portion applies to all wages.

The original maximum employee tax of $30 per year has also increased dramatically. The employer/employee tax rate is 6.2 percent for the OASDI portion and 1.45 percent for the HI portion. That amount is paid by both the employee and the employer, resulting in a combined FICA tax of 15.3 percent. The self-employed tax is also 15.3 percent—12.4 percent for OASDI and 3.9 percent for HI. In 1999, the Social Security tax on the $72,600 wage base was over $5,550 for the employee alone and over $11,000 for a self-employed person.

Social Security was designed to be a self-supporting program and has largely succeeded in that goal. In the early 1980s, when policy makers feared the Social Security system would become bankrupt, a special Social Security reform commission recommended several changes, which Congress adopted, including the creation of a trust fund for the wave of baby boomers expected to retire after 2010. The Social Security trust fund is invested solely in special U.S. Treasury bonds.

Each year the Social Security Board of Trustees projects the solvency of the system, based on three different sets of assumptions, one using lowest expected costs, one using highest expected costs, and one using moderate costs. The soundness of the Social Security system depends on which actuarial and demographic assumptions are used. According to the 1998 Social Security Board of Trustees' Report, under the lowest-cost set of assumptions, the system continues to take in more money than it pays out for the next seventy-five years. But under the highest-cost set of assumptions, the system shows the trust fund being depleted in 2022. The most realistic scenario, using the moderate assumptions, calculates that the trust fund will be depleted in 2032, but estimates that 75 percent of all benefits can still be paid.[1]

Changes in the 1980s Increased Retirement Age

Part of the 1980s changes involved adopting the expanded and indexed wage base and higher rates we have had in recent years. Another important change was in the increase in retirement age at which full Social Security benefits would be paid. While the increase is gradual and relatively small, it represented a major change in Social Security philosophy. The age 65 retirement limit for full benefits had not been changed since adoption of the Social Security Act in 1935. In 1935 the life expectancy for a 65-year-old then was only another two years, while today the life expectancy of a 65-year-old is another nineteen years for females and fifteen years for males. In 1935 when Social Security was enacted, most males never reached age 65.

Full Social Security Retirement Age Today

Today full benefits still begin at age 65 and reduced benefits are available at 62 for those born before 1938. Alice can still retire with full benefits. But Susan, Bonnie, and Jennifer will be under a new schedule to receive full benefits. Those born between 1938 and 1943 will have to add two months to age 65 for every year born after 1937 before they can retire with full benefits. Susan will have to be age 65 and ten months for full benefits to begin.

If you were born between 1943 and 1954, you must reach age 66 to receive full benefits. Bonnie is in this group. Those born between 1955 and 1960 again begin the two-month addition for each year born after 1954. Those born after 1960 will not receive full benefits until age 67. Jennifer is in this age group.

Retiring Before the "Normal" Retirement Age Reduces Benefits

You can begin receiving Social Security benefits at age 62, regardless of your birth year. But if you do, you will receive a permanently reduced benefit for the rest of your life. There is an actual reduction in your benefit made by the Social Security Administration ranging from 20 percent at age 62 for those born before 1939 to 30 percent at age 62 for those born after 1959. The reduction for those born in 1939 and thereafter is based in part on the older retirement age and in part on your age when you retire. The benefit you would receive at your normal retirement age will be reduced by five-ninths of 1 percent for each month between the time you actually retire and your normal retirement age; the closer to your normal retirement age, the smaller the reduction. This reduction applies to workers. If you are considering receiving benefits based on your spouse's benefit, a different reduction factor will be used.

Table 8.2
Age to Receive Full Social Security Retirement Benefits

Year of Birth	Age to Retire
1937 and earlier	65
1938	65 and 2 months
1939	65 and 4 months
1940	65 and 6 months
1941	65 and 8 months
1942	65 and 10 months
1943–1954	66
1955	66 and 2 months
1956	66 and 4 months
1957	66 and 6 months
1958	66 and 8 months
1959	66 and 10 months
1960 and later	67

Two additional factors will indirectly further reduce your early retirement Social Security benefit. First, you will probably be earning less at age 62 than you would have earned if you had continued to work until age 65. As a result, your Social Security benefit will not reflect those higher years of pay you could have earned had you not retired. Second, Social Security is based in part on the number of years you worked and early retirement will mean fewer years to count toward your benefit.

Suppose Alice decides to retire at 63½. Her normal retirement age is 65, and she will be retiring eighteen months before that age, so her benefit will be reduced by 18 times ⅝, or 10 percent. But her benefit will also be smaller because had she worked for another eighteen months she would have almost certainly received a raise and would have had another year and a half of earnings on which her Social Security benefit would have been calculated.

Retiring After the "Normal" Retirement Age

You may also permanently *increase* your benefit for each month you delay retirement past your normal retirement age. The Social Security Administration will increase the amount of the normal retirement benefit from 3 percent to as much as 8 percent per year, depending upon when you were born. This increase is designed to compensate you for the years you did not receive Social Security.[2] You also may receive a higher benefit because your wages at retirement are higher, increasing the overall wage base for your benefit calculation.

Delaying the payment of Social Security benefits past age 65 is usually thought not to be a wise financial move. But for women, delaying retirement may be worth it. This depends on a number of factors.

- If you haven't worked the number of years for full Social Security credit when you reach normal retirement age, working a few more years will raise your earnings base considerably, thereby raising the benefit you receive.
- If your salary during those last years is high, this will also increase your earnings base and thus increase your benefit.
- Remember that women live longer than men. As a result, you are likely to be receiving benefits longer than a man would on average, even if you delay receipt of Social Security benefits past age 65.
- Finally, Congress recognized that the small increase in Social Security benefits for delaying retirement was not a sufficient incentive and the incentive is being increased slowly over the years.

In the future, retirees like Susan, Bonnie, and Jennifer will have more incentive to delay retirement.

How Social Security Benefits Are Calculated

Your benefits are calculated on your wages and the number of quarters during which you paid Social Security taxes. Let's walk through how the benefits are derived.

You may qualify for Social Security benefits as a wage earner or as spouse of a wage earner, even if you are divorced, so long as you were married ten years or more. If you have been married, you need to look at your Social Security qualification as both a wage earner and a spouse. Even though you have worked for many years and qualify on your own earnings, if your spouse's earnings are much higher than yours, you may be entitled to higher monthly Social Security benefits as a spouse. Let's look at qualification and benefits as a wage earner first. Then we will discuss qualification as spouse and why that may give you higher benefits.

Qualifying for Social Security as a Wage Earner

To qualify for Social Security as a wage earner you must have 40 quarters of coverage. (If you were born before 1929, you need fewer quarters, but by now you are probably receiving Social Security and you know that.) You must earn a minimum amount of wages in each year. In 1999 a quarter of coverage was granted for each $740 earned, so $2,600 earned in a year entitled you to four quarters of coverage. Prior to 1978 you had to earn a minimum amount each quarter, but now the law only requires an annual amount. This change is especially helpful to women who may have taken the summers off to be with the children and earned enough to meet the annual minimum for coverage, but did not meet the minimum earnings test for a particular quarter.

Get Your Earnings History and Your Benefits

The key to any of your Social Security benefits is your Personal Earnings and Benefit Estimate Statement—PEBES. The PEBES contains the Social Security Administration's records of your average indexed monthly earnings, frequently called by its acronym, AIME. This is your lifetime earnings history and the estimates of your expected retirement benefits. Beginning in 1999, the Social Security Administration will mail this history to you on a periodic basis. But you also can get a copy of this record at any time, and you should do so. It can be requested by sending your name, address, and Social Security number and signing the request with a statement that you are requesting your own Social Security record. Send the request to: Social Security Administration, Wilkes-Barre Data Operations Center, P.O. Box 20, Wilkes-Barre, PA 18711. You can also use Form SSA-7004, reproduced here as Figure 8.1, to request this information. Or you can obtain a copy from the Social Security Administration Internet site, *www.ssa.gov.* You can also call the Social Security Administration at 800-772-1213 between 7 A.M. and 7 P.M. ET and request the form as well as other information on Social Security.

This information is free. A popular scam has been charging for the form or charging to complete the form and submit it. Don't pay for the form or for anyone to submit the form for you.

Take AIME Throughout Your Career

You should send for your Personal Earnings and Benefit Estimate Statement every three years to be certain the Social Security Administration has accurate information, including your accurate average indexed monthly earnings (AIME). You will receive the PEBES, which lists a history of your Social Security earnings each year through your previous year's wages. It also gives you the current value of your Social Security benefit at the retirement age you designated on Form SSA-7004, as well as the benefit at your normal retirement age and at age 70. The statement will also tell you what your survivors would receive if you died and what you and your family would receive if you became disabled. The information on survivors and disability benefits is helpful right now to determine how much additional insurance you need to buy for adequate disability benefits and for your dependent survivors should you die.

In most cases, the Social Security Administration by law can correct errors only up to three years, three months, and fifteen days after they occur. If you don't get a copy of your earnings history every three years and review it, you won't catch errors in time for the Social Security Administration to correct the problems.

Years Needed for Maximum Benefits

If you were born after 1928, you will use your highest-paid thirty-five years of work to determine your AIME. Those born in 1928 may use thirty-four years and those born earlier may use even fewer years. If you did not work the minimum number of years, you will be adding zeros into the average, which greatly reduces your AIME and your subsequent benefit amount, called the primary insurance amount, or PIA.

Basically, the Social Security system assumes a forty-year career and allows you to use the thirty-five years with the highest earnings. This works well for a career like Bonnie's where she works in a job with earnings exceeding the Social Security wage base and she takes less than five years off. But if a woman today takes ten years to raise her children and perhaps a year or two to deal with elderly parents, she may have only twenty-eight years of the needed thirty-five years. She has to count seven years as zero. Each year counted as zero reduces the average yearly Social Security retirement benefit by about $260. With only twenty-eight years of earnings, the average Social Security benefit would be only about $7,500 per year, rather than the average $9,500 a year for a worker with a thirty-five-year earning history.

Fortunately, Alice will estimate her benefit based on her expected forty-three-year career. Alice uses thirty-five years to calculate her AIME. Because Alice will have worked all but three years during her career, the zeros for those three years will not hurt her. She can drop those three years and the first five years of her career, which were the lowest paid, and still have thirty-five years of earnings to calculate her AIME.

What if Alice had taken ten years off to raise her children? Based on the same figures, Alice would have had only thirty-three years of earnings to count. She would have had to add in two years of zeros and to have included all years of earnings including those early low-paid years. Those two years would reduce her yearly Social Security benefits by about $520.

Social Security Basic Assumptions Versus Women's Career Patterns

Both the Older Women's League and the Congressional Caucus for Women's Issues have criticized the Social Security system for its impact on women. Social Security was designed for different demographics in which a family had one wage earner and one caregiver. Benefits are earned under Social Security for both the wage earner and the "dependents," which include a spouse and minor children. But today's demographics show that, for the vast majority of families, two wage earners are supporting the family or, if only one wage earner supports the family, there is no spouse.

Inequities for Two-Wage-Earner Families

There are grave inequities in the system for two-wage-earner families. Table 8.3 eloquently shows how two working couples, the Tudors and Stuarts, compare

Request for Earnings and Benefit Estimate Statement

[ ] Please check this box if you want to get your statement in Spanish instead of English.

Please print or type your answers. When you have completed the form, fold it and mail it to us. (If you prefer to send your request using the Internet, contact us at http://www.ssa.gov)

1. Name shown on your Social Security card:

_____   _____
First Name   Middle Initial

_____
Last Name Only

2. Your Social Security number as shown on your card:

[ ][ ][ ] – [ ][ ] – [ ][ ][ ][ ]

3. Your date of birth (Mo.-Day-Yr.)

[ ][ ] – [ ][ ] – [ ][ ][ ]

4. Other Social Security numbers you have used:

[ ][ ][ ] – [ ][ ] – [ ][ ][ ][ ]

[ ][ ][ ] – [ ][ ] – [ ][ ][ ][ ]

5. Your sex: [ ] Male   [ ] Female

Form SSA-7004-SM Internet (6-98) Destroy prior editions

For items 6 and 8 show only earnings covered by Social Security. Do NOT include wages from State, local or Federal Government employment that are NOT covered for Social Security or that are covered ONLY by Medicare.

6. Show your actual earnings (wages and/or net self-employment income) for last year and your estimated earnings for this year.

A. Last year's actual earnings: *(Dollars Only)*

$ [ ][ ][ ] , [ ][ ][ ] . [0][0]

B. This year's estimated earnings: *(Dollars Only)*

$ [ ][ ][ ] , [ ][ ][ ] . [0][0]

7. Show the age at which you plan to stop working.

[ ][ ]
(Show only one age)

8. Below, show the average yearly amount (not your total future lifetime earnings) that you think you will earn between now and when you plan to stop working. Include performance or scheduled pay increases or bonuses, but not cost-of-living increases.

If you expect to earn significantly more or less in the future due to promotions, job changes, part-time work, or an absence from the work force, enter the amount that most closely reflects your future average yearly earnings.

If you don't expect any significant changes, show the same amount you are earning now **(the amount in 6B).**

Future average yearly earnings: *(Dollars Only)*

$ [ ][ ][ ] , [ ][ ][ ] . [0][0]

9. Do you want us to send the statement:
   • To you? Enter your name and mailing address.
   • To someone else (your accountant, pension plan, etc.)? Enter your name with "c/o" and the name and address of that person or organization.

_____
Name

_____
Street Address (Include Apt. No., P.O. Box, or Rural Route)

_____
City   State   Zip Code

Notice:
I am asking for information about my own Social Security record or the record of a person I am authorized to represent. I understand that if I deliberately request information under false pretenses, I may be guilty of a Federal crime and could be fined and/or imprisoned. I authorize you to use a contractor to send the statement of earnings and benefit estimates to the person named in item 9.

Please sign your name (Do Not Print)

_____
Date   (Area Code) Daytime Telephone No.

Request for Earnings and Benefit Estimate Statement

Thank you for requesting this statement.

After you complete and return this form, we will--within 4 to 6 weeks--send you:

- a record of your earnings history and an estimate of how much you have paid in Social Security taxes, and

- estimates of benefits you (and your family) may be eligible for now and in the future.

We're pleased to furnish you with this information and we hope you'll find it useful in planning your financial future.

Social Security is more than just a program for retired people. It helps people of all ages in many ways. Whether you're young or old, male or female, single or with a family--Social Security can help you when you need it most. It can help support your family in the event of your death and pay you benefits if you become severely disabled.

If you have questions about Social Security or this form, please call our toll-free number, 1-800-772-1213.

Kenneth S. Apfel
Commissioner of Social Security

Mailing Address

Social Security Administration
Wilkes Barre Data Operations Center
PO Box 7004
Wilkes Barre PA 18767-7004

About The Privacy Act

Social Security is allowed to collect the facts on this form under Section 205 of the Social Security Act. We need them to quickly identify your record and prepare the earnings statement you asked us for. Giving us these facts is voluntary. However, without them we may not be able to give you an earnings and benefit estimate statement. Neither the Social Security Administration nor its contractor will use the information for any other purpose.

Paperwork Reduction Act Notice and Time It Takes Statement

The Paperwork Reduction At of 1995 requires us to notify you that this information collection is in accordance with the clearance requirements of section 3507 of the Paperwork Reduction Act of 1995. We may not conduct or sponsor, and you are not required to respond to, a collection of information unless it displays a valid OMB control number. We estimate that it will take you about 5 minutes to complete this form. This includes the time it will take to read the instructions, gather the necessary facts and fill out the form.

Figure 8.1 Request for Social Security Earnings and Benefit Estimate Statement (SSA-7004)

Table 8.3
Comparisons of One-Earner Versus Two-Earner Families: Social Security Taxes and Benefits

	Yorks— One Earner	Tudors— Two Earners, Wife Earning 1/3 of Family Income	Stuarts— Two Earners, Equal Income
Family Income $34,200: About One-Half the Late 1990s Social Security Wage Base			
Husband's Income	$34,200	$22,800	$17,100
Wife's Income	$0	$11,400	$17,100
Annual Social Security Tax	$2,120	$2,120	$2,120
Couple's Monthly Benefit	$1,623	$1,340	$1,340
Widow's Monthly Benefit	$1,082	$810	$674
Widow's Benefit as % of Couple's Benefit	67%	60%	50%
Family Income $68,400: Approximate Late 1990s Social Security Wage Base			
Husband's Income	$68,400	$45,600	$34,200
Wife's Income	$0	$22,800	$34,200
Annual Social Security Tax	$4,241	$4,241	$4,241
Couple's Monthly Benefit	$2,031	$2,030	$2,164
Widow's Monthly Benefit	$1,354	$1,219	$1,082
Widow's Benefit as % of Couple's Benefit	67%	60%	50%
Family Income $102,600: About 150% of Late 1990s Social Security Wage Base			
Husband's Income	$102,600	$68,400	$51,300
Wife's Income	$0	$34,200	$51,300
Annual Social Security Tax	$4,241	$6,361	$6,361
Couple's Monthly Benefit	$2,036	$2,436	$2,517
Widow's Monthly Benefit	$1,357	$1,354	$1,258
Widow's Benefit as % of Couple's Benefit	67%	56%	50%

Source: Based on data from Anna M. Rappaport, "Improving the Financial Status of Elderly Women: Issues in Savings, Pension Plans and Social Security," paper prepared and distributed to the National Summit on Retirement Savings, Washington, D.C., June 4–5, 1998, exhibits 7–10.

with the one-wage earner family, the Yorks. Two-wage-earner families where both spouses earn an average wage are especially hard hit, when you compare the amount those families pay over the years in Social Security taxes. Table 8.3 illustrates the disproportionate burden of Social Security taxes in relation to both the original amount earned by such a family and the benefits they ultimately receive.

The Stuarts, with both husband and wife making the same salary, pay about the same or more than the Yorks and the Tudors, even though all families earn about the same income. Mrs. York never pays Social Security tax, yet she will receive a greater percentage of Social Security benefit as a survivor than Mrs. Stuart, who always paid tax, will receive as a survivor drawing on her workers' benefits.

As a practical matter any changes to Social Security that will increase benefits will have to be financed by increased taxes, and no one is eager to increase taxes. There may also be the unstated fear that correcting the injustices of the system to the two-wage-earner family where both spouses have paid Social Security taxes can be done only by reducing dependent spouse benefits for women who have not worked outside the home and have not paid Social Security taxes.

Receiving Social Security Benefits as a Spouse

If Alice had worked only before her children were born and after the youngest child left home at eighteen, she would have been in the work place only twenty years. In calculating her AIME she would have to include fifteen years of zeros. Depending on her husband's earnings, Alice might be entitled to receive a higher Social Security benefit as his spouse than she could on her own earnings.

Any wage earner—male or female—who is married and widowed or was married for ten years and is divorced is entitled to receive benefits based on her own earnings or the spouse's earnings. A spouse who has never worked outside the home is entitled to draw benefits based on the wage earner's work record.

Once the wage earner begins receiving benefits and the spouse reaches normal retirement age, she is entitled to a dependent's benefit equal to 50 percent of the wage earner's Social Security benefit. A spouse may choose to receive a reduced benefit beginning after age 62. Currently, at age 62 the spouse is entitled to 37.5 percent of the wage earner's benefit. As the normal retirement age increases above 65 over the years, the spouse may still begin receiving a benefit at 62, but she will receive less than 37.5 percent. As with wage earner benefits at early retirement, this reduction is permanent.

Retirees with Children

A spouse at any age with a child under 16 or a disabled child can also receive a 50 percent benefit when the wage earner begins to receive Social Security benefits. The child may also receive a benefit of 50 percent of the wage earner's benefit, if she is under 18, is under 19 and still in high school, or, regardless of age, became disabled before age 22. The total amount of benefits any family can receive based on one wage earner's work record is limited. But if both you and your spouse worked and you still have dependent children at home when you retire, you may be able to receive higher benefits if you use both of your work records. You can receive benefits for the children under the higher work record of the two of you. The second worker's benefit is not subject to the higher-paid worker's "maximum family benefit," as the limit is called.

Using Both Your Wage History and Your Spouse Benefits

A spouse may also retire early based on her own wage earnings. She would receive a reduction in her benefits for early retirement. Then, when her spouse retires at normal retirement age and she reaches normal retirement age, she could shift to receiving benefits as a spouse, if those benefits are larger. If she has not worked continuously in the work force or has worked for very low wages, as we saw from the Yorks in Table 8.3, it is possible to receive a higher spouse benefit than a wage earner benefit. Under this scenario, her spouse benefit would not be reduced for early retirement, because she did not begin receiving the spouse benefit until she reached normal retirement age.

Benefits for Divorced Spouses

If you are divorced, you may receive benefits based on your spouse's earnings, but the rules are a little different. So long as your former spouse is eligible to receive Social Security benefits, regardless of whether the former spouse is actually receiving benefits or not, you can receive benefits once you and your former spouse have reached age 62. But if your spouse is only 62, you must have been divorced for at least two years before benefits can begin. The benefits percentages will be the same as a married spouse's and you will be subject to the same reductions in benefits as married spouses. Your benefit will stop if you remarry, unless you remarry someone who is receiving benefits as a dependent of a wage earner.

Special Social Security Rules

Minimum benefits are available for individuals who have worked for many years at low wages. These minimum benefits are paid only if they are higher than the benefits that would be received under ordinary calculations.

If you are entitled to a pension as an employee of a local or state government or the federal government and, when you retire from that job, you are not covered by Social Security taxes, in most cases Social Security benefits you receive as a spouse or as a widow will be reduced by two-thirds of the amount of your other pension. Because government employee pensions are usually relatively generous, this two-thirds offset rule generally eliminates any benefit from Social Security. Any Social Security benefit you receive based on your own wage record is not affected by this rule.

If you were in the military or you are relying on benefits received as a military spouse, your Social Security benefits may be increased by credits counted toward the earnings record.

Receiving the Social Security Benefits

Social Security checks don't just magically appear. You must apply for your Social Security benefits. Depending on the area of the country in which you live, this can take from one month to three or four, so you are wise to begin the application process a few months before you hope to retire. The application process is detailed in Chapter 16. Generally, most of the application process can be done by phone, although you will have to mail in relevant documents.

How Wage Earnings Affect Benefits

You may continue to work after you begin receiving Social Security benefits, but until you reach age 70 you will be subject to an *earnings test.* Your benefits (and your family's benefits, if any) will be reduced if you earn more than the limit.

The limit changes annually by law. In 1999, recipients between the ages of 65 and 69 could earn $15,500 and those under 65 were limited to $9,600. The future limits for those age 65 to 70 are set as follows: in 2000, $17,000; in 2001, $25,000; and in 2002, $30,000. Future limits for those under 65 will be set each year. If you hit the limit and you are under 65, your Social Security benefits will be reduced by $1 for every $2 over the limit you earn; if you are over 65 your benefits will only be reduced $1 for every $3 you can earn over the limit. Once you reach age 70, your Social Security payment is not affected by your earnings.

For example, in 1999, Jean is 66 and earned $18,000 at her receptionist job. Her Social Security benefit of $10,000 for that year will be reduced by $834 (one-third of the $2,500 over the earnings cap). She may also pay income tax on part of her Social Security benefit because of her wages.

"Earnings" for purposes of the earnings limitation are generally compensation received for services. Usually, the type of income a retired person could expect to receive, such as pensions, interest, dividends, and so on, are not "earnings" subject to this limitation, so you are not penalized for saving and investing before retirement. Noncash payments for domestic service are also not included in earnings. So if you receive a rent-free apartment in exchange for management services, it is not "earnings."

If a family member receiving benefits earns more than the limit, only that family member's benefits will be reduced. For example, you and your husband are 68. He is receiving benefits as a wage earner and you are receiving Social Security benefits as a spouse. If your husband exceeds the earnings limit, both of you will have benefits reduced. But, under the same circumstances, if you each are receiving benefits based on your own wage-earning records, *your* benefits will not be reduced if *his* earnings exceed the limit. Likewise, if you were working, but he was not, any of your earnings exceeding the limit would not limit his benefits.

Doing the Math on the Earnings Limit

If you are considering working after beginning your Social Security benefits, you need to consider carefully the amount of income earned and whether the additional income is worth the trade-off. Also remember that the amounts you are earning are subject to income taxes and Social Security taxes. The Social Security earnings limits are applied on a pretax basis. But generally, Social Security benefits are not taxable. Once the taxes are calculated, you may earn very little, especially if you are working between ages 62 and 65, when the reduction is $1 of Social Security benefit for every $2 earned over the limit.

If you are considering beginning Social Security benefits before your normal retirement date and are going to continue to work, you should look at the numbers very carefully. You may be choosing a permanently reduced Social Security benefit for the rest of your life and then see that benefit further reduced because of your wages earned between ages 62 and 70.

Let's say Alice decides to go through with her plan to retire at age 63½, but continues to work half-days. She would have received a Social Security benefit at age 65 of approximately $14,400. But because she retired eighteen months before her normal retirement age of 65, that amount will be reduced during her entire retirement lifetime by 10 percent (5⁄9 times 18 months). Her Social Security base benefit will be only about $13,000. But by working half-time she will earn $18,500 in 1999. This exceeds the 1999 earnings limitation of $9,600 by $8,900. Her Social Security benefit in 1999 will be further reduced by $4,450 ($1 for every $2 earned over the $9,600 limit). So Alice's Social Security benefit will be only about $8,500 for 1999. Between the permanent reduction for retiring early and the reduction for earnings, Alice will be receiving just over half of what she could have received had she waited until age 65 and completely retired or worked only enough to earn around $15,500. Alice may want to rethink her plan.

Social Security Benefits Taxed for the "Wealthy"

Social Security benefits are nontaxable if you are single with a yearly income of $25,000 or less or are married with a yearly income of $32,000 or less. Note that the income limit here is not "earnings" like that used in the earnings limitation test. Income for determining the taxability of Social Security counts one-half your Social Security benefit and all non–Social Security income, including earnings and all the pension benefits, interest, and dividends from your preretirement savings and tax-free bond interest. Also, these amounts do not increase for inflation.

If this income exceeds these thresholds, you pay income tax on 50 percent of a base amount over $25,000 for singles or $32,000 for marrieds and tax of up to 85 percent of your Social Security benefits, if you exceed an "adjusted base amount of income" of $34,000 for singles and $44,000 for marrieds. Table 8.4 shows how your Social Security benefits are included in your taxable income.

The tax structure is fairly complicated for at least two reasons. First, in calculating the tax, you base your tax on 50 percent of Social Security benefits if you exceed the first "base amount" income threshold and on 85 percent of those

Table 8.4
Amount of Social Security Benefits Subject to Income Tax

Yearly Income (Including 50% of Social Security)	No Tax on Social Security	Tax on the Lesser of (1) 50% of Social Security or (2) Excess Income Amount	Tax on the Lesser of (1) 85% of Social Security or (2) Excess Income Amount
Single			
$25,000 or less	X		
$25,001 to $34,000		X	
Over $34,000			X
Married			
$32,000 or less	X		
$32,001 to $44,000		X	
Over $44,000			X

Table 8.5
Alice's Taxing Threshold

Income Source	Amount
Pension	$4,600
Savings income	8,000
Part-time job	4,000
Half Social Security	7,200
Total	$23,800

benefits if you exceed the second income threshold, or "adjusted base amount." Second, you pay tax based on the *lower* of the percentage of Social Security benefits subject to tax or the amount of income that exceeds the base amount or adjusted base amount. Confused enough? Some examples may clear up the confusion.

In Alice's case, at 65 she will have a pension of approximately $4,600 a year. She hopes her own savings can generate another $8,000 a year and for a time she hopes to have a part-time job paying $4,000. Her Social Security benefit will be approximately $14,400. Her taxing threshold is calculated in Table 8.5. She has includable income of $23,800 per year, well below the $25,000 "base amount" for taxing Social Security benefits for single individuals, so she will pay no income tax on her Social Security benefits.

But suppose her savings income generated $11,000. Then her income (includ-

Table 8.6
George and Harriet's Taxing Threshold

Income Source	Amount
Pension	$25,000
Savings income	12,000
Half Social Security	9,350
Total	$46,350

ing one-half of her Social Security benefits) would be $26,800, exceeding the $25,000 base amount for singles by $1,800. She would then pay income tax on the *lesser* of $1,800 (the amount in excess of the first income threshold) or $7,200, which represents 50 percent of Social Security benefits. Clearly, $1,800 is less, so she will pay income tax on that amount of her Social Security benefits.

Her neighbors, George and Harriet, are not so lucky. Their includable income is shown in Table 8.6. George and Harriet will now do three different calculations and pay tax on the *lesser* of those three amounts.

Calculation 1: 50% of all excess over married base amount, plus 35% of adjusted base amount
($14,350 × 50%) + ($2,350 × 35%) = $7,175 + $823 = $7,998
Calculation 2: 85% of Social Security benefits (85% × $18,700) = $15,895
Calculation 3: 50% of Social Security benefits, plus 85% of excess over adjusted base amount
$9,350 + (85% × $2,350) = $9,350 + $1,998 = $11,348

George and Harriet will have to pay income tax on the lesser of three amounts, or $7,998.

Supplemental Security Income (SSI)

The Social Security system, along with some states, makes available supplemental security income (SSI) to those over 65 and to disabled persons, if they have assets less than $2,000 for an individual or $3,000 per couple.

Your home, burial plots, burial funds of up to $1,500, and, usually, your car and home furnishings do not count toward the asset limits. Income from other sources reduces SSI benefits, but the first $65 per month of wages is ignored, as is half the amount over $65. The basic payment to those over 65 is about $500 per month for an individual and about $750 for a couple. Payments may be higher, depending on how much the state adds to the SSI benefit. Or payments may be lower, depending on your earnings. Obviously, SSI is available to you only if you are in truly desperate circumstances. More information on Social Security and SSI is available on the Internet at *www.ssa.gov.*

Medicare

Medicare is the federal health care reimbursement system that pays for a portion of medical care for those age 65 and over. Medicare is administered by the Health Care Financing Administration (HCFA), part of the U.S. Department of Health and Human Services. Medicare becomes an important source of retirement "income" because health care costs represent an unusually high percentage of retired persons' incomes. The average American spends about 5.4 percent of her expenditures on health care. But Americans between 55 and 64 spend about 5.9 percent on their expenditures on health care, those age 65 to 74 spend 10.3 percent, and those 75 and older spend over 14.4 percent.[3] The average Medicare reimbursement for retirees was about $5,300 per enrollee in 1995. About half of that amount is spent for inpatient hospital care.[4] Of course, this is a somewhat misleading figure because a significant amount of Medicare expenditures is spent on people in the last six months of their lives. Nevertheless, Medicare reimbursements or payments constitute a substantial portion of the elderly's "income."

Medicare Part A: Hospitalization Coverage with No Premium

Medicare has two parts. Medicare Part A is hospital insurance, paying some of the costs of hospital stays, some related care while you are there, and certain home health care. Medicare Part A is financed by the "hospital insurance" portion of the Social Security tax. If you or your spouse is eligible for Social Security, you pay nothing additional for Medicare Part A coverage. It is automatically provided when you apply for Social Security. Even if you don't qualify for Social Security, you may buy Medicare Part A insurance for a fee after you reach age 65.

Medicare Part B: Other Medical Services, Additional Premium

Medicare Part B, also called supplementary medical insurance benefits, covers other medical services such as doctors' fees and outpatient services. Part B is financed in part by monthly premiums deducted from your Social Security check. You may opt out of Part B coverage. The monthly premiums, which are designed to cover only about one-fourth of the cost of Part B, are adjusted each January. The premiums are calculated for those who enrolled when they were first eligible. If you enroll after you are first eligible or drop in and out of Part B, your premiums will be higher when you do enroll in Part B. In 1999 Medicare premiums were $45.50 monthly for those who enrolled at age 65. These premiums are adjusted each year.

You may begin to receive Medicare at age 65, regardless of whether you are applying for Social Security. However, even if you begin receiving Social Security benefits at age 62 you will not become eligible for Medicare until you are 65. Medicare is also available for the disabled and for those with chronic kidney disease.

Even if you plan to continue working past age 65, you should enroll in Medicare coverage. Depending on your age, health, and the benefits your employer is providing, you may opt out of Part B, but if you do, remember you will pay a higher premium later. It is unlikely that you will find a health insurance policy covering the same services for less money—if you can find an individual policy at all.

What Does Medicare Pay?

Medicare does not pay all medical expenses. Like other health insurance plans, you pay a "deductible" and a "co-payment" for most services. These deductibles and co-pays are linked to the increases in medical costs and go up each year. For example, in 1999, hospital benefits required a $768 initial deductible and $192 per day after the first sixty days. After ninety days you pay the full amount for hospitalization or you may choose to pay $384 per day for up to sixty "lifetime reserve" days. This means over the course of your entire lifetime you will have only sixty days of hospitalization at this rate for those periods when you are in the hospital more than ninety days at a time. If you are in a skilled nursing care facility receiving treatment you will pay $96 per day for the twenty-first through the hundredth day of each benefit period during which you are receiving treatment.

Ordinary nursing-home care, in which the services provided are custodial care rather than for rehabilitation or treatment, is *not* covered by Medicare. Custodial care becomes a source of serious income depletion for some elderly people when they are unable to care for themselves at home, but have no treatable illness. This is when the long-term care policies discussed in the next chapter become crucial. Unfortunately, many younger people still do not realize that Medicare does not cover custodial care.

Medicare Part B pays for doctors' services, x-rays, diagnostic tests, physical therapy, necessary ambulance services, drugs that cannot be self-administered, and so on. You must pay the first $100 of Medicare-recognized charges annually. After that Medicare will pay for 80 percent of covered expenses, but only at the "customary" or "prevailing" charge level established by Medicare. If the Medicare prevailing charge for a specific service is $100, but your doctor charges $130, Medicare will pay only $80 for the service. You must pay the remaining amount up to a government-imposed limit.

Medicare now covers some preventive benefits, including mammograms, pap smears, and pelvic exams, without a deductible. But most other preventive tests and procedures are subject to a deductible.

Medicare Assignment: Paying Doctors for Medicare Services

Most doctors accept Medicare assignment, meaning they will bill Medicare directly. The doctor is limited to charging the Medicare set amount for the procedure and may ask you to pay your share immediately.

If you use a doctor that does not accept Medicare assignment, the doctor may charge a higher fee, but the fee will still be limited by Medicare. The doctor will also likely ask for payment in full at the time the service is rendered. You will then have to send the bill to Medicare and receive reimbursement for only that part that Medicare will pay.

Private contract doctors may also opt out of Medicare completely. In such cases the doctor will ask you to sign a private contract when you receive services. Medicare will not pay for any part of the fee and most other insurance coverage, such as any "Medigap" policy you may have, will not pay for such fees either.

Medicare and Managed Care

Medicare also will pay for enrollment in managed care health programs such as health maintenance organizations (HMOs) and networks of health care providers that have contracts with Medicare. These programs are offered also in part through a new program begun in 1999, called Medicare + Choice. Additional information and updates on Medicare are available at *www.hcfa.gov* and at *www.medicare.gov*.

Supplemental Insurance

As you can see, you can still incur significant medical expenses in retirement, even with Medicare. Many retirees want additional insurance coverage beyond Medicare. If your employer offers retiree medical insurance designed to supplement Medicare after you retire or, if you retire early, to cover you after you leave the employer but before you become eligible for Medicare at age 65, be sure you sign up for it. Chances are it will be the cheapest health insurance available—and you will not have to meet insurability tests for coverage.

For those retirees whose employers do not offer retiree medical coverage, so-called Medigap health insurance policy from a private health insurance company will cover additional medical expenses such as co-pays and deductibles. "Medigap" policies do not cover custodial nursing home care. Only a long-term care policy specifically designed for custodial care will cover nursing homes as a rule. "Medigap" policies became a scandal in the 1980s and some progress was made in regulating them. The area still remains subject to abuse, although criminal penalties apply for those selling such policies in violation of the regulations.

If you consider a "Medigap" policy, either for yourself at retirement or for your parents, shop slowly and ask lots of questions. The National Association of Insurance Commissioners and the Health Care Financing Administration provide the following tips.

■ Don't believe statements that the insurance is government sponsored; policies to supplement Medicare are not sold by the federal or state governments.

- Compare several different policies and companies.
- Don't buy more insurance than you need and don't buy several different policies.
- Check for "pre-existing condition" exclusions that will not pay for treatment of a medical condition you already have or had perhaps years ago. By law, the application of pre-existing condition exclusions is prohibited if you have had continuous health care coverage. But if you have had gaps in health coverage, pre-existing condition exclusions can, and probably will, apply.
- Be alert for maximum benefit limits. Many policies have limits on the number of days or amounts they will pay.
- Be suspicious of any suggestion that you give up a current policy and buy a replacement; the new policy may have waiting periods or pre-existing condition exclusions.
- Check your right to renew; buy only policies that have an automatic right to renew (most states now require this by law).[5]

Financial Future of Medicare

In 1997 Congress undertook a number of changes to Medicare to help preserve its solvency. These included placing further limits on payments to health care providers, increasing the focus on fraud and abuse, and encouraging Medicare recipients to use "managed care" programs such as HMOs and the new Medicare + Choice program. But Medicare will continue to face significant cost problems.

What the Medicare program may look like twenty years from now when the age wave begins to retire is pure speculation. The nation as a whole is concerned about health care availability and affordability. We have gone from a nation spending about $800 per person annually for health care in 1978 to one spending over $3,600 per person in the late 1990s, excluding research and facilities construction.[6] Through the 1990s, health care inflation has slowed dramatically from the 14 percent rates of increase seen in the 1980s to as low as 4 percent in the late 1990s.

Most health care, even that provided by private systems through employer insurance or individually purchased health care, is "managed" through health maintenance organizations or medical providers who agree to discounts through "preferred provider" organizations or networks.[7] The managed care system has been credited with some of the success in limiting the increase in health care costs, but the system is increasingly criticized for limiting access to care. At the same time, the 1997 changes in Medicare are moving that system toward more managed care.

In some form Medicare will be available to future retirees, but its use is likely to be more regulated. And Medicare could become more means-tested, with higher-income retirees paying more, or certain medical procedures could be rationed as they are now in other countries providing national health care deliveries.

Conclusion: Strategy Steps for Social Security and Your Retirement Saving Program

Social Security will be a part of your potential income when you retire, but as you have seen, it is not likely to be sufficient to provide a secure retirement—nor was it ever intended to be. It is also almost certain to be changed in order to preserve benefits, but contain the cost to taxpayers. But what those changes may be are unclear. Nevertheless, while you are still young enough to save for retirement, seeing your projected Social Security benefit will be important "reality therapy" for calculating the additional retirement income you will need to maintain your life style.

- Examine the Personal Earnings and Benefit Estimate Statement (PEBES) you received from the Social Security Administration to see what your benefits may be under the current Social Security system and to be sure your earnings history is correct. If you have not received a recent PEBES, order it now, no matter how old you are. Use the form on pages 122–23.
- Once you have your recent PEBES, check it carefully for any errors. It is important to check regularly for errors because the Social Security Administration cannot correct old errors in most cases.
- Use the estimated Social Security benefits in your current planning and budgeting for retirement saving.
- Look carefully at the estimated benefit at retirement. It will be given to you in current dollars. Obviously, unless you are very close to retirement, the current dollar figure is not likely to be the same as your actual retirement benefit. But the current dollar figure will give you an idea of the buying power of your Social Security benefit at retirement. As inflation goes up, so does your Social Security benefit, at least under current law. Theoretically, the benefit you actually receive at retirement will have the same buying power as the benefit amount shown to you in your various estimates.
- Recognize that your PEBES estimates assume you will continue to work and to earn approximately the same salary. If you stop working, your ultimate benefit will be lower than the estimates. If you begin to receive a higher salary, your final retirement benefit will likely be higher than the estimates you receive.
- Order your PEBES about every three years. Having these statements will enable you to check for errors and get them corrected within the legal period for corrections, as well as see how much your expected Social Security benefit at retirement is changing.
- Pay attention to the debate about changes to Social Security. Social Security is extremely important to women given their long life spans and life-long lower wages.

Your Individual Savings
for Retirement

Your own individual savings are the most important segment of your retirement income security program. You cannot control government policy on Social Security. You cannot control the retirement plan or the rules of the plan your employer may adopt. You may not always have an employer. But you can control the amount of money you set aside in savings for retirement. Your individual retirement savings include obvious investment accounts like IRAs, but we will also look at other retirement security planning devices, such as disability insurance, annuities, universal life insurance, Keogh plans, long-term care insurance, and, possibly, your home.

Paying Yourself

Saving is a habit. As with any habit, the more often you do it, the more likely you are to continue. If you haven't started saving, start today. Don't be discouraged if you can only put aside small amounts. Most habits start small and then begin to grow.

Pay yourself first, using a method that is automatic. Don't tell yourself you will do this by writing a check to your investment account each pay period. You won't. You will have the best of intentions, but in month one, the dentist's bill is due. In month two, the car needs new tires. In month three, the house insurance bill is due. . . . You begin to get the picture.

If your employer has any sort of payroll deduction plan, use it. If your bank will make automatic withdrawals from your checking account into a savings account, use that option. An even better option is to have your paycheck deposited directly into a money market fund that is your short-term savings account.

Then write a check to your checking account for living expenses. You have reversed the psychology of saving. Under this approach everything you take out of your "savings account" is clearly drawing down on your savings. The point is, if you never see the money, you never seem to miss it. If you absolutely need the money at the end of the month, you can always withdraw more from your savings account.

Finding Money to Save

You may feel that there is simply nothing left to spare after covering current necessities. You may be right. But think about current spending you could eliminate or reduce so that you could use that money for savings. Skip lunch one day a week. Even a carry-out lunch these days can cost $5. That's a saving of $260 a year—with interest at 8 percent it's $280.80. Granted, that's a small start, but it *is* a start. Chances are, once you start looking for expenses to eliminate, you will find more. Wash those silk blouses and iron them yourself; take public transportation to work instead of paying for parking; walk to work instead of taking public transportation.

Some financial planners even advise keeping track of literally every penny you spend for a week or two to see where the money goes. This kind of tracking may show you spending $10 a week in the junk food vending machines or $70 a week on eating out or $10 a week on magazines at the drug store. From those figures you can see how seemingly insignificant purchases add up. While you might not want to eliminate them entirely, if you cut them in half you would give yourself $45 a week to save.

Among women who are currently not saving for retirement, 60 percent say they could afford to save $20 a week; among those who are saving, 70 percent say they could save another $20 per week.[1] If $20 a week sounds insignificant to you, think about the fact that $20 a week, saved over forty years and earning a modest 5 percent, would buy you an annuity paying $200 a week at retirement.

All of this probably sounds like the conventional wisdom you've heard a hundred times before. It is. But there is a reason why it's "conventional wisdom." It works.

Put Your Money to Work: Enjoy the Wonders of Compound Interest

Chapter 3 showed us the time value of money. Money you have saved is growing into more money through the interest or investment growth it earns. And the interest earns interest. When Albert Einstein was queried about his opinion on the greatest invention in the world, he replied, "compound interest." Perhaps he had heard compound interest described by one of the Rothschilds as the "eighth wonder of the world."

Compound interest also explains why you should start saving early. When you begin saving at age 30 for retirement, your early money has thirty-five years to earn compound interest before you retire at age 65. If you wait until you are 55 to start saving, you have only ten years of interest-earning time. If you invest $1,000 at 7 percent in ten years it will grow to $1,967, but after thirty years, it will have grown to $7,612. At 7 percent, investing $1,000 a year for ten years will give you $13,816, or $3,816 earned on the $10,000 investment. But $1,000 a year invested for thirty years gives you $94,461, which is earnings of $64,461 on your $30,000 investment over the years.

Any sort of savings program is good, but as we learned from Chapter 6, tax-favored savings plans (where taxes are deferred or where the amounts are exempt from tax) yield much higher returns. The rest of this chapter focuses on tax-deferred retirement savings vehicles that you as an individual can use.

Individual Retirement Accounts (IRAs)

Individual retirement accounts—IRAs—are the primary tax-favored individual retirement saving vehicle. There are four types of IRAs.

- *Tax-Deductible Traditional IRAs.* These are limited to no more than $2,000 per year. They are tax deductible if you do not accrue benefits under an employer-provided retirement plan that year or if you earn less than that year's earnings limit, regardless of whether you have an employer plan that year.
- *Nondeductible Traditional IRAs.* These are limited to no more than $2,000 per year. They are available if you are building up benefits under an employer-provided retirement plan that year, but are earning more than that year's limit for deduction.
- *Roth IRAs.* These IRAs are limited to no more than $2,000 per year as a nondeductible contribution, but the earnings are tax-free at withdrawal.
- *Rollover IRAs.* This type of IRA has no annual limit; it receives and holds the taxable portion of money distributed from an existing IRA or from an employer's retirement plan when you leave the employer.

The bad news: you cannot contribute more than $2,000 a year to all your IRAs, whether they are traditional IRAs or Roth IRAs. The good news: rollover IRAs are not subject to the $2,000 limit and are not included in calculating the $2,000 limit for other IRAs.

You may—and you should if possible—put the $2,000 into your Roth IRA or Traditional IRA on January 1 of the year for which you are contributing. But you have until April 15 of the following year to put money in your IRA for the past year. Just remember, if you put $2,000 in your IRA for the current year on January 1, after thirty years you will have about $245,000, but if you wait to fund your current-year IRA until December 31 each year, you will have about $227,000. That's an $18,000 reward for acting in January.

Traditional IRAs

Anyone who earns compensation or who has a spouse who earns compensation can establish and contribute to a traditional IRA until they are age 70½. The earnings on the money in the IRA will be tax-deferred until you begin withdrawing the money from the IRA.

Deductible Traditional IRAs

Whether you may deduct the amount you contribute to a traditional IRA depends on two factors in any given year:

- your *modified adjusted gross income* for income tax purposes and
- whether you earned a benefit from an employer plan for that year.

If your employer does not sponsor a retirement plan, your traditional IRA will be fully deductible to you that year, regardless of how high your compensation for the year. If you earn less than the earnings limit shown in Table 9.1 for the specific year, your IRA will be fully deductible regardless of whether your employer sponsors a retirement plan or whether you actually earn a benefit under that plan.

DETERMINING THE DEDUCTION IF YOU ARE COVERED
BY AN EMPLOYER RETIREMENT PLAN

If your employer sponsors a retirement plan, whether you can deduct your IRA contribution for a specific year will depend on two things: your modified adjusted gross income and whether you actually accrued a benefit under that plan for the tax year. "Modified adjusted gross income" for this purpose includes any income you receive during the year, not just compensation. For example, it includes interest, dividends, foreign income, or foreign housing allowances you may receive.

In 1999, if you are single and have an adjusted gross income of $31,000 or less, or if you are married and have an adjusted gross income of $51,000 or less, your traditional IRA (and your spouse's traditional IRA) will be fully deductible. The deduction is available regardless of whether you (or your spouse) have an employer-provided retirement plan. If you are single with income between $31,000 and $41,000 or married with an income between $51,000 and $61,000, a portion of your IRA will be deductible.

Table 9.1 shows the income levels over the next few years. For each year, if your income is the lower amount, your IRA contribution and, if you are married, your spouse's contribution are deductible. If your income falls in the range given each

Table 9.1
Traditional IRA Deductibility: Income Limits and Phase-Out Range for Individuals Participating in an Employer-Provided Retirement Plan

	Earnings Limit and Deduction Phase-Out Range	
Tax Year	*Single Taxpayer*	*Married Filing Jointly*
1999	$31,000–$41,000	$51,000–$61,000
2000	$32,000–$42,000	$52,000–$62,000
2001	$33,000–$43,000	$53,000–$63,000
2002	$34,000–$44,000	$54,000–$65,000
2003	$40,000–$50,000	$60,000–$70,000
2004	$45,000–$55,000	$65,000–$75,000
2005	$50,000–$60,000	$70,000–$80,000
2006	$50,000–$60,000	$75,000–$85,000
2007 and after	$50,000–$60,000	$80,000–$100,000

year, your contribution will be partially deductible, and if your income is above the range for that year, your IRA contribution will not be deductible.

Are You an Active Participant in an Employer Plan?

Assuming that your modified adjusted gross income exceeds the figures above and your employer sponsors a retirement plan, the next question is to determine whether you are an *active participant* in that plan for the tax year in question. If you are, your IRA contribution will not be deductible for that year, or may be only partially deductible if your income falls in the "phase-out" range.

The IRS defines "active participant" or "coverage" by an employer plan very strictly. The rules are complicated and subject to change. In fact, the IRS primarily suggests you rely on your W-2, which will tell you whether you are covered by a retirement plan.[2]

Recall that in many employer plans you do not become a participant until you have worked for the employer for a year. So, in most cases, if your previous employer did not have a plan or you were not in it yet, the first year you join a new employer you will probably not be an active participant in any plan for that year.

The moral of the story here is to contribute to your IRA early in the year. Don't wait to find out whether the contribution is tax deductible. You will have an additional fifteen months, at a minimum, to earn tax-deferred interest as opposed to your dilatory colleagues who wait until April 15 to fund the previous year's IRA. In most cases you will know before you file your income tax whether the IRA is, in fact, deductible. (If you find out later in the year that your traditional

IRA is not deductible, you can decide whether you want to convert that year's IRA contribution to a Roth IRA. We'll discuss that wrinkle in the section on Roth IRAs.)

Active Participant Status Depending on the Plan

According to the IRS's publications, whether you are an active participant in an employer-provided retirement plan for purposes of deducting your contributions to a traditional IRA varies depending on whether the employer plan is a defined benefit or defined contribution plan.

"ACTIVE" IN A DEFINED CONTRIBUTION PLAN

If the plan is a defined contribution plan, you are covered if a contribution is made to your account during the plan year that ends in your tax year. Assume you quit working for Acme on December 1, 1998. Acme has a defined contribution profit-sharing plan with a plan year running from July 1 to June 30. On March 31, 2000, Acme declares a profit-sharing allocation for the July 1998–June 1999 plan year. You are considered covered by Acme's employer plan in 1999 and, depending on your income in 1999, you may not be able to deduct your 1999 IRA. This could be a big problem if you have already filed your 1999 return before the allocation is announced on March 31, 2000. If your employer's plan is a profit-sharing plan and no profits are shared for your tax year, you are not considered covered by a plan for that year.

"ACTIVE" IN A DEFINED BENEFIT PLAN

You are considered covered by a defined benefit plan if you are eligible to participate in a plan year that ends in your tax year. You are *not* considered covered by a plan if you are not eligible to participate in the plan at the end of your tax year. For example, you join Acme December 1, 2000, at a salary of $60,000. Your previous employer had no retirement plan, but Acme has a pension plan, which requires a year of service before you become a participant. You can deduct your IRA contribution for tax year 2000. You become a member of Acme's plan on December 1, 2001. You cannot have a tax-deductible IRA for tax year 2001 because you are an active participant in that year and your income exceeds the income limits for deductible IRAs.

Even if you did not work enough during the plan year for your employer to credit service to you that year, you are considered an active participant. For example, if you worked less than 1,000 hours in a year and the plan requires at least 1,000 hours or more to credit service to you for the year, you will still be treated as an active participant.

You are not considered an active participant in an employer-provided retirement plan if you are actually receiving benefit payments from the plan. So if you have taken early retirement and are receiving benefits from a retirement plan, but are working, you may still be eligible for a deductible IRA.

If You Are an Active Participant and Your Income Exceeds the Deduction Limit

If you are an active participant in an employer plan and your income falls in the deduction "phase-out" range, you will have to calculate your partial IRA deduction. The deductibility of the $2,000 IRA limit is phased out as your income increases. The deduction is reduced by multiplying $2,000 by a fraction in which the top number is the amount in excess of the deduction limit and the bottom number is $10,000. (The bottom number in the fraction is scheduled to increase to $20,000 for marrieds after 2006.)

For example, let's assume that in 2000 you are single and are earning $35,000, which is $3,000 over the full-deduction limit. You make a $2,000 traditional IRA contribution on January 2, 2000, for your 2000 tax year. Your deduction calculation is

$2,000 − ($3,000/$10,000 × $2,000) = $1,400$

You may deduct $1,400 of your $2,000 IRA contribution.

Or let's assume that in 2001 you are married and your joint income is $59,000, which is $6,000 above the limit. You make your traditional IRA contribution on January 2, 2001, for your 2001 tax year. Your deduction calculation is

$2,000 − ($6,000/$10,000 × $2,000) = 800

You may deduct only $800 of your $2,000 IRA contribution. If your husband contributes $2,000 to a traditional IRA, he may also deduct $800.

Roth IRAs

Roth IRAs, which follow many of the same rules that apply to traditional IRAs, have been available since 1998. In a Roth IRA, you may contribute up to $2,000 or the amount of income you earned for the year if you earned less than $2,000. The contribution is not deductible, but the earnings from the Roth IRA are never taxed, as long as they are not withdrawn from the Roth IRA within five years from the tax year the Roth IRA was established. This includes both the amounts originally contributed—on which you have already paid taxes—as well as the amount of earnings on which you will never pay tax.

Roth IRA Advantages

Roth IRAs have a number of advantages over traditional IRAs in addition to the fact that you never pay taxes on the earnings in the account.

- Unlike traditional IRAs, you are not required to take minimum distributions from your Roth IRA when you reach 70½. This enables you to save your IRA money until you think you need it and continue deferring tax on its earnings.
- It also avoids the chances you would be hit with the 50 percent—yes, 50 percent!—excise tax that applies if you fail to take the minimum required distribution from your IRA or any other retirement plan you have each year after you reach age 70½.
- Because the amounts withdrawn from Roth IRAs are not treated as income, Roth withdrawals, unlike traditional IRA withdrawals, are not included in calculating income when determining whether you will pay income taxes on a portion of your Social Security benefits when you retire.

Roth IRA Income Limits

But there are a few catches. First, you may not contribute to a Roth IRA in any year when your annual income exceeds certain caps. For single tax filers, the income limit for a full $2,000 contribution is $95,000 and phases out proportionately as income reaches $110,000. Singles earning $110,000 or more cannot contribute to Roth IRAs. For marrieds filing jointly, the income limit for a full $2,000 contribution is $150,000, phasing out proportionately as income reaches $160,000. Married individuals filing separately are limited to an income range of $0 to $10,000. If your income falls in the Roth IRA phase-out range you may fund the proportional amount in a Roth IRA and the remainder in a traditional IRA. But the contributions to both IRAs cannot exceed $2,000 in any one year.

Roth Five-Year Holding Period

If you take earnings out of your Roth IRA within five years of the tax year for which the Roth IRA was established, you will pay tax on the earnings and a 10 percent early withdrawal penalty. The 10 percent early withdrawal penalty tax on earnings will be due even though you meet one of the exceptions from the penalty—for example, that you are over 59½ or have become disabled.

Should You Use a Traditional IRA or a Roth IRA?

Assuming that your income qualifies you to set up a Roth IRA, should you use it or a traditional IRA? Definitely use the Roth IRA, if you are not eligible for a deductible traditional IRA but are eligible for a Roth IRA. You aren't getting a deduction for the traditional IRA, and with the Roth IRA you will have the advantage of withdrawing tax-exempt earnings at retirement, so long as you have the money in a Roth IRA that has existed for five tax years.

If you are entitled to both a deductible traditional IRA and a Roth IRA, the choice isn't so obvious. You have to make assumptions about several factors, including:

- your tax bracket after retirement,
- how long you can keep the money in the IRA, and
- whether you will need all the money in your IRA at retirement or will be able to leave most of your IRA to relatives.

Roth IRAs have significant advantages for wealthy individuals who want to leave money to their heirs. They are also useful for those who believe their tax bracket will be as high when they retire as it was during their working lives. If you start early in retirement planning, you may be one of those individuals. But for most women, the advantage of the Roth IRA is clear only if you earn so little money that the actual value of the deduction you would receive under a traditional deductible IRA would be very small.

When a Traditional IRA Is Better

If you qualify for both a traditional deductible IRA and a Roth IRA, in general you would want to use the deductible traditional IRA only if you would *not* have enough money to fully fund a Roth IRA and pay the taxes on that $2,000 contribution to the Roth IRA. For example, suppose your budget has only $2,000 left and you also still have to pay income taxes at a 28 percent rate on that amount. This means that after you pay the $560 of tax on this $2,000 you could only put $1,440 after taxes in the Roth IRA. But with a traditional IRA, you would have the full $2,000 to invest that year because you would deduct that amount rather than paying tax on it. Since you would not have enough left after taxes to put $2,000 in the Roth IRA and you could put the full $2,000 in the traditional IRA, use the traditional IRA. Because you are likely to be in a lower bracket after you retire, you will likely earn more money in the traditional IRA to offset the fact you will have to pay tax on the earnings when they are withdrawn.

When a Roth IRA Is Better

If you think your tax bracket will be the same (or perhaps even higher) when you retire than it is now, the Roth IRA will be a better investment. Roth IRA earnings will also be better if:

- You use the standard deduction on your income taxes now, so that you would receive no benefit from a traditional IRA deduction.
- You think you will earn enough money in retirement that your Social Security benefits may be taxable (the general income thresholds for taxing a

portion of Social Security benefits are $25,000 for singles and $32,000 for married individuals).

■ You will not need to make significant withdrawals from your IRA until you are older than age 70½ or you will not need to make withdrawals from your IRA at all.

Spousal IRAs: Traditional or Roth

If you are married, but one of you doesn't earn an income or earns less than $2,000 for the year, the earning spouse can set up an IRA for the nonearning spouse of up to $2,000 per year. This can be a traditional IRA. Or the spouse's IRA can be a Roth IRA, if the couple's income does not exceed the annual limit ($150,000 in 1999 and adjusted for inflation for later years). This is an ideal retirement planning strategy for those years when one member of the couple is staying home to care for children or elderly relatives.

The Rollover IRA: Transferring Employer-Plan Money

IRAs also can preserve the tax-deferred sheltering of money received from employer retirement plans. When you receive a lump-sum distribution from an employer plan, don't even think of putting the money anyplace other than a rollover IRA. If you have your employer put the money in an IRA in a process called a *trustee-to-trustee transfer* or a *direct rollover,* no taxes are due until you begin to withdraw the funds from the IRA. If you take the retirement plan distribution and don't put it in an IRA within sixty days, you will pay tax on all pretax contributions and on all earnings in the plan. If you are under age 59½ you will also pay a 10 percent early withdrawal penalty on that amount.

A rollover to an IRA is one area where the IRS laws are fairly simple. Lump-sum distributions from your former employer's plan must go directly from that plan into an IRA or another employer's plan or be issued as a check payable to your IRA account or a new employer's plan. Otherwise, the distributing plan must withhold 20 percent of the taxable amount for federal income taxes before it distributes the remainder of your account to you.

Even if the old plan withholds the 20 percent amount, you may still transfer the full taxable amount of your account to an IRA or your new employer's plan within sixty days of receiving the amount. The problem is you will have to use other savings to come up with the 20 percent that has been withheld. You will be due a refund of the 20 percent withheld amount from your income taxes, but you almost certainly won't receive it within the sixty-day time limit.

For example, Sarah Goodthyme, age 30, is leaving Midnight Banking. She has $10,000 in her Midnight 401(k) plan account. She has several options. She can set up an IRA with a bank, savings and loan, mutual fund, stockbroker, or insurance company before she receives the money. She can then instruct the plan administrator at Midnight Banking to transfer her 401(k) funds directly to that IRA. Alternatively, the plan administrator can give Sarah a check for the full $10,000 payable to the "Sarah Goodthyme IRA" (not to Sarah) and Sarah can deposit the check in the new IRA. Midnight Banking will make no withholding from the amount and Sara owes no tax or penalty on the amount.

Sarah's friend, Sally DeLay, age 35, is also leaving Midnight Banking and has $10,000 in her 401(k) plan. But Sally doesn't get organized. The Midnight Banking plan issues a check payable to Sally DeLay for $8,000. Sally gets the check on June 1. This represents the amount remaining after the mandatory 20 percent withholding. The addition of $8,000 to her income this year would put Sally in the 28 percent income bracket, and she will owe a 10 percent early withdrawal penalty on the $10,000. So in addition to the $2,000 already withheld, Sally will need to pay an additional $1,800 on the distribution, leaving her just $6,200 from her original $10,000. But if Sally acts quickly—by July 30—she can still put the entire $10,000 in an IRA and keep the money growing with tax-deferred earnings. She won't pay taxes on the original $10,000 or on its earnings until she begins to withdraw money from the IRA.

Transfer to a Traditional IRA, Then to a Roth IRA

Generally, you cannot roll over money from your employer plan directly to a Roth IRA. But you can transfer plan amounts to a traditional IRA and immediately convert the traditional IRA to a Roth IRA. Then rules for a Roth IRA will apply. That means you will owe tax immediately on the amount you have converted to the Roth IRA, but after the Roth IRA has been in existence for five years, money you take out of it, including the untaxed earnings from the account, will not be subject to tax. Of course, this assumes that you meet the general rules for IRA distributions.

Life on the Grates: Why You Should Never Spend Lump Sums

When you leave an employer, *never, never, never* spend the money you may have coming to you from the retirement plan. Even if you are actually retiring, you won't want to spend a lump-sum payment at once. Put any taxable amount of the lump-sum payment into an IRA. That way you won't pay tax on it all at once and it will continue to earn income on a tax-deferred basis. Remember, this is the money you need to live on during retirement. If you spend it, the money is gone, the potential earnings are gone, and the tax deferrals on the money and its earnings are gone. Further, if you are under 59½, a 10 percent federal tax penalty will be added to the bill.

A quick example will reinforce this warning. At 35 you leave dear old Acme and receive the $10,000 in your profit-sharing plan. You spend it on a wonderful vacation. Well, actually you spend the remainder after taxes. If you are in the 28 percent bracket and your state income tax is a mere 2 percent, you will pay $3,000 in state and local taxes. You will also pay another $1,000 for the 10 percent early withdrawal penalty. You have $6,000 left for your vacation.

Have a good time, because here's what you miss. If you had rolled $10,000 into an IRA, no taxes would be due until you begin to withdraw the money from your IRA. If that IRA earns 8 percent annually, when you retire at 65, your $10,000 rollover will now be worth $100,630. If the money had earned 9 percent, by the way, you would have $132,680. Now that will buy a *great* vacation—complete with vacation house. Alternatively, it will pay you an annual annuity of nearly $9,500 a year until you are 90, if it continues to earn 8 percent, or about $13,500 if it continues to earn 9 percent.

Few Restrictions on Lump-Sum Rollovers

Any lump sum you receive from an employer's tax-qualified retirement plan can—and should—be placed in an IRA. There are only two restrictions on retirement plan lump-sum distributions. First, any after-tax contributions you may have made to the plan cannot be rolled over to an IRA. Only money you contributed on a pretax basis, such as 401(k) contributions, employer contributions, and earnings on the account can be rolled over into an IRA. By law the employer must give you a brief description of the tax treatment of the money you are receiving from the plan.

Second, rollovers of pretax money from employer plans into IRAs must take place within sixty days of your receiving the money. This time limit is not within sixty days of your terminating employment or of the date on the check. It is sixty days from the time of actually receiving the check or other assets. The IRS is very strict about the time limit. It has disallowed rollovers made sixty-five days after receipt. However, where individuals have sent the assets to a bank, broker, or other IRA custodian within sixty days and the bank or custodian neglected to get the account set up within sixty days, the courts have required the IRS to allow the rollover IRA in spite of the agent's delay.

Obviously, the smarter approach is to set up the IRA before you take the money from your former employer's plan and have the plan transfer the money directly to the new IRA. Then the sixty-day limit is immaterial. The plan is not bound by the sixty-day rule because the account is held by the old plan trustee and then transferred to the new IRA trustee. You never receive it, so the sixty-day clock never starts running.

Where to Set Up an IRA

IRAs can be set up in a number of places—banks, thrift institutions, stockbrokers, mutual funds, insurance companies. You may have any number of IRAs. Where you set up your IRA depends on the type of investments you wish to make and how you wish to make them. Banks and savings and loan associations will issue you certificates of deposit with no additional charge for an IRA account. Some saving institutions offer higher rates on CDs placed in IRAs. Brokerage houses and mutual funds usually have a small charge for handling IRA accounts. These charges are frequently in the $20–$30 range, although for accounts over $100,000, the fee may be waived. Most mutual funds will reduce the minimum amount of investment required for IRAs. Chapter 13 provides more advice on how to invest.

Advantages of an IRA

- The earnings on the money in the traditional IRA are tax deferred; in the Roth IRA, the earnings are tax exempt once the Roth IRA is five years old. Your savings grow faster because you are not paying tax on the earnings.
- You may also be able to deduct all or part of the initial contribution, if you use the traditional IRA.
- The savings are locked up. They cannot easily fall prey to impulse spending.
- IRAs are controlled only by you. Your employer does not have control over the fate of this retirement plan. You won't fail to get a contribution because the company had a bad year and your IRA cannot be "terminated" because the employer finds the program too expensive.
- IRAs are immediately vested. It's always your money. You won't lose IRAs if you move to a new job or take time out of the job market.
- IRAs are easy to set up and to maintain. There's a bank on every corner and brokers or mutual funds will set up accounts by phone or mail.
- IRAs can invest in almost any financial instrument. This even includes U.S. minted gold coins. Investments that are unattractive because they lock up money for too long are perfect for IRAs. IRA investments are locked up until your retirement anyway. Investments that produce a lot of income annually are good for IRAs because the tax is deferred on that income.
- IRAs can be used for short-term loans. Use this advantage with extreme caution, but you may withdraw money from your IRA without tax consequences as long as it is replaced within sixty days. You may only do this once a year with the same money or the same IRA. And you should never do it unless you are absolutely positive you can repay the money within sixty days. For example, if you go to closing on your new house in June, but don't go to closing on your old house until July 10, it may make sense to use IRA money in the first closing. If you don't repay the loan within sixty days, you will pay tax and possibly a penalty on the amount borrowed and you cannot put the amount back into the IRA.
- IRAs can be the last resort for income in certain emergencies. If you die or become disabled, IRA funds can be used by your family or you without penalty, in most cases. IRAs can be used to pay medical insurance premiums

when you are unemployed for more than twelve weeks, medical expenses if they exceed 7.5 percent of income, and higher education expenses. Up to $10,000 may also be used for first-time home purchases.

Disadvantages of an IRA

- The law on IRAs has changed frequently. Congress seems to want to use the IRA as both a carrot and a stick. Usually, Congress does not make the changes retroactive, but still it is confusing when one year the money is deductible and the next year it isn't unless you satisfy various criteria.
- The savings are locked up. If you withdraw the money from the IRA (other than to roll it into another IRA) before you are 59½, the earnings on money and any contributions you deducted from income tax will be taxed at ordinary income tax rates plus a 10 percent penalty. (The only exceptions are your death or disability, expenses for medical care, health insurance during unemployment, and up to $10,000 for first-time home buying.) The only way to avoid this is to take the money out in equal payments over the course of your expected lifetime. However, from a retirement security point of view, this "lock-up" is not a disadvantage; it's an advantage. Retirement savings should be used at retirement, not before.
- IRAs cannot be borrowed against or otherwise used to secure loans. (The short-term sixty-day loans don't count because they are treated as though you were only moving from one IRA to another IRA during the sixty-day grace period for such moves.) Unlike an ordinary savings account or brokerage account, which may serve as collateral for a short-term loan or other borrowings, IRAs may never be used as security. If you do so, the amount will be treated as though it was distributed and you will owe income and penalty taxes.

Retirement Plans for the Self-Employed and Moonlighters: Keoghs, SEPs, and SIMPLEs

If you are self-employed, work as a freelancer, or have your own business in addition to being employed by another, you could always set up your own retirement plan, like those discussed in the chapter on employer-provided retirement plans. But as you have seen, the rules for these employer plans are very complicated.

Consider the more manageable plans designed for small employers or the self-employed, such as SEP-IRAs and SIMPLE IRAs or SIMPLE 401(k)s, all discussed in Chapter 7, or a favorite of the self-employed, a tax-deductible Keogh or H.R. 10 plan. The earnings from this plan's investments are tax deferred until you begin to withdraw them at retirement. Keoghs are designed to provide self-employed individuals, sole proprietorships, and partnerships with the same types of retirement plans corporate employers can establish, including the same tax advantages.

Retirement Funding for the Self-Employed: Keoghs

Who Can Contribute to a Keogh?

You are eligible to set up a Keogh if you are self-employed. This option is usually available even if you have a conventional job but have additional income from self-employment. The IRS gives as an example an attorney who is employed by a corporation during the day, but has her own law practice in the evening.

Full-time insurance salespeople, members of religious orders, or ministers are examples of "employees" who cannot set up Keoghs even though their earnings are deemed self-employment income for Social Security purposes. But such people may also be self-employed, in addition to being insurance salespeople or ministers. For example, a minister may receive a regular salary from her congregation, which is treated as self-employment income for Social Security tax purposes. She may also be "self-employed" for fees reported on Schedule C for performing marriages, baptisms, and other personal services, and the fees for these services may be self-employment income for Keogh plan purposes.[2]

If you have other employees in your business, you will probably need to include them under the Keogh plan. Keoghs are subject to many of the same rules applied to other employer plans discussed in Chapter 7, so if your employees meet the age and service rules, you will need to include them in your plan.

How Your Employment Status Affects Your Keogh

Keoghs can be especially useful for women. During times when we are "out of work" officially, we may be working at home on various paying projects. Keoghs offer a way to save for retirement even when you are officially off the payroll. For example, if you take a leave of absence, you may be able to convince your employer to engage you as a "consultant" with independent contractor status to finish up a project in progress or to help out with work overflows. From this self-employment income you can set up your Keogh.

Independent Contractor Status

If you are shifting to part-time work for an employer and as a part-timer you would not receive or accrue retirement benefits or service credits, consider whether you could work as an "independent contractor" rather than as a part-time employee. You are then self-employed. You can save in your own Keogh retirement plan rather than have no retirement savings growing. As we have seen, growing retirement savings amounts, even if small, can become significant sums over the years.

There are drawbacks to becoming an independent contractor, however. You will pay 15.3 percent Social Security taxes as a self-employed person, rather than the 7.65 percent you pay as an employee. You will be responsible for calculating and paying estimated income taxes. The employer cannot withhold for you. Additionally, you really must be "independent" and control your work performance, a status the IRS has not specifically defined. In determining independent contractor status, the IRS weighs a number of factors, such as setting your own hours, using your own equipment, working in your own premises, working for other clients, and being free to turn down assignments.

For example, suppose you are a graphic arts designer. Your employer's business slows down, making it necessary to cut work hours. You and she agree you will go off the payroll, but be available to do projects for her on an as-needed basis. Together you draft a contract. You work at home, at hours you determine, using your own desktop publishing software. You pay your own expenses and hire any assistants you need without consulting your former employer. The IRS would probably agree that you are a self-employed independent contractor, eligible to set up your own Keogh plan.

But if the same facts applied, except you are expected to be available to your employer every work day between 9 A.M. and 12 and you may not work for other clients, the IRS would almost certainly consider you to be an employee and not eligible to set up a Keogh plan.

Setting Up the Keogh

You may set up a Keogh at any time before the end of the year. You do not need to contribute to the plan when you set it up. Once the plan is in place by the end of the year, you may contribute to it for that tax year until your tax return filing date, including extensions. In fact, if you choose a defined contribution plan, you probably will not be able to fund the Keogh fully until after your tax year closes, because your contribution must be based on net earnings. You generally won't know that figure until you calculate your year-end income and expenses. In order to maximize the growth of your money, you should be placing some money in the Keogh during the course of the year.

Should Your Keogh Be a Defined Benefit or a Defined Contribution Plan?

Keogh plans can be defined benefit or defined contribution plans, like corporate employer plans. For example, if your Keogh is a defined contribution plan, your contributions are limited to the section 415 limits, discussed in earlier chapters, of $30,000 or 25 percent of compensation, whichever is less. The $30,000 figure will be indexed for inflation in coming years.

Also, if you set up your defined contribution plan as a profit-sharing plan, your tax deduction is limited to 15 percent of compensation for employees, or 13.043

percent of compensation for you as a self-employed person. And you have the discretion not to contribute to the plan each year. If you set up a "money purchase pension" defined contribution plan, you may make a higher contribution of up to 25 percent of your compensation. But under a money purchase plan you must contribute a fixed percentage of compensation each year, regardless of profits. Of course, if you are the only person in the plan, the net income of the business is your compensation, so there is little problem. But if you have employees, the money purchase pension plan may pinch in lean business years.

If you set up a defined benefit plan, you will need an actuary to calculate the amount you must contribute to the plan. You must make payments to fund the benefit at least quarterly. The benefit you ultimately receive cannot exceed $90,000 adjusted for inflation ($130,000 in 1999) or 100 percent of compensation, whichever is less. When you retire, if the plan has been in existence for less than ten years or if you retire before your Social Security retirement age, these limits will be actuarially reduced.

Maximizing Contributions to Your Keogh

If you are lucky enough to be concerned about exceeding these contribution and benefit limits, you should recognize that while you are young the defined contribution limit will permit you to make a greater contribution to your Keogh plan, all things being equal. After you reach middle age you can probably contribute more money under a defined benefit plan. Whether a defined contribution plan or a defined benefit Keogh allows you to contribute more money depends on your age when you start contributing. Remember, these are simply rules of the growth pattern of money. If you want $1 million at age 65, you can contribute less money each year if you start when you are 30 than you can if you start when you are 40.

The compensation for you as a self-employed plan participant is your net earned income from the business, minus the deduction allowed for self-employment taxes *and* the deduction you take for your contribution to the Keogh. Compensation in excess of a set amount (this figure is indexed each year; in 1999 it is $160,000) cannot be taken into account.

Keogh Compliance

Keogh assets must be in a trusteed account with a formal, written plan document like other employer-provided retirement plans. There are many *master plan* or *prototype plan* documents approved by the IRS and offered without additional charge by banks, mutual funds, insurance companies, and brokerages when you set up a Keogh account with one of these organizations. Just be sure to read the plan document to be certain its provisions are the provisions you want. Alternatively, you could have a lawyer draw up your own Keogh plan document, but there are few significant advantages to such an individualized document.

As with your IRA, the organization you use to hold your Keogh assets depends on the investments you want. If you simply want certificates of deposit, use a bank or thrift. If you want only mutual funds, deal directly with the mutual fund company. If you have enough money in your Keogh to diversify investments, a brokerage house makes sense. The broker can purchase stocks and bonds for you, as well as CDs and mutual funds. You also may buy annuities with your Keogh assets. If you buy annuities or certificates of deposit from an insurance company, the Keogh does not require a trustee.

Prohibited Transactions with the Keogh

Keogh plan assets may not be invested, loaned, or otherwise used for the benefit of any corporation, partnership, or business that is more than 50 percent owned by you, members of your family, or any fiduciary of the Keogh. If you ignore that rule, you have engaged in a prohibited transaction and must pay a tax of 15 percent of the value involved in the prohibited transaction. This amount increases to 100 percent if the violation transaction is not corrected after the first year.

IRS Filings for Keoghs

Keoghs, like other employer-provided plans, are generally required to file annual reports with the IRS on Form 5500. For single-employee plans, the IRS made available Form 5500EZ, which requires minimal information and is easy to complete. In the past few years, the IRS has announced that Keoghs with less than $100,000 in assets can omit filing even Form 5500EZ except upon termination of the plan. The absence of a filing requirement should encourage more eligible parties to set up the accounts.

Advantages of Keoghs

- Keoghs are the primary way for self-employed individuals to save substantial retirement benefits in a tax-sheltered plan. The $2,000 permitted to an IRA contribution is simply not adequate to build a substantial retirement savings account.
- Keoghs are easy to set up and require little reporting until your account contains substantial assets.
- Keoghs can offer a way to keep investing for retirement even when you are officially off the payroll, if you earn money freelancing in your profession.

Disadvantages of Keoghs

- The Keogh contribution can be difficult to calculate. IRS Publication 560, "Retirement Plans for the Self-Employed," will give you instructions. Call

1-800-TAX-FORM [829-3676]. Instructions can also be retrieved from the IRS Internet site: *www.irs.ustreas.gov,* under "Publications.")
- Unless the Keogh is a profit-sharing plan—that is, if it is a money purchase plan or a defined benefit plan—you must fund it each year or terminate the plan. If you have no income in a year, you may either have to borrow money to fund the plan or terminate the plan. Because the plan is supposed to be permanent, the IRS will look with disfavor on plans that are terminated after a few years. Of course, since the funding is usually based on your income, the contribution will coincide with the income, except in a defined benefit plan.
- If you have other employees you will need to include them in the Keogh.

Small Business Pension Plans: SEPs and SIMPLEs

Simplified Employee Pensions—SEPs—can also be used as individual retirement accounts, in so-called SEP-IRAs, and SIMPLE IRAs can also be used for the self-employed. The same rules apply for these individual SEPs and SIMPLEs as for employer-provided SEPs discussed in Chapter 7 on employer plans. Recognize that if you set up a SEP or a SIMPLE plan for yourself and you later acquire employees, they will most likely have to be covered by the plan as well—and the benefits will be vested immediately.

Annuities: Your Home-Grown Pension

Individual annuities are investments designed to pay out over your lifetime, much like creating your own pension plan. Basically, you and an insurance company enter into a contract in which you invest an after-tax amount of money, generally at least $5,000, to earn a stated rate of interest over the contract period. When the contract expires, usually timed to coincide with your retirement, you begin to receive payments from the annuity.

The earnings on the amount you originally invested, frequently referred to as *inside buildup,* are not subject to taxes until you begin to receive payments from the annuity. The portion of the money you originally invested, referred to as your "basis" in the contract, is not subject to tax at all because you have already paid taxes on it.

Usually, there are no direct commissions charged for annuities, because commissions are built into the plan's cost. The annuity issuer may impose substantial early withdrawal penalties should you wish to get your money out of the investment before the end of the contract. You will also face the IRS's 10 percent early withdrawal penalty tax if you receive the money before you are age 59½ in a form other than a periodic stream over the course of your expected lifetime. This IRS early withdrawal penalty will not apply if you become disabled and begin to withdraw the money.

Variations in Annuities

Annuities have literally hundreds of variations. Each insurance company selling annuities has several different plans and several variations in each plan.

- You may be able to add to the investment each year.
- The interest rate may be changed each year.
- The interest rate may be tied to a stock or bond index.

Variable annuities, sold by insurance companies, mutual funds, and others, permit you to invest money in mutual funds and usually permit you to choose among and move in and out of various mutual funds in the "family" of funds covered by your annuity. The basic advantage of a variable annuity is that your investment in mutual funds is allowed to grow without paying current taxes on the earnings in the mutual funds. As with any other annuity investment earnings, tax is not paid until you begin to withdraw the money.

Receiving Payouts from Annuities

Once the annuity contract has reached the payment date, you may be able to choose a number of ways to begin receiving the money. The traditional form of payment under an annuity is—no surprise—annuitizing, which guarantees equal periodic payments over the course of your life. Under such a payment plan, you receive a fixed amount as long as you live, just as you do with an employer-provided pension. If you die a short time after payments begin, the insurance company pockets the money. But if you exceed your life expectancy, the insurance company must keep paying you as long as you live, even if the original investment and earnings have been exhausted.

But there are many other ways to receive payment, including variations on the annuitizing method. For example, you may elect a *joint and survivor annuity,* which will reduce your monthly payments, but will pay out as long as you or your named beneficiary is alive. After the death of both you and the beneficiary, no further payments will be made. Any remaining amount is kept by the insurance company.

Another form of annuity payment is the *life-with-years-certain annuity.* This form of payment guarantees you a lifetime income, but also permits you to elect payments for a certain period, even if you die before the end of that period. For example, you could elect a *life-with-ten-years-certain* payout. As long as you are alive, you will receive the established payment, but if you die before ten years have passed, your estate or a beneficiary would collect the payments for the remaining portion of the ten-year period.

Alternatives to Lifetime Guarantees

Some annuities promise a higher interest rate on your investment, but limit you to receiving the money only in the traditional annuity form. Some companies will allow you to take payout under a schedule you set up. This plan of withdrawal is usually referred to as the *systematic withdrawal plan*. With this approach, you can raise, lower, or stop the payments whenever you wish. You could also switch the remaining sum of money into an annuitized form of payment. But you pay for this flexibility. First, you lose the guarantee of lifetime payments. In most cases, you also will pay tax on the total payment each month until the earnings on your investment are considered to have been exhausted.

You may also take your annuity payment in one lump sum and invest it in some other investment vehicle. Some investment advisers suggest shopping again for an annuity at retirement with the lump sum from your original annuity. You may be able to receive a higher rate of return with a new company, thus increasing the monthly payment you begin to receive.

Safety of Annuities in the 1990s

For years, annuities were considered to be among the safest of investments. Experts viewed them as highly appropriate for conservative investors, especially those 50 and over who did not mind having their investment locked up until retirement. But in the 1980s and 1990s things began to change as a few annuity companies failed. In the early 1990s, Executive Life Insurance in California and Mutual Benefit Insurance in New Jersey all but collapsed, leaving annuity holders, among other creditors, in doubt as to whether they would ever see all their money. After state insurance regulators stepped in most holders received most of their money either directly from these companies or through state insurance pools.

The moral of the story: *carefully* investigate any annuity and its offering insurance company. Use an independent insurance broker or a financial planner, not an insurance company agent, to evaluate both the companies and various annuities. If you use an agent who represents only one company, she can offer you only the annuities her company sells, which may not have the highest rates or all the features that are available.

Insurance companies are regulated by the states. Investigate what the state regulatory agency says about the company. But don't rely on state agencies. A few months before the collapse of Executive Life the state of California was still rating the company positively. Go to a library and look at insurance company rating services such as A. M. Best Company, Standard & Poor's, or Moody's Investors Service. You might also consult *Annuity Shopper* (800-872-6684), a semiannual newsletter that publishes annuities' rates. Individual copies of the newsletter are $25; an annual subscription is $45.

Be particularly wary of any annuity that offers interest rates much higher than those generally available. This can be a sign that the company desperately needs your money to keep the wolf from the door. If the annuity guarantees the interest rate for only one year, ask what rate the same type of annuity purchased in the previous year paid then and is paying this year. Ask about the rates for the company's similar annuities over the past five years. The answers at least will give you an idea of whether the company lures customers in with high rates and then drops the rates drastically in subsequent years.

Beware of Annuity "Resales"

Even if you choose a company that is sound, problems can arise because in most states an insurance company may sell your annuity contract to another company, which could be less sound. Theoretically, this should not happen without your knowledge and consent. Annuities are, after all, contracts between you and the company and one party to a contract cannot assign the contract's performance to a new entity without consent of the parties to the original contract. This practice of selling annuities to other companies is sometimes referred to as *assumption reinsurance* and is increasing, according to state insurance officials.[3] At this point there appears to be little defense against such resales other than to watch your statements and your mail closely. If you receive notice of an impending sale, contact the original annuity insurer immediately and withhold your consent until you can review the status of the purchasing company. It may not be all bad news. There is a chance that the purchasing company is more sound than the original company.

Annuity Advantages

- In spite of the bad publicity of the early 1990s, most annuities are safe and can provide a steady income at retirement.
- Annuities don't need to be "managed"; the investment return can be totally controlled by the insurance company.
- If you choose an annuity that permits you to make periodic payments, you will be encouraged to add to your savings because the "payment" seems like a bill that must be paid.
- Annuities can provide a guaranteed income for life, if you choose that option of payment at retirement.

Annuity Disadvantages

- Your money is tied up in a specific investment. If the interest rate falls, your only recourse is to withdraw from the annuity and that involves substantial penalties in most cases. When you withdraw from the annuity, you will also have to pay tax on any money the annuity investment earned.

- Check the annuity fees carefully, especially if the annuity involves mutual funds. Total fees may be higher than you expected, with the result that the real income on assets in your annuity is less than expected after subtracting all the fees.

- Your annuity is only as safe as the insurance company sponsoring it. If the company becomes insolvent, you may receive some minimum payments from state reinsurance funds or you may receive nothing.

Nontraditional Retirement Savings Investments

Universal life insurance, disability insurance, long-term care insurance, and home ownership are not typically thought of as investments for retirement savings. But in many cases for women they fulfill an important role in saving and investing for retirement.

Universal Life Insurance

Universal life insurance is not an ideal retirement savings vehicle and it generally is not sold for retirement saving. But if you are a single mother on a limited budget, it may be the best retirement investment you can afford. Universal life insurance can provide life insurance to protect your dependents and build future value for retirement. The policy uses your premium payment both to cover life insurance, which would provide money to your children if you die, and to cover an investment, giving you a cash value in the policy. The premiums can be divided to purchase different amounts of life insurance and investments, and the premiums can be varied. In the first years of the policy, while the children are small and so is your salary, you might want most of the premium to go to insurance. As the children grow up, more of the premium can move to the investment side of the policy.

The changes in divisions of the premium might be more up and down. For example, suppose you get a job providing you with twice your salary in life insurance, at no cost to you, and permitting you to buy even more life insurance cheaply, if you wish. You can shift most of your universal life policy premium to the investment side. Six years later you move to a job without that automatic life insurance benefit and the children have just started college. It's time to move more of the premium back to the life insurance side of the policy.

Policies will vary from company to company, so be sure you understand the exact operation of any policy you buy. As always, working with an independent agent should give you the best range of options.

Advantages of Universal Life Insurance

- If you have dependents, universal life insurance enables you to buy life insurance to provide for those dependents and invest at the same time.
- The premiums are a "bill" that is likely to be paid even in financially tight months when savings deposits otherwise might not be made.
- The earnings on the invested portion of your premium are not taxed until you withdraw the money.
- You may be able to borrow against the policy.
- Your employer may offer universal life insurance at a group rate that would be lower than other policies and premiums and would be automatically deducted from your paycheck.

Disadvantages of Universal Life Insurance

- The return on your investment may be low compared with other returns you could be receiving on the money.
- Your "investment" is locked up.
- If you don't have dependents, you don't need the life insurance.

Disability Insurance

Disability insurance is not usually thought of as part of "retirement" planning. But if you become permanently disabled, you are retired—without the ability to have planned for retirement. Most likely in this situation, you also lack the years of private savings and accruals of employer retirement benefits you had counted on.

Disability insurance should be one of the most important parts of your financial planning, indeed, the number one priority after a roof over your head and a job. Most individuals need more disability insurance than that provided through either an employer plan or Social Security.

Disability benefits are usually divided into short-term disability, in which there is the expectation you will recover and work again, and long-term disability, under which you are presumed to be incapable of ever rejoining the work force. Disability claims and benefits are also divided into work-related and nonwork-related types.

Work-Related Disability Controlled by State Programs

If your disability is directly work-related, you may be covered by worker's compensation. Every state has laws requiring worker's compensation benefits. These laws vary widely from state to state. If you have questions about worker's compensation, you should talk with a local expert. Begin with the state office in charge of worker's compensation enforcement. If the disability is nonwork-related, you will not be covered unless you have some form of disability insurance. The following discussion focuses on nonwork-related, long-term disability.

Social Security Disability Benefits

Social Security may provide some disability benefits. But the qualifications for receiving the payments are rigorous. Social Security disability payments are subject to the following requirements.

- You must prove you are unable to perform any "substantial" gainful employment, not just that you are unable to conduct your usual employment.
- Your impairment must be expected to last at least twelve months.
- There is a five-month waiting period after you become totally disabled before benefits begin.
- You must have worked a specified number of quarters, depending on your age, to qualify and some of those work periods must have been recent.

Social Security also has strict disability standards, which you will have to meet. Be prepared to prove your disability. You will not receive benefits for the five-month waiting period. You can expect the Social Security review to take a number of months, but you will be paid retroactively for Social Security's delay in processing your case for any time after the five-month waiting period.

You must have been covered by Social Security for forty quarters—ten years—to be eligible for disability benefits. If you were born before 1929, you need fewer quarters. Obviously, if you are just starting out in the job market, you will receive nothing under Social Security if you become disabled. Also, some of those quarters must have been earned recently. That number depends on your age. If you were born between 1948 and 1959, you must have earned twenty quarters in the past ten years. If you were born after 1960, you must have earned six quarters in the past three years.

Social Security disability benefits will be reduced if you are receiving worker's compensation or other disability benefits. Total disability benefits may not exceed 80 percent of your pre-disability compensation.

Employer-Provided Disability Insurance

Your employer may provide some long-term disability insurance or may give you the opportunity to purchase such insurance. Only 42 percent of employees employed by companies with more than one hundred workers had disability insurance in 1995.[4] Small employers are even less likely to provide such benefits. If the employer does provide disability insurance, purchase as much as you can.

Ideally, you would buy enough to cover your current salary if you become disabled. Usually if you are disabled you will need more money to live, not less. Services you once performed for yourself will now have to be done by others who must be paid. However, many policies limit the amount they will pay to a percentage of your compensation before disability. Policies may also offset their payments by disability benefits from other sources such as Social Security, worker's compensation, or your own privately purchased insurance. Check these features carefully. Also check whether benefits cease if you earn a limited income under a new profession. You don't want to be punished for becoming rehabilitated and working at a lower-paying job.

Privately Purchased Disability Insurance

If you are self-employed or your employer does not provide disability insurance, purchase it on your own. If you belong to a trade association, such as the American Bar Association or a local chamber of commerce, you may be able to purchase a policy through the group at a lower rate. It may be worthwhile to join an organization just to get the group rates for the disability insurance. One way to reduce the cost of disability insurance is to buy a policy that does not begin payments for six months or a year after disability. If you have savings that could support you for a time, think of buying this type of policy.

Investigate several policies. Ask about the same features we discussed with employer-provided insurance, but be even more alert.

- Determine what sort of disability is covered.
- Must you be totally disabled from all gainful employment or only from your usual occupation?
- Who decides—one doctor, a team of doctors?
- Is there an appeals procedure?
- Do they use the Social Security standard? Given Social Security's tight standards, beware of policies that rely on Social Security's definition.
- How long must you be disabled before payments begin?
- How long will benefits last?
- Do you have to submit to periodic examinations?

Weigh the answers to each of these questions carefully. Don't decide just on price.

Long-Term Care Insurance

Long-term care insurance—coverage for nursing home or in-home custodial care—is another item you might not ordinarily include in retirement planning. Certainly long-term care insurance is nowhere near as important as disability insurance, and, unlike other forms of disability and health insurance, it is relatively new.

Long-term care insurance is truly a middle-class issue. If you are wealthy you will "self-insure" because you will have enough money to pay for custodial care in your older years. If you have no assets in your retirement years, Medicaid generally will pay for nursing home care. But if you are in the middle, long-term care without help from insurance could bankrupt you and/or your family.

Long-term health insurance pays for custodial care if you are incapacitated by an illness or accident, or if age simply makes it impossible for you to care for yourself. Medicare and most other health insurance programs do not pay for custodial care that merely helps with your ordinary living activities and does not purport to treat an illness.

Long-term care insurance policies should not be one of the elements of your retirement planning if you are under 40 or if you have limited savings. Unless you have extraordinary medical conditions, such insurance should be a part of your retirement assets only after you have invested close to your maximum savings in other retirement programs.

You might also consider the purchase of long-term care insurance for an elderly parent for whom you have responsibility. Even if you are not paying for the policy, your parent may wish to consult with you on the purchase of the policy.

Important Tax Breaks for Long-Term Care Premiums and Benefits

Since 1997, long-term care policies also may offer some important tax breaks. First, a portion of the premiums for long-term policies and the expenses of long-term care may be treated as tax-deductible medical expenses. While medical expenses are deductible only if they exceed 7.5 percent of income, in some years the deduction may be available. Premium deduction limits are shown in Table 9.2.

Second, long-term care benefits received from qualified long-term care policies are exempt from federal tax, and per diem amounts of up to $190 per day in 1999 are also exempt. This amount is adjusted each year for inflation.

Some Employers Offer Long-Term Care Insurance

Some employers offer long-term care policies covering the employee and her spouse or partner and, in some cases, even the parents and parents-in-law of the employee. Such policies usually require contributions by the employees. The older the policy beneficiary, the higher the premium. Employer-provided long-term care insurance is a tax-free benefit (as long as the premiums are not paid by your salary reduction). If you have any bargaining power at all with your employer, try to get long-term coverage as a "perk" since neither the coverage nor the benefits when eventually paid are taxable.

Table 9.2
Maximum Amount of Deduction for Long-Term Care Insurance Premiums, 1999

Age before Year End	Eligible Annual Premium Limit[a]
40 or less	$210
41 to 49	$400
50 to 59	$800
60 to 69	$2,120
70 or more	$2,660

[a]Adjusted annually for inflation.

Individual Long-Term Care Policies

Individual long-term care policies are also available. Insurance companies have been wary of offering such policies because of the many uncertainties involved, including the period of years in which the need could arise and over which it could last and the rapid changes in medical technology. But many reputable companies are offering long-term care policies and revising them frequently based on the company's experience. Nevertheless, caution must be your watch word as you look at such policies.

The National Association of Insurance Commissioners has produced a *Shopper's Guide to Long-Term Care Insurance* that includes a number of recommendations, as well as the addresses and phone numbers for every state's insurance departments, insurance counseling agencies, and agencies on aging. The booklet also offers a worksheet to help you learn the availability and costs of long-term care facilities in your area and another worksheet to help you compare the provisions and costs of long-term care policies.[5] NAIC notes that most states have a "free look" period after you purchase the policy during which you may cancel the policy.

Questions you should specifically ask include:

- What is the nature of the benefit—a fixed dollar sum, a percent of costs? Is there any inflation protection?
- How long will care last?
- Is there a days per year maximum?
- Can premiums be raised once care begins?
- Can the policy be canceled? Why, when, for what reasons?
- Where can the care be delivered, at home or only in an institution?
- Is Alzheimer's disease covered?
- Are other types of cognitive impairments covered?

- Is there a requirement that you first be hospitalized before you can begin receiving long-term care? Frequently, patients don't require hospitalization before requiring custodial care. You don't want to be forced to be hospitalized as a prerequisite to beginning long-term care.
- What is the "trigger" for the policy? Inability to complete basic tasks such as dressing, eating? How many such tasks?
- Who decides whether these criteria have been met?
- What is the level of care? It should be skilled, intermediate, and custodial. Custodial care covers basic needs such as feeding, dressing, and so on. Skilled care involves the services of licensed medical professionals. Intermediate care is the "day care" approach, requiring some care every day, but not round-the-clock service.
- Does the policy qualify for favorable federal income tax treatment for both the premiums and any benefits paid up to the dollar limits outlined by the IRS?

In addition to these questions, be certain you are dealing with a reputable and financially stable company. The chances are you will not begin to collect on your long-term insurance for decades. You want to be certain the insurer will still be there when you do need your benefits. As with investigating insurance companies for annuities, look to the independent insurance rating services such as Moody's Investors Service or Standard & Poor's. Consult with your state's insurance regulatory agency as well.

Home Ownership as a Retirement Investment

At one time any self-respecting book on financial planning—especially one on retirement financial planning—would have started with the advice to buy the most expensive house you can afford and let it be the primary source of your "savings" in your early working years. Such books would have told you that the first priority after feeding yourself should be a home purchase. Today no less an authority than the National Association of Realtors recommends you purchase a house for shelter, not for investment, according to Linda Goold, the realtors' director of federal tax programs.

Depending on where you live, buying a home may be risky business. Starting in Texas in the early 1980s, we saw the old "buy a big house" advice go very wrong. People bought houses and a year or two later their value had declined 25–50 percent—if they could sell the house at all. Jobs were lost, mortgage payments were missed, and people with previously sound financial records simply walked away from their mortgage and their home, not to mention the savings they had invested in their home. In the early 1990s the same scenario was played out on the east and west coasts. Women in Los Angeles, Boston, New York, and Washington, D.C., saw their life savings eroded as the overheated value of their homes melted down. If these women also had the misfortune to lose their jobs, their financial security melted, too.

If the same woman had bought a more modest house than she could afford and invested the difference in mortgage payments in an IRA or 401(k) plan, even if she had lost her job, there would have been smaller mortgage payments. As a last resort, she could have used her IRA or 401(k) retirement savings to live on until she found another job. Granted, one still has living expenses even with small or no mortgage payments. Still, it is easier to pay a smaller mortgage or to break the lease on a three-bedroom apartment and move into an efficiency than it is to sell a five-bedroom, six-bath house in a down economy.

Don't Be "House Poor"

Moreover, at retirement you may find yourself house poor. A large portion of your net worth could be tied up in your home, and the market may or may not be good. You may find the steady investment in upkeep eating away at your retirement savings. You may want to move to a different locale, or you may want a smaller yard and less house to heat, cool, and paint.

Buying a home still can be a wise financial move. You have to live somewhere and you might as well be paying yourself rent. You also get a tax deduction for the interest you are paying on your mortgage. But ignore any advice to invest all your savings in the down payment. Don't "stretch" to buy a house a bit more expensive than you can afford on the theory that inflation will increase your income and in two or three years you can easily afford the mortgage payments that first seemed gargantuan.

In considering buying a house—especially in a high real estate market—do your financial calculations on a worst-case scenario, considering the cost of the house, the closing costs, the interest rate, and the monthly payments. After the down payment, closing costs, and incidentals, will you still have enough money to pay the mortgage payments for six months if you lose your job? Will you still be able to save at least enough to fund your employer-provided 401(k) or contribute the maximum to your IRA next year?

If the answers aren't "yes," think long and hard—and very realistically—about whether your job or business is likely to be secure two years from now. Look at the housing market in your area. Has it been stable for the last decade? Has it increased dramatically? How does it compare with the rest of the country? Some of this will be guessing. If you have evidence to suggest your job is safe and the housing market in your area has been stable or is just beginning to climb, you may want to make the investment in a home even if it will deplete your savings.

Remember that homes priced at the lower end of the scale have better resale potential in any kind of market. The three-bedroom, two-bath house near a good school, while more modest than the five-bedroom with master bath and Jacuzzi that you really want, may be the better investment. As a bonus, you may find that when you retire it is the home you really want to live in instead of the five-bedroom white elephant eating all your retirement income in lawn service fees and new roofs.

Conclusion: Recognize the Importance of Personal Saving— and Start That Saving Now

Accept the fact that you are the single most important source of your retirement savings. It is the source you can control and plan around. Recognizing the importance of your own retirement savings now and taking steps to begin building those savings—no matter how small at the start—is the single most important thing you can do for your retirement planning. Starting *today:*

- Begin an automatic payroll or checking account deduction savings program with an eye toward retirement; don't worry if it seems small.
- Open an IRA and put as much money as you can afford into it up to the $2,000 limit. Start with a certificate of deposit, if you feel uncomfortable with mutual funds or stocks, but an equity or balanced mutual fund is probably the best investment for growth.
- Find out whether you have disability insurance through your employer. If your employer offers disability insurance but doesn't pay for it, buy it. If you don't have access to it at work, buy it on your own.
- If you are self-employed, research and set up a Keogh or SEP even if the initial contribution must be small.

Let's move on to look at the role of benefits in taking or leaving a job and to see how you can maximize your personal retirement investing success.

PART THREE

HOW MUCH TO SAVE AND INVEST

The Role of Benefits in Taking or Leaving a Job

Jennifer has just received a call from her boss's colleague, who needs an experienced secretary. The colleague has seen Jennifer's work and wants to offer her $2,000 more a year than her current salary of $21,000. Jennifer knows the colleague and the business. She needs the extra money, so she accepts the job. Jennifer just lost over $1,000 in annual compensation. She confused "salary" with compensation and she didn't ask about health, disability, or retirement benefits. What happened?

In this chapter we will see how to estimate the value of benefits in calculating your total compensation package. We will also discuss how to protect your benefits when you leave a job for any reason.

If Jennifer had asked, she would have learned the new job does not provide health, disability, or retirement benefits. At her current job she has health insurance benefits worth $2,000 a year; she pays for 25 percent of the cost of health care benefits with pretax dollars. Automatically she has lost $1,500 in health benefits paid by her original employer. She currently pays only a small amount to buy group disability insurance through her employer. Buying it as an individual will cost much more.

Jennifer has a defined benefit retirement plan under her current job that will pay her $8,000 per year at retirement. There is no retirement plan at the new job. She will have to save over $700 per year for thirty years to make up for the loss of the retirement benefit. Worse, she is only a few months away from vesting in the benefits she has accrued under her current employer's plan. Because she is leaving before she vests, she has lost the current lump-sum value of the benefits she has earned to date. That amount, $543, seems small, but $543, which could be in-

Table 10.1
Comparison of Total Compensation: The Value of Salary Plus Benefits at Jennifer's Jobs

	Current Job	New Job
Salary	$21,000	$23,000
Health Benefits	$1,500	—
Retirement Benefit Current Value Equivalent	$700	—
Subtotal	$23,200	$23,000
Loss of Accrued Retirement Benefit		(543)
Total Compensation	$23,200	$22,457
Difference before Tax Advantages	**$743**	

vested in a tax-deferred IRA at 6 percent for the next thirty-five years until she retires, would grow to $4,175. If the amount were invested at 9 percent it would grow to $11,080.

Table 10.1 shows the balance sheet for Jennifer's old job and her new job.

Jennifer has lost approximately $2,750 in benefits this year in return for a $2,000 annual increase in salary, for a loss of about $750 this year.

But her net loss is really greater when you account for the tax consequences. The $2,000 of additional salary at the new job is subject to at least 22 percent in taxes, leaving her with a net salary increase of only $1,560. The $1,500 of health benefits she received at her former job was not subject to tax, and her contribution of $500 toward the health care plan was made with pretax dollars. The equivalent value of the retirement benefit she was accruing is about $700 and that value was tax deferred. She will need over $3,462 in pretax earnings to replace the tax-favored employer-provided benefits she was receiving at her former job.[1] So Jennifer has actually lost $3,462 minus her after-tax salary increase of $1,560 for a total compensation loss of $1,902.

Remember: Compensation Equals Both Salary and Benefits

Jennifer's situation is dramatic, but not unusual. Too many employees realize too late that they are working for more than salary. Other important benefits need to be counted. Employers are partly to blame for employees' lack of benefits awareness. Each year employers spend literally billions of dollars on retirement, health, disability, and other benefits. ERISA requires employers to disclose information about these benefits, and employers comply. But most employers do little in either the ERISA-mandated communications or other employer communications to emphasize the value of those benefits. It's not surprising, but it is regrettable that most employees receiving employer-provided benefits have little, if any, concept of the after-tax value of those benefits.

When questioned about this lack of publicity, employers give two common responses. If we talk about the cost of benefits, employees fear that we are preparing to reduce benefits. We spend enough on benefits as it is. We don't want to spend more money publicizing them. Both answers are self-defeating.

Unless the annual benefits statement for a defined benefit plan includes an estimate of the present value lump sum of the benefit under the plan, it is virtually impossible for an employee to know the dollar value by doing her own calculations. Employers rarely provide such present value calculations, because they are based on too many variables. With defined contribution plans, determining the value of the annual employer-provided benefit is easier. The employee usually knows what the profit-sharing plan or 401(k) matching contribution was for last year. And the employer usually includes the value of employer contributions in the annual benefit statement. But still the employer rarely stresses the total amount of benefits and the tax advantages of those benefits.

It is not surprising that Jennifer didn't think about the value of the retirement plan. No one had ever given her a clue about the estimated costs. But you shouldn't repeat her errors.

What to Ask During the Job Interview

The time to learn about benefits—retirement, disability, health, and dependent care—is during the interview process. The health, disability, and dependent care benefits are important, because the less money you need to spend for those items, the more money you have to save for retirement.

Job candidates are often reluctant to ask many questions about benefits, perhaps for fear of seeming too greedy. But you can pose your questions and still avoid seeming greedy. At an appropriate point in the interview, usually when the interviewer casually and rapidly lists the benefits, say something like, "I recognize that labor costs, including the benefit costs, are an important part of any business's expenses. I really appreciate that and I know that compensation is more than just salary; it includes those benefits. I'll consider the value of benefits when weighing just what my compensation is."

You have conveyed both your awareness of the employer's expenses and your appreciation of benefits. You don't look greedy. You look cost-conscious for both you and your employer. Then go on to ask specifics about the benefits plan. Asking about the retirement plan should suggest that you are a serious, long-term-oriented person, not just someone who is passing through. As the interview concludes, ask for the "new employee" packet. Tell the interviewer it will save important work time if you review the packet now rather than taking the time to do so on your first day. Get a copy of the SPDs and be sure they tell you when you are eligible for the plans and when you vest. If it isn't clear from the materials you receive, call and ask the personnel or human resources office.

What If No Benefits Are Offered?

What if the answer is, "There are no benefits"? Clearly, you are not going to turn down a wonderful job you want, or even a not-so-great job you need, because benefits are not included. But bear that in mind in your budgeting and, most important, in your salary negotiations. When the discussion begins to focus on salary, remind your potential employer that the job comes without benefits. Give an estimate of how much that is going to cost you out of your paycheck. Have fairly specific figures—that is, individual health insurance will cost so much, additional savings for retirement will need to be so much, and so on. Share the information with your employer.

Also point out that if the employer had provided retirement or health benefits, those benefits would be tax free or would be tax deferred. Because you will be paying for them yourself, you will be buying benefits with after-tax dollars, further reducing your income. Your potential employer may not have realized that the full value of your benefits is $2,000 to $3,000 before taxes. (You may not have thought about it either before now.) This lesson on the value of employer-provided benefits may give you some leverage to get a higher starting salary. Again, you will appear to be a serious person who is inclined to think ahead and prepare for the future, important qualities every employer wants.

Obviously, acquiring retirement and other benefits cannot drive your career. Still, when weighing and considering jobs, benefits may be the factor that tips the balance in staying with your current employer or shifting to a new job. Benefits' value works both ways. A new job at the same salary, but with retirement and health benefits, may give you much more compensation than your current job even though there appears to be no more in your pay envelope at the end of the month.

Benefits Issues When You Leave a Job

Having a firm grasp of the benefits in the job you are leaving is as important as knowing about the new job's benefits. First, you cannot compare existing compensation to the benefits and compensation at the new job unless you are knowledgeable about your current benefits.

Check Vesting Schedules

Like Jennifer you may walk out just before benefits are due to be vested. Leaving a job four years and eleven months after you arrived could cost you thousands of dollars of tax-deferred retirement benefits. Those benefits could be transferred directly to an IRA to continue growing on a tax-deferred basis until your retirement. Check vesting schedules for benefits. Doublecheck your years of service and any breaks in service you might have had that would reduce that service. Do these things well before you give any hint of resigning. In fact, right now would be a good time to ask the benefits department about the status of your retirement benefits, regardless of whether you are thinking of moving your career.

If a new employer has pursued you, but the job move would mean a loss of nonvested benefits at your present employer, negotiate with your new employer on the issue. Ask the new employer to "buy out" those nonvested benefits you are losing by giving you a "hiring on" bonus or increasing your salary. Even if the new employer offers you the value of the nonvested benefits you are forfeiting at the old job, remember you will not be able to shelter that money in a tax-deferred retirement account. To receive the exact equivalent of the benefits you are forfeiting, the bonus should be "grossed up" for the taxes you will pay on the amount and adjusted for this lack of tax deferral.

Understand the Payout Options on Your Old Job's Benefits

Before you leave your current job, be sure that you understand all the payment options for your vested retirement benefits. Some retirement plans do not release benefits before you reach the plan's retirement age. In that case, you have no decisions to make when you leave the employer. Do remember that the burden will be on you to keep the retirement plan administrator informed of your current address until you retire. Be sure you have the address of the plan administrator too.

Most plans today are eager to "cash out" departing employees because it lowers the plan's administrative costs. In fact, if you have less than $5,000 in accrued benefits, you can be "cashed out" of the plan without your permission. This simply means the plan will issue you a check for your accrued benefit, which you will then roll into an IRA to permit continued growth of your retirement benefit. If the plan permits preretirement distributions or if you are going to be "cashed out," begin thinking about where and how you want to invest the money well before the distribution date. Go back and look at the discussion about rollover IRAs in Chapter 9.

Defined Contribution Plan Distribution Decisions

If the plan is a defined contribution plan and the investment managers have a good record or there are several plan investment options you like, you may want to consider leaving the money where it is. Be sure that as a former employee you have the same investment choices and rights as current employees. The IRS won't let the plan just sweep former employees' accounts into a single low-risk, low-return investment option, but plans can place some restrictions on former employees' accounts. Check to see whether former employees are charged a management fee or other fees different from those charged current employees. Leaving the money in the plan should avoid your having to pay fees to manage the money in an IRA.

If you decide to take the money out of the defined contribution plan, learn whether you can take your benefit in cash or in the assets you have in the plan. If your account is heavily invested in company stock and the stock is at a record low, you won't want to sell the stock and take cash now. You will want to take it as stock and wait for the price to increase. Frequently, when companies announce massive layoffs the stock is in the doldrums. The announcement may have an artificial effect on the price, either up or down. If the price goes up, the higher price is likely to last only a few days and not continue through the long period it may take for the plan to sell the stock. If you must sell the assets in your account and they are at an unusually low value, that fact alone may argue for leaving your account in the plan.

If the plan does require you to sell the assets or you want to sell the assets and take the distribution as cash, be certain you know the date for setting the sale price of the stock or other assets. This is the "valuation date" under the plan. Some plans have valuation dates based on a past date, such as the last day of the previous quarter. In this case you will know the exact value of the assets before you have to decide whether to take your account out of the plan. But other plans use the actual date of the sale transaction, which might be weeks after you have elected to cash out the assets. The value of those assets, especially if they are employer stock, may fluctuate dramatically between the time you decide to sell and the time the plan actually executes the sale. In most cases you, not the plan, bear the risk of loss or gain. This is another reason why you may want to take your benefit as assets rather than cash, if you can. You can roll the assets into an IRA with a bank or brokerage firm and you will control the date on which the assets are sold.

Defined Benefit Plan Distribution Decisions

If the money is in a defined benefit plan, your task will be even more complicated. First, don't take a lump sum, if the defined benefit plan has a cost-of-living adjustment (COLA) that will increase your benefits for inflation during retirement. Among large employers, more than a quarter of these plans have COLAs,[2] but if you take your money as a lump sum, you will not be eligible for the COLA.

If you withdraw your benefit as a lump sum before retirement, the amount will be reduced by a "mortality factor," as discussed in Chapter 7. But the earning assumptions used to calculate the present value of the lump sum are usually modest. This means you may be able to make the lump sum earn more than the plan assumed, even after the mortality reduction. If you can, the lump sum will provide a larger benefit at retirement under your own management than you would receive under the defined benefit plan payments.

For example, Carla's pension fund assumes a 6 percent earnings rate in calculating the lump-sum amount needed today to equal the value of her accrued benefit when she reaches retirement age. Carla thinks she may be able to make the money grow at the rate of 9 percent. The lump-sum value of her defined benefit plan today is $20,000 and she has twenty years until she reaches retirement age. If left in the plan, the benefit would have a lump-sum value at retirement of $64,140. But the lump sum would be worth $112,000 at retirement if she takes the amount and achieves her expected 9 percent rate of return. That's almost twice the value, if Carla can manage the sum and earn the 9 percent.

Before you make your decision, get both the lump-sum value and the retirement benefit monthly annuity figure at the age you intend to retire. Use the time value of money tables in the Appendix to see how the money would grow at different interest rates. Ask your employer about date of death assumed in calculating the value of the benefits. Take the number of years from the date of retirement to the date of death the employer used and, using the tables again, see how much you could pay yourself each month from the lump sum you have by investing the money at different rates of return. Compare that amount to the monthly benefit you would receive from the retirement plan. Then assume that you will live to age 95 and, using the tables again, see how much you could pay yourself over those years from your desired date of retirement to age 95. This amount will result in a lower figure because you will be paying yourself over a greater number of years. Of course, the longer you live the greater the odds you would earn more by taking monthly benefits at retirement rather than the lump sum. How lucky do you feel?

Transferring the Benefits from the Previous Employer: Using the Rollover IRA

Of course you won't even *think* of doing anything with the money you receive other than having your employer transfer it into an IRA or your new employer's plan, if that plan accepts such transfers. Remember our example from Chapter 9. You can take a $10,000 distribution from your plan and spend it—you'll have less than $6,000 after taxes and penalties to spend—or you can put it in an IRA. Leave it there for thirty years at 9 percent and it will then begin to pay you a little under $13,500 a year until you are 90. This is a choice?

You must give your former employer's plan the information necessary to transfer your assets directly to an IRA or another employer's plan (or give you a check payable only to your IRA or to the employer's plan). If you don't give the plan this information, the former employer's plan must withhold 20 percent of the taxable amount in your account for federal income taxes. Review the rules on transferring to an IRA from an employer's plan discussed in Chapters 7 and 9.

I Lost My Job: I Need That Money, Not an IRA

No, you don't. Even if you are out of work and know you will have to spend the money from your former employer's retirement plan, put the money in an IRA first. As long as the money is in the IRA, its earnings are tax deferred. As soon as the money is placed in a taxable account, the ability to earn tax-deferred money is lost forever. Why pay taxes before you have to, especially when you are out of work? Withdraw amounts from the IRA as slowly as possible so that you only pay taxes and penalties on the amount you absolutely need to live.

In fact, if you can draw it out in a steady stream based on equal amounts paid over your life expectancy, you will even be able to avoid the 10 percent penalty, but not the income tax, of course. Realistically, unless the amount in your IRA is quite large, this life stream payment option probably won't give you enough to live on if it is your sole source of income. Additionally, once you begin this form of payment, you must continue it until you reach age 59½ and at least five years have elapsed since you began receiving the life stream payments from the IRA. For example, you started the life stream of payment when you were laid off from a job at age 53. You could stop that form of payment when you reached age 59½ because you had received five years of payments and you are 59½. But if you were 55 when you began receiving the payments, you could not stop them until age 60.

Continue Your Health Insurance Coverage: A Friendly COBRA

If you have current health insurance with your employer when you leave your job, you are entitled by law to continue that coverage at your expense, unless you will receive the same coverage from your new employer immediately. This health care continuation requirement is sometimes referred to as COBRA, an acronym for the Consolidated Omnibus Budget Reconciliation Act, which contained the law. Employers with fewer than twenty employees are not subject to COBRA.

You are entitled to the coverage whether you quit or are fired for any reason other than "gross misconduct." The employer may charge the full cost of the coverage plus as much as 2 percent for administrative costs. Unfortunately, health care coverage is so expensive without any employer contribution that many terminated employees find they cannot afford COBRA coverage.

Because the penalties for not complying with COBRA are so strict, most employers try diligently to comply. But the COBRA law is as difficult and wily as the snake. The law has been amended several times since its inception in 1986 and the rules are not familiar to all employers. If you think you will need coverage under COBRA, inform your former employer and ask for the COBRA election form before you leave. Elect the coverage and pay the premium even if your former employer thinks you are not eligible. If you find out that you are covered at the new employer for all your needs or you really are not eligible for COBRA, your former employer may have to return the premiums you paid. So pay first and ask questions later if you have any doubt about your coverage with your new employer.

If You Are Laid Off

The decade of the nineties has already proved to be the decade of downsizing, right-sizing, and plain old massive job eliminations. No matter what it is called, it hurts just as much and the financial bind is the same. But if you find yourself right-sized out of a job, keep your wits about you as you negotiate your severance or examine your package. You never needed rational planning more than now. Take all the steps outlined above to determine your benefits.

If the layoffs are massive enough, the retirement plan may have undergone a "partial termination" that would entitle all plan participants who were affected by the layoffs to immediate vesting in their accrued benefit. If so, you will be eligible for retirement benefits even though you were not vested. Ask your employer about this. Also, even if you are told no such partial termination occurred, insist the benefits department keep your address and tell you the amount of the benefit you had accrued to date. The Pension Benefit Guaranty Corporation (PBGC) or the courts have been known to declare a partial termination even when the plan sponsor disagreed. If this happens, you want to be easily reached so that you can receive your benefits. And you will want to have evidence of what the employer told you those benefits were before the legal actions declaring a partial termination occurred. There may be some differences because interest rate assumptions change over time, but major differences should be brought to PBGC's attention.

Even when not required by law, some companies vest retirement benefits as part of the severance package. Early retirement packages may be available. If you qualify, investigate the packages closely, even if you have no intention of retiring. These packages frequently are very generous. But you may have a fairly short time limit to decide whether to take the package, and you may have to sign waivers agreeing not to sue the employer. If you have a very short time frame and substantial amounts of money are involved, it may make sense to consult a lawyer, an accountant, or an actuary to help you understand the proposals and options and to calculate your benefits under certain options.

COBRA health care continuation applies in layoffs, unless the company shuts down all health care plans. Such total shutdowns are rare, so chances are good that you can buy continuation coverage if you are laid off.

If You Are Fired

Unlike health care benefits, even if you are fired for "gross misconduct," your retirement benefits are unaffected. If you are vested in your retirement benefits, the reason for your dismissal is immaterial. The fact that you were embezzling from the company and caught red-handed in no way reduces your retirement benefits. However, do not embezzle from the retirement plan itself. Some courts have allowed reductions or eliminations in retirement benefits as restitution to the plan when the individual acted as a fiduciary and stole money from the plan. In general, "bad girl" clauses are ineffective. Violating a noncompete clause you may have signed also cannot affect the payment of your retirement benefits under an ERISA plan. Of course, any bad girl clauses contained in a non-ERISA plan, such as an executives-only plan or contract, may deny you benefits under that plan.

Strategy Plan for Benefits When Changing Jobs

- In examining any new job offer be sure to think in terms of compensation, not just salary, including retirement benefits, health insurance, disability benefits, and dependent care. Include the after-tax value of these benefits from both your current and expected job before you make any decisions.
- Contact your present employer's benefits office and get an up-to-date record of your accrued benefits and your vesting status.
- Find out what your current retirement plan's payout options are.
- Compare the options carefully. If the sums are very large, consider hiring an expert such as an accountant or actuary to calculate the differences in plan payments.
- Decide whether you need health care continuation insurance from your former employer. Be sure your new employer's coverage meets all your needs if you decide against the continued coverage from your former employer.
- If you are laid off from your job and are not vested in your accrued retirement benefits, check to see whether a partial termination of the plan has occurred that would vest you in the benefits.
- If early retirement options are offered, examine them carefully. Again, hire an expert if necessary to help you calculate your numbers.
- Remember that you cannot lose vested retirement benefits under ERISA regardless of your conduct or the reason for your dismissal. If anyone representing your employer attempts to tell you differently, report him or her to the Department of Labor.

How Much Do You Need for Retirement?

In order to have a retirement savings goal, you have to know how much you will need. Conventional wisdom says that you need from 60 percent to 90 percent of your preretirement income. But that analysis does not fit women's retirement planning very well because it assumes a man's life expectancy and a man's higher income. Women live longer and their benefits will be more vulnerable to the ravages of inflation. Also, the less you earn during your working life, the more likely you are to spend most of your income on the basic necessities such as food and shelter—needs that don't change after you retire.

In this chapter we will discuss the factors affecting your estimates, such as tax rates, inflation, rates of return on your investments, as well as how to estimate your needed savings rate. We will also walk through retirement savings calculators, both the old-fashioned paper-and-pencil type and the computer program versions.

Basic Questions

Your retirement savings goals will depend on several things. Some we can know now; some we can't. Basic questions include:

- When do you want to retire?
- What will inflation be like?
- Will you own your home by retirement?
- Is your health likely to be good?
- Do you want to work part-time when you retire?
- Do you want to travel extensively?

- Do you want to go back to school?
- Do you want to indulge expensive hobbies?
- What sort of life style do you want? Will you be content to say good-bye to expense-account restaurants or will you still want to frequent them? Can you switch to having a new car every seven years when you have always had a new car every two years?

Ignore the Conventional Wisdom About Needing Less Money After You Retire

The advice that you need less income in retirement is based on the traditional male career and life span. That advice doesn't work for women for the reasons already explained. But the advice really may be wrong for both sexes. The idea that you need less in retirement is usually supported by reasoning that you will spend less on clothes, lunches, and commuting to work, you will be in a lower tax bracket, and your Social Security benefits will not be taxed. Alas, each of these factors is at best subject to review or probably just plain wrong.

Myth 1: You Will Spend Less Because Work Expenses Will Be Reduced

Will this difference be significant enough to reduce your cash need appreciably? Granted, if you are commuting thirty miles by car each way to work, your savings in commuting costs after retirement will be considerable. If you eat lunch out daily and spend even $5 or $6 for each meal, you may reduce your costs when you retire. Lunch at home can be less than that, but it still costs something. And from time to time you may *want* to lunch out. Certainly, you may need fewer clothes suitable for work. But let's face it, if you were a clotheshorse while working, you are unlikely to be content in retirement with buying one new outfit a year. If you weren't concerned about clothes while you were working, you probably didn't spend that much anyway, so any savings from buying fewer clothes after retirement is likely to be small.

Myth 2: Will You Be in a Lower Tax Bracket? Not If You're Lucky

Falling into a lower tax bracket after retirement may have been common in the 1970s and early 1980s when there were fifteen tax brackets that ranged up to 70 percent. But now that there are only five tax brackets, it is less likely that your federal income tax rate will drop dramatically. Unless you are very near retirement now, it is impossible to know what the tax rates may be when you retire. But realistically, it is unwise to count on lower taxes for your entire retirement. While it is true that the huge federal deficits of the late 1980s and early 1990s seem to be under control, the United States still has a national debt of over $4 trillion and a looming need for baby boomer Social Security and Medicare payments.

Table 11.1
Federal Income Tax Rates, 1999

Tax Rate	Annual Income		
	Single	*Married, Filing Jointly*	*Head of Household*
15%	$0–25,750	$0–43,050	$0–34,550
28%	$25,750–62,450	$43,050–104,050	$34,550–89,150
31%	$62,450–130,250	$104,050–158,550	$89,150–144,400
36%	$130,250–283,150	$158,550–283,150	$144,400–283,150
39.6%	$283,150 and up	$283,150 and up	$283,150 and up

Note: Federal income tax rates are adjusted annually for inflation.

To fall into a lower bracket at retirement under current income tax rates, most people would need to reduce their income by 50 to 100 percent. True, Alice, Susan, and Jennifer would each be in a lower tax bracket if they retired with only their employer-provided benefit and Social Security, but they each would also be living on less than half of their former income if that happened. Most people would not consciously strive to reduce their income by half when they retire.

One reduction in your taxes after retirement will be the elimination of Social Security and Medicare Insurance employment taxes. These taxes apply only to wages, so these taxes will not be applied to your pension, Social Security, or personal savings income. That saves at least 7.65 percent of your earnings, or 15.3 percent, if you are self-employed.

Myth 3: Your Social Security Won't Be Taxed

That is only partially correct, as we saw in the chapter on Social Security. If you have income (including half of your Social Security benefits) of more than $25,000 if single, or more than $32,000 if married, you may be taxed on as much as 85 percent of your Social Security benefits. While Social Security benefits were not subject to income tax until the 1980s, the amount of Social Security benefits subject to income tax has gradually increased. Chances are good that all Social Security benefits will be subject to income tax before the baby boomers retire. In part the additional revenue will be needed to help pay for the boomers' retirement.

Myth 4: You Won't Be Saving After You Retire

Once you retire, it is true that you need not save for retirement, so you won't be saving as much of your preretirement income as you did before retirement. But if you started saving early, the portion of income going into retirement saving shouldn't have been that large just prior to retirement. At the start of your retirement you should still be saving, even if that saving takes the form of paying yourself less than you could from your own retirement savings. Your life expectancy after retirement may be another two decades or more. To make your retirement savings last that long, you will need to be cautious in the early years of retirement. Also, in retirement, as in the rest of your life, emergencies may occur or special opportunities like an exotic trip come up. Having a fund for those occasions requires some savings.

Assume You Need at Least 100 Percent of Preretirement Income

Certainly in the early stages of your retirement planning, assume you will need 100 percent of the income you were earning immediately before you retired. Use your current income and the Appendix time value of money tables to project it forward at a realistic rate. For the cases of Alice, Bonnie, Susan, and Jennifer, salary increases were projected at 6 percent a year. The only sure reduction in expenses after retirement will be the elimination of Social Security and Medicare Insurance employment taxes, assuming you are not working then. Using at least 100 percent of preretirement income is a good rule for planning in your twenties, thirties, forties, and early fifties, because your actual desired life style in retirement is impossible to predict so far in advance.

Refine Your Estimates as Retirement Nears

As you get nearer to retirement, you can begin to refine your estimates for financial needs at retirement, based on better knowledge of what you want to do with the rest of your life and your current assets. By the time you reach 55, the house that seemed cramped when you were in your forties may seem impossibly large and troublesome or it may be the only place you could ever be happy living. But you will know those things more certainly as you get closer to actual retirement age. Also remember to think carefully about your possible circumstances in retirement. Will you still have children in college? How is your health likely to be? Will you be contributing to your parents' or your grandparents' support?

Even When You Own the Home, Housing Isn't Free

Assuming you will need 100 percent of preretirement income is prudent, but if you absolutely know certain expenses will change, then adjustments can be made. If you know that you will own your home, you can reduce your income needs by the amount of mortgage or rent you now pay. But don't make the mistake of assuming your housing costs will be zero. Remember, taxes, insurance, and utilities continue. And they will increase over the years with inflation.

For an easy dose of reality therapy on housing costs, if you are in your thirties or forties now, ask your parents or retired neighbors what their mortgage payments used to be. Then ask them what they now pay in real estate taxes and utility bills—but be prepared for a long conversation, perhaps peppered with strong language.

Condo fees and homeowners' association dues will continue and increase. Repairs will still be needed, and painting and other routine maintenance will be necessary, especially as property ages. In your early years of retirement you may find that you have the time and energy to do maintenance you used to pay for, such as yard work and painting. But as you age, things you used to do yourself routinely will be less appealing or impossible for you to do safely. These service costs need to be counted. And if you are one of those ambitious people who always did all the painting, repairs, and gardening yourself, you will be unpleasantly surprised how much your labor was worth and how much those things cost when others do them.

Health Care Costs Go Up

Statistics tell us that health care costs will be taking a larger portion of your income in retirement. The average American spends about 5.4 percent of her expenditures on health care. But Americans between 55 and 64 spend about 5.9 percent on their expenditures on health care, those age 65 to 74 spend 10.3 percent, and those 75 and older spend over 14.4 percent.[1] Certainly, health care costs constitute a large portion of older retirees' expenses and Medicare payments constitute a large portion of the average retiree's income.

Medicare Part A, which charges no premium, covers hospitalization. But there will be Medicare Part B premiums, which cover medical services. Don't even *think* of passing up this insurance. Of every 1,000 retired Americans eligible for the Part B program, 793 receive benefits under Part B. You can't get it cheaper because you pay only one-fourth of the cost, and even if you have excellent health, uncovered medical costs aren't worth the risk. But those costs have risen rapidly. In 1992 those premiums were $31.80 per month; in 1997 they were $43.80 per month, and in 1999 they are $45.50. Assume Medicare Part B premiums will increase faster than inflation.

Medicare requires copayments and deductibles for most services, so you may also wish to purchase additional Medigap insurance, another costly item. Also remember that Medicare does not cover long-term care, such as nursing homes or in-home custodial care. You may want long-term care insurance and the premiums will be high if you didn't purchase this insurance when you were younger.

Be realistic about how your health might be in retirement and the costs of health care beyond what Medicare covers. You won't fall apart as soon as you hit 65, but by 75 health problems are likely to arise. The health and longevity of your parents and older siblings are your best guide. If your mother developed diabetes late in life, there is a good chance you will, too. But if she was severely overweight in her later years and you have maintained a normal weight and exercise frequently, those chances go down considerably.

Factor in Fun Money

Also factor in the money necessary to do the things you really *want* to do. If you have always dreamed of completing your master's degree in Shakespeare's works, factor in the cost of tuition, books, and so on. If creating the prize garden is a goal, that costs money, too, so include those fertilizers, exotic seedlings, and the cost of travel to flower shows.

While you will be better able to estimate expenses as you near retirement, it is too late then to adjust your retirement savings significantly if you have not saved enough in your thirties to early fifties. That's another good reason to assume you will need at least 100 percent of your preretirement income in projecting your savings needs.

Planning for Inflation

The time value of money tables in the Appendix show the way money grows at varying interest rates. Those same tables also show how the purchasing power of money erodes at various inflation rates. The principle is the same. This is one of the reasons you must assume you need at least 100 percent of your preretirement income to survive in retirement.

For example, Ruth is earning $50,000 when she retires. Her pension, Social Security benefits, and personal savings will provide her $50,000 annually in retirement. If the inflation rate after she retires is 7.1 percent, the average inflation rate in the 1970s, in five years she will need slightly more than $70,000 to have the same purchasing power. If the average inflation rate is 5.5 percent, as it was in the 1980s, she will need more than $65,000 to purchase the same goods in five years. But if inflation remains at 3.4 percent, the average over most of the 1990s, she will still need $59,000 to maintain the buying power she had only five years before. Only Ruth's Social Security will be adjusted for inflation.

A woman of 65 today can expect to live another nineteen years.[2] If she were earning $50,000 when she retired and inflation stayed at a low 4 percent per year each year during the next nineteen years, she would need approximately $105,000 to maintain the same purchasing power in her last year of life as she had when she retired. At a 6 percent rate, the average inflation rate for the 1970s and 1980s, she would need about $151,000 to maintain purchasing power after nineteen years.

Inflation is the retiree's greatest enemy. You must understand its effect and plan for it as you save and invest for retirement. As you can see, inflation means that even having a retirement income of 100 percent of your preretirement income may not keep you financially secure. Very few employer-provided retirement benefits are adjusted automatically for inflation. The exceptions are certain federal, state, and local government retirement plans. These plans are usually adjusted for inflation, either directly through increases tied to a cost-of-living index or indirectly through payments based on a percentage of the current salary being paid to the position you held while you worked for the government.

Private pensions do occasionally provide inflation adjustments to pensions on an ad hoc basis. Such cost-of-living adjustments, or COLAs, as they are frequently called, seem to be dwindling even among employers who have provided them in the past. Forty-four percent of retirees who first received pensions before 1975 reported receiving some sort of pension increase after retirement. But the numbers have steadily declined, with only 9 percent of those retiring after 1993 reporting such increases. Among all retirees receiving pensions, 31 percent of men reported pension increases after retirement, but only 24 percent of women reported such increases.[3] If you should receive a COLA under your pension plan, celebrate. But in your preretirement planning, don't assume there will be increases in your pension benefits for inflation, even if your employer has made such increases in the past. Clearly the trend is away from inflation adjustments.

Social Security Provides Some Inflation Protection

You can take steps to insulate your retirement savings and later income from inflation, at least partially. First, Social Security benefits are adjusted for inflation, at least for the present time, so a part of your retirement income is protected from the scourge of inflation. Ironically, the less income you had during your working years, the higher proportion of your retirement income will come from Social Security benefits. Consequently, more of your retirement income will be protected from inflation.

Some economists argue that because entitlements, including Social Security benefits, are such a large part of the U.S. economy, linking these payments to inflation in fact exacerbates inflation. While a majority of Congress has yet to embrace this concept, as more and more retirees are supported by fewer and fewer workers in the twenty-first century, the least obvious way (and hence the most politically acceptable way) to reduce the Social Security burden would be to limit inflation adjustments. One could also argue that such limits would fight inflation and increase or at least stabilize income for both retirees and workers. On balance, the strong protection against inflation that Social Security provides for today's retirees may not be guaranteed to future retirees.

Choose Investments to Ride with Inflation

Once again, your investments from your own savings are probably your best protection. Your investments for retirement, especially in your twenties through age 50 or so, should contain primarily assets that will benefit from inflation, such as stocks and other investments that give you equity in the asset. The single biggest mistake people make with employer-provided plans that allow the employee to choose among investments is choosing too safe an option. Chapter 12 will discuss in greater detail the relationship between risk and rate of return. For now, recognize that the safer the investment, the lower the rate of return. But if the rate of return is so low that your savings are being dissolved by inflation, the investment isn't really safe. It's a waste of money.

Investments That Are Too Safe Can Make You Very Sorry

Suppose Jennifer's employer institutes a 401(k) plan with three investment options: a stock mutual fund, a government securities fund, and a fixed-interest investment option, commonly called a *guaranteed income contract*. As the mutual fund prospectuses always say, "Past performance is no guarantee of future investment return," but over the years the mutual fund has had an average return of 10 percent, some years losing as much as 10 percent in value and other years earning as much as 30 percent. The government securities fund averages about 7 percent annually, some years going as low as 3 percent and as high as 12 percent. The "guaranteed income contract" (GIC) is guaranteed only by the assets of the insurance company offering it and its only real "guarantee" is to pay 4 percent for one year on the money invested. At the end of the year the GIC will set a new interest rate based roughly on similar interest rates for certificates of deposit.

Faced with those investment options, too many people go with the GIC because they think they understand it (they probably don't) and because they think it is safer than the mutual funds (it probably isn't). GICs' safety is based solely on the financial security of the insurance company underwriting it.

At age 30 Jennifer has a lot of time to let her money grow, so even small amounts can become significant. Because she will not need her money for many years, ups and downs in the market have plenty of time to even out. Jennifer decides to put $1,000, about 5 percent of her current salary, in the 401(k) plan each year until she retires at age 60. How much she will have at retirement varies dramatically depending on the investment mix she chooses. Assume over the next thirty years the funds achieve their historic rates of return.

Table 11.2 leaves no doubt about the critical difference the rate of return has on the growth of your investments. Depending on the investments she chooses now, Jennifer's annual $1,000 contribution may give her an annual retirement income from her 401(k) plan of $5,250 a year, or about three times that much, $15,400. If Jennifer follows the lead of many unsophisticated employees and "safely" invests her money in the lower rate of return, but presumably lower risk, she is likely to have a very risky retirement. She simply won't have enough money, even with Social Security and her employer-provided pension, to maintain her life style.

As a 30-year-old, Jennifer has decades before she will retire. She can wisely invest in the "riskier" stock mutual fund because, even when the fund loses money in a bad year, she can wait for the value to build up again. In contrast, at 60

Table 11.2
Jennifer's Retirement Savings: Comparison of Retirement Savings Earned from Different Investment Options

Investments Chosen	Lump Sum at Retirement	Annual Income for 25 Years[a]
100% Stock Mutual fund–10% return	$164,494	$15,400
100% Gov't Securities fund–7% return	94,461	8,850
100% GIC–4% return	56,085	5,250
50% Stock Mutual Fund/50% GIC	110,289	10,300
50% Government Securities Fund/50% GIC	75,272	7,050

[a] Assumes an 8 percent rate of return on lump sum after retirement.

Alice cannot wait for the fund to regain value over decades. Alice should invest a larger part of her assets in less volatile assets such as a large portion in the government securities fund and perhaps 40 percent or so of her 401(k) in the stock mutual fund. She should be invested in the GIC only if she believes her retirement is imminent and she knows she will need money immediately.

One basic rule for retirement savings is to invest heavily in the assets with higher rates of return and risk early in your career and shift to the lower risk and return assets only as you near retirement. Even during the early retirement years, some of your funds should be higher-return assets to protect against inflation during your long years of retirement. The less risk tolerance you have, the more money you must save to reach the same dollar retirement savings goals. The next chapter discusses investment strategies in more detail.

Look at the Real Rate of Return: Subtract Inflation

As you plan for inflation, look at investments in terms of their *real rate of return.* An investment earning 8 percent per year is really only growing at the rate of 8 percent minus the inflation rate. From 1990 to 1996, when inflation averaged 3.4 percent, this 8 percent investment is really only giving us 4.6 percent of real return. The real rate of return is the earnings rate minus the inflation rate.

Of course, as inflation increases, so do nominal rates of returns in many investments. That's why buying a thirty-year bond toward the end of an inflationary cycle is a very good investment. Chances are that it will be paying 10 percent for the next thirty years, which will provide a very good real rate of return when inflation is 4 percent. But in the years in which inflation spirals to 11 percent, you are losing 1 percent per year on your money. The other problem is knowing when we are at the end of the inflationary cycle. If the financial experts, the White House, and the Federal Reserve Board can't figure it out, you may have a bit of a problem discerning the end of an inflationary trend, too.

Beware of the Optimistic Financial Adviser

Many retirement adviser projections do not adequately account for inflation. Several of the mutual fund families and stock brokerage houses produce very worthwhile retirement financial planning guides, but these forms often assume unrealistically low estimates of inflation. Some of these guides even provide you with charts showing inflation averaging 5.5 percent for the 1980s and then merrily tell you on the next page that their examples and projections will assume a 4 percent inflation rate. They were right so far in the 1990s, when inflation has averaged under 4 percent and, in the 1960s, only averaged 2.3 percent. But remember you will be planning for and living in the next two to four decades, too. Just two decades ago, in the 1970s, inflation averaged 7.1 percent. And remember the five years from 1978 to 1982, when inflation averaged just under 10 percent.

A History of Inflation

Table 11.3 shows you inflation rates for 1960 through 1996 based on two common indices. The consumer price index, or CPI, is the most popularly used guide to inflation; however, changes in the gross domestic product are more comprehensive because they cover everything. Table 11.3 gives you inflation's history. Decide for yourself on its future. Unlike most other areas of life, in retirement financial planning pessimism is a better trait than optimism. Think about inflation in all your calculations.

Calculating Savings Needed to Reach Your Goals

If you are under 55 now, start by assuming you will need at least 100 percent of your current income. Then subtract Social Security taxes (7.65 percent up to $72,600 and 1.45 percent on the remainder in 1999) from your present income. There are vast differences in the projected amounts needed, depending on the retirement financial planning method you use and the inflation factors you assume.

Included here are two pencil-and-paper ways to calculate your retirement needs and the amount you need to be saving.

Retirement Planning for the Twenty-first Century: Surfing the Net for Retirement Calculators

If you have access to a computer or the Internet, there are many sites that will help you with your planning and do the math for you. Also, retirement planning software can be purchased. Quicken Financial Planning software and Microsoft Money are two programs that provide retirement planning as well as other saving advice, but you pay for these.

Retirement planning sites abound. Try some of these, but before you do, a

Table 11.3
Common Indices for Rates of Inflation, 1960–1997

Year	Consumer Price Index (%)	Gross Domestic Product (%)	CPI Decade Average (%)
1960	1.7	1.6	
1961	1.0	1.0	
1962	1.0	2.2	
1963	1.3	1.6	
1964	1.3	1.5	
1965	1.6	2.7	
1966	2.9	3.6	
1967	3.1	2.6	
1968	4.2	5.0	
1969	5.5	5.6	2.3
1970	5.7	5.5	
1971	4.4	5.7	
1972	3.2	4.7	
1973	6.2	6.5	
1974	11.0	9.1	
1975	9.1	9.8	
1976	5.8	6.4	
1977	6.5	6.7	
1978	7.6	7.3	
1979	11.3	8.9	7.1
1980	13.5	9.0	
1981	10.3	9.7	
1982	6.2	6.4	
1983	3.2	3.9	
1984	4.3	3.7	
1985	3.6	3.1	
1986	1.9	2.5	
1987	3.6	3.3	
1988	4.1	3.8	
1989	4.8	3.4	5.5
1990	5.4	1.2	
1991	4.2	−0.9	
1992	3.0	2.7	
1993	3.0	2.3	
1994	2.6	3.5	
1995	2.8	2.0	
1996	3.0	2.8	2.2
1997	2.3	3.8	

Source: Based on data from the *1991 Statistical Abstract,* tables 765 and 767, and *1998 Statistical Abstract,* tables 718 and 772.

word of caution. Some sites are excellent; others leave a great deal to be desired. Sometimes the sites make assumptions or fail to ask all the relevant questions. Use the sites, but be careful.

The following are among the many Internet sites for retirement planning:

www.asec.org	The American Savings Education Council offers an interactive Ballpark Estimate for retirement planning. The paper version is included here.
www.financialengines.com	Financial Engines offers asset allocation advice.
www.morningstar.net	The well-known investment publication offers personal advice too.
www.personalwealth.com	This is Standard & Poor's asset allocation program.
www.vanguard.com	This mutual fund provider offers detailed advice on Roth IRA conversions too.
www.fidelity.com	A fairly basic retirement calculator is provided, along with other planners.

Old-Fashioned Paper-and-Pencil Approaches

We will use two approaches and suggest ways you can construct your own approach using the time value of money and your own assumptions. Susan's retirement planning will serve as an example, and there are blanks for your own calculations.

The Ballpark Estimate

The American Savings Education Council has been working diligently since 1996 to help Americans understand their retirement planning and savings needs. Along with the Employee Benefits Research Institute and numerous other supporters, ASEC has organized the Choose to Save ad campaign, pushed for legislation and then helped organize the National Retirement Savings Summit, and released *Not Your Mother's Retirement: Women and Saving in 1998: Results of the 1998 Women's Retirement Confidence Survey.* One of its most helpful projects has been the "Ballpark Estimate" worksheet for retirement savings calculations.

Using both ASEC's Ballpark Estimate worksheet (pages 192–93) and a more complex calculation sheet based on *Money* magazine's approach, you can see what a difference various assumptions can make. We will use Susan, our 50-year-old manager. The Ballpark item 1 helps determine how much Susan will need. The Ballpark assumes Susan only needs 70 percent of her income in retirement and it assumes she will earn a constant rate of return of 3 percent on her money. For the Ballpark, 70 percent of Susan's annual $25,200 salary, equal to $17,640, goes under item 1.

WHAT SUSAN HAS SO FAR FOR RETIREMENT

The calculations under item 2 help Susan calculate how much she already has for retirement from possible Social Security benefits, employer plans, and personal savings. For the Social Security entry under item 2 we will use the $8,000 annual figure, because Susan barely earns over $25,000 and we want to be more conservative. Susan will have $4,695 in today's dollars each year from two employer retirement plans and that amount goes under item 2. Susan doesn't want to work part-time when she retires and she doesn't think she will have income from other sources, so no other amounts are added under item 2. Subtracting Social Security of $8,000 and retirement benefits of $4,695 from the estimated needed retirement amount of $17,640, Susan will need an additional income of $4,945 a year during retirement. Let's call it $5,000 per year.

THE ADDITIONAL AMOUNT SHE NEEDS TO SAVE

Under item 3, we determine how much additional money Susan will have to save to build enough to generate the additional $5,000 per year in retirement. We multiply $5,000 by the factor of 16.4 since Susan intends to retire at age 65 and find she will need about another $82,000 to generate the additional amount. Under item 5 we consider the $30,000 Susan has already saved and multiply that by 1.6 since she has another fifteen years before she wants to retire. That amount will grow to $48,000, so she will need about $34,000 more for retirement. Under item 6, we use the factor for fifteen years to find that Susan only needs to save about $1,768 each year until retirement to reach her needed goal.

But consider how things would change if Susan thought she needed 100 percent of her current income in retirement. Then she would need approximately $8,500 additional income each year in retirement. She would need personal savings of $139,400 before retirement. With her current savings of $30,000, Susan has to save about $4,752 a year, or almost 20 percent of her annual income.

The More Precise Estimate for Susan

Let's see what happens using the more complex worksheet derived from *Money* magazine. We will follow our 100 percent rule. We did subtract Social Security taxes from that amount. Remember that you don't pay Social Security taxes on non-wage income such as the Social Security benefits themselves or pensions and interest income, so you won't need that amount of money in retirement. But at 50 Susan is too far from retirement to have an exact idea of her retirement income needs to outline a budget and use that budget figure.

We have begun with Susan's current income of $25,200 and current dollar figures for salary, Social Security, and her pension benefits. We have also used a more precise estimate of her Social Security benefit, which results in her receiving $10,320 annually, or about midway between the Ballpark Estimate's high and low

BALLPARK E$TIMATE™

Planning for retirement is not a one-size-fits-all exercise. The purpose of Ballpark is simply to give you a basic idea of the savings you'll need when you retire.
So let's play ball!

1. How much annual income will you want in retirement? (Figure 70% of your current annual gross income just to maintain your current standard of living. Really.) $ _____

2. Subtract the income you expect to receive annually from:
   - Social Security—If you make under $25,000, enter $8,000; between $25,000 - $40,000, enter $12,000; over $40,000, enter $14,500   -$ _____
   - Traditional Employer Pension – a plan that pays a set dollar amount for life, where the dollar amount depends on salary and years of service (in today's dollars)   -$ _____
   - Part-time income   -$ _____
   - Other   -$ _____

   This is how much you need to make up for each retirement year: =$ _____

Now you want a ballpark estimate of how much money you'll need in the bank the day you retire. So the accountants went to work and devised this simple formula. For the record, they figure you'll realize a constant real rate of return of 3% after inflation, you'll live to age 87, and you'll begin to receive income from Social Security at age 65.

3. To determine the amount you'll need to save, multiply the amount you need to make up by the factor below. $ _____

Age you expect to retire:	Your factor is:
55	21.0
60	18.9
65	16.4
70	13.6

4. If you expect to retire before age 65, multiply your Social Security benefit from line 2 by the factor below.

Age you expect to retire: Your factor is: +$ _____

        55   8.8

        60   4.7

5. Multiply your savings to date by the factor below (include money accumulated in a 401(k), IRA, or similar retirement plan).

        If you want to retire in: Your factor is: -$ _____

                  10 years   1.3

                  15 years   1.6

                  20 years   1.8

                  25 years   2.1

                  30 years   2.4

                  35 years   2.8

                  40 years   3.3

Total additional savings needed at retirement: =$ _____

Don't panic. Those same accountants devised another formula to show you how much to save each year in order to reach your goal amount. They factor in compounding. That's where your money not only makes interest, your interest starts making interest as well, creating a snowball effect.

6. To determine the ANNUAL amount you'll need to save, multiply the TOTAL amount by the factor below.

        If you want to retire in: Your factor is: =$ _____

                  10 years   .085

                  15 years   .052

                  20 years   .036

                  25 years   .027

                  30 years   .020

                  35 years   .016

                  40 years   .013

See? It's not impossible or even particularly painful. It just takes planning. And the sooner you start, the better off you'll be.

This worksheet simplifies several retirement planning issues such as projected Social Security benefits and earnings assumptions on savings. It also reflects today's dollars; therefore you will need to re-calculate your retirement needs annually and as your salary and circumstances change. You may want to consider doing further analysis, either by yourself using a more detailed worksheet or computer software or with the assistance of a financial professional.

ASEC/EBRI-ERF
Suite 600
2121 K Street NW
Washington, DC
20037-1896

202-775-9130 or
202-659-0670
Fax 202-775-6312
www.asec.org
www.ebri.org

1/98

Figure 11.1 ASEC Ballpark Estimate Worksheet

Figure 11.2
Retirement Savings Projection Worksheet Based on the
Money Magazine Approach in 1999 Dollars

	Susan	You
1. Salary	$25,200	_____
2. Social Security taxes	−1,928	_____
3. Income needed at retirement (line 1 minus line 2)	23,272	_____
4. Annual Social Security retirement benefits (estimated)	10,320	_____
5. Annual pension benefits from defined benefit plans	4,695	_____
6. Annual income needed from personal savings (line 3 minus lines 4 and 5)	8,257	_____
7. Amount to be saved before retirement (line 6 times factor A)	158,534	_____
8. Amount saved for retirement to date, including IRAs, etc.	30,000	_____
9. Projected value of current savings at time of retirement (line 8 times factor B)	45,900	_____
10. Amount of retirement capital still needed (line 7 minus line 9)	112,634	_____
11. Annual savings needed to reach retirement goal (line 10 times factor C)	6,082	_____

estimate for Social Security for those near Susan's income. The real figures will be slightly higher, but this method gives you an idea of where she stands today. The assumptions for Susan's calculations are:

Current salary (increases only with inflation)	$25,200
Total savings to date	$30,000
Annual employer-provided retirement benefits in today's dollars, based on continued service to age 65 and salary increases at 5%	$4,695
Annual Social Security in today's dollars, assuming continued service to age 65	$10,320
Rate of return on savings	8%
Inflation rate	5%

SUSAN'S ESTIMATE LINE BY LINE

Worksheet line 1 shows Susan's current salary of $25,200. Line 2 shows her current Social Security taxes (7.65% × $25,200). Line 3 shows 100 percent of her salary and subtracts the Social Security taxes she won't have to pay when she retires, leaving the amount of income we assume she will need each year in retirement. Line 4 is Susan's projected income at age 65 from Social Security based on current law estimates for a person of Susan's age, income, and work history.

Line 5 shows the total amount Susan will be receiving annually from her

Table 11.4
Money Magazine Projections

Age at Retirement	Factor A	Years to Retirement	Factor B	Factor C
55	23.3	5	1.15	0.188
56	22.9	7	1.22	0.131
57	22.6	9	1.29	0.099
58	22.2	11	1.36	0.079
59	21.8	13	1.44	0.065
60	21.4	15	1.53	0.054
61	21.0	20	1.76	0.038
62	20.5	25	2.02	0.028
63	20.1	30	2.33	0.022
64	19.6			
65	19.2			
66	18.7			
67	18.2			

Note: These factors assume an 8 percent rate of return on money invested and a 5 percent rate of inflation.

Source: This worksheet and the factor tables are based on similar table and factors appearing in *Money* magazine and used by permission of the publisher, Time-Warner, Inc.

employer-provided retirement plans that we discussed in Chapter 2. Then subtract the Social Security payments (line 4) and the employer retirement benefits (line 5) she will receive from the amount of income she needs (line 3), and line 6 shows the amount Susan needs each year from other sources. Unless Susan wins the lottery, this line 6 amount must come from her own individual savings.

Line 7 shows the total individual savings amount Susan needs ($158,534) to generate the amount on line 6 each year during her retirement. To see how much of that individual amount she already has, line 8 shows her current individual savings of $30,000. Line 9 estimates how much this $30,000 will have grown by the time she retires by multiplying $30,000 times the fifteen-year growth factor B to reach a sum of $45,900. Line 10 subtracts the projected value of her savings, $45,900, from the total amount of individual savings and reports that Susan must save $112,634 between now and the time she retires. Line 11 then estimates how much she must start saving now and save each year to reach her goal. Line 11 shows that Susan will need to save $6,082 this year and every year from now until her planned retirement at age 65.

Susan Needs to Save Much More

Based on these projections, Susan has a very difficult task before her. She will have to save about 24 percent of her pretax income in order to meet these goals.

Of course, in Susan's case, if the law remains unchanged it is not likely that she will have to pay taxes on the Social Security benefits she receives. She can live without the income she would have needed to pay taxes on $10,320 of Social Security income. Also, because Social Security is indexed to meet inflation and because Social Security will make up a large part of her income after retirement, she will have some built-in inflation protection. Her employer-provided benefit is stated in today's dollars and will in fact be higher at retirement.

The projections also assume that Susan has saved $30,000 to date. The other difficulty is that these projections do not factor in inflation erosion. There is no guarantee that even with 100 percent of today's salary, she will still be able to maintain her lifestyle. However, to partially account for inflation, both Susan's Social Security benefit and her employer-provided pension values used here are based on the buying power of today's dollar. The actual amount Susan receives at age 65 will be higher, at least under current law. Additionally, under current law the Social Security payments will be increased annually based on an inflation factor.

Saving Only Five Percent Each Year Would Have Met the Goal

Susan needs so much individual savings for two primary reasons. First, her employer-provided pension will supply only about 16 percent of her preretirement income. Second, she started her own personal savings so late in her career. If Susan had started saving 5 percent of her earnings at the beginning of her career, those savings would provide her with an annual income of $10,600 (in today's dollars) when she retired. Combined with Social Security and her employer-provided pension, her income in retirement would be $25,615 a year, in today's dollars. This income does not exceed the $25,000 threshold for taxing some portion of Social Security benefits because only half of Social Security income is counted in that threshold. As a result Susan would have a considerably higher after-tax income during retirement than she had while working. The income from her small, but early and consistent personal savings would give her a greater annual income than either the employer-provided benefit or Social Security and, more important, would reach her retirement income goals.

From Susan's case, you can see why retirement planning financial advisers are tempted to assume unrealistically low inflation rates and unrealistically high earnings rates on your savings and investments. Otherwise, they fear, you will be so discouraged by the amount you need to save that you will abandon the idea of retirement savings completely. But don't fall into either the trap of unrealistic assumptions or the slough of despondency over the large sums projected for retirement needs. It is better to know the bad news while you are working and young enough to save something; if you bury your head in the sand you may learn how much you should have saved after it is too late to do anything about it.

Work the Examples for Your Planning

Now it's time go through your own calculations. You can use an electronic planner, going to the ASEC web site, where you enter the information and the calculations will be done for you, or simply use a pencil, a pocket calculator, and one of the worksheets reproduced here. You can construct your own projection sheet, using your own assumptions on inflation rates and rates of return by using the time value of money tables in the Appendix and choosing the appropriate factors, rather than relying on the assumptions and factors used in the worksheet.

Your Step-by-Step Through the *Money* Worksheet with Other Assumptions

For the most precise calculations, short of using a very sophisticated computerized retirement planner, use the *Money* magazine worksheet and your own estimates about inflation and rates of return, taking factors from the time value of money tables in the Appendix, and your specific financial information. Begin with your current salary. The number for Social Security taxes on line 2 can be calculated from your paycheck stub or by multiplying your salary by 7.65 percent for amounts up to $72,600 (in 1999) and 1.45 percent for all amounts above that. Your Personal Earnings and Benefit Estimate Statement ordered from the Social Security Administration will supply the number for line 4. For line 5, use your annual benefit statement for any pension benefits from a defined benefit plan. If you don't have this statement, you will need to look at the SPD for that plan and calculate your expected amount. For line 8, include all amounts you have in employer-provided defined contribution plans, such as 401(k), 403(b), or profit-sharing plans, as well as amounts in your IRAs, Keoghs, and any other savings you have set aside solely for retirement. Don't cheat by including in line 8 money you have saved for your children's education or money you intend to use for a house.

If you want to assume an 8 percent return on your investments and a 5 percent inflation rate, you can use the factors listed in Table 11.4. You can also construct your own projection sheet, using your own assumptions on inflation and rates of return by using the time value of money tables in the Appendix. For example, assume you have twenty years until retirement and think your earnings on line 8 will earn 10 percent, but inflation will be 4 percent (the average rate for the 1980s and 1990s to date). You will have a real return on your savings of 6 percent (a 10 percent return minus 4 percent inflation). Using the real rate of return helps to correct for inflation. When you retire, the amount you will have actually saved will be larger than the amount you projected here, but the buying power of that amount (which is what you really care about) should be close to what you projected using this approach.

Use Appendix Table A.1 and apply a factor of 3.207 (the multiplier for 6 percent over twenty years). Multiply line 8 by that factor and put the result on line 9. Once you have a figure on line 10 for the amount you still need to save, go to

Table A.3, the Future Value of an Annuity. Using your 6 percent real rate of return and knowing you will be saving for twenty years, find the factor for 6 percent over twenty years, which is 36.786. Here it gets a little tricky. You know the future value of the amount you need to save each year: that's the amount on line 10. So to find how much you must save each year you *divide* line 10 by 36.786.

As we saw with Jennifer's choices in Table 11.2, it is obvious what a difference a few points on rate of return or inflation make in the amount you need to save and the amount you will ultimately have for retirement.

Don't Be Overwhelmed: You Don't Need It All Today

Don't be discouraged if your projected sums seem astronomical. Maybe you won't be able to save that much, but at least you know what your goal should be. Remember, some savings are better than no savings. Also, as you get nearer to retirement, you can calculate your actual needs more accurately. If you begin to see you can live on less than 100 percent of your current salary, but you have saved based on needing 100 percent of your current income, you will find you have all the savings you need before you retire, as well as a cushion for retirement.

Seeing what you need to save for retirement well in advance of your retirement will help your planning in other ways. If the amount you need to save seems impossible when you have assumed retirement at age 60, recalculate planning retirement at age 62 or 65. You will be surprised at the difference. Delaying retirement helps two ways. You have more years to save and there are fewer years when you are drawing down capital. Or plan to work part-time after retirement so that you will have some earned income during your first years of retirement. If you begin planning for part-time work before retirement is actually upon you, you have time to plan for a different type of work or a second career.

Recalculate Every Few Years

Project your retirement needs and savings requirements every few years. These numbers change dramatically at different inflation rates or rates of return on savings. Hopefully your employer-provided retirement benefits should be growing, too. As the employer-provided benefit grows, you will need less personal savings. But remember, for planning purposes, use the worst-case scenario and set your savings goals based on that scenario, even if you cannot meet the goals. At a minimum you will be safe in most scenarios. If you assumed inflation at 7 percent and a real rate of return on your retirement investments of 3 percent in your early saving years, but in fact inflation was only 4 percent and you received a real rate of return of 4 percent, then recalculate your needs after a few years. Even if you don't change your future assumptions, your projected needed savings rate will be much lower because you will have already oversaved in the early years and will be earning money on a larger pool of assets than you had originally projected.

Strategy Plan: Calculating Your Own Retirement Needs

■ For retirement savings purposes, assume that you need about 100 percent of your income to live comfortably in retirement.

■ Today, estimate the amount you will need for retirement. Use the worksheets in this chapter, the ASEC Internet site, or software, but do it!

■ If you think your salary will increase over time by more than inflation, project your salary forward using the Appendix Table A.1 factor for the amount of noninflationary growth you expect in your salary. Use that amount to recalculate your estimates. But don't be overly optimistic about salary increases.

■ Don't panic when you see the amount you may need to save. Keep saving. It only gets easier because savings are compounding—and saving is habit-forming.

■ Remember the effects of inflation in calculating your needed retirement income and the savings to produce that income.

■ In your early years of retirement saving, invest heavily in assets that will give you a higher rate of return and track inflation such as stocks or stock mutual funds. The difference in the amounts you must save when you are getting a 9 percent rate of return are vastly lower than the amount you need to save when you are only receiving a 5 percent rate of return.

■ Let your projections inspire you to save more than you thought you could. And remember, future raises will make saving easier, as long as you don't count on them and don't spend the raise before it occurs. Resolve to save every windfall, such as a bonus or an income tax refund you weren't expecting.

■ Finally, you may have to adjust your expectations to better fit reality. You can't retire at 55 if you didn't start saving until you were 50.

12

Becoming Familiar with Investment Vehicles

Nike's advice for an exercise program applies equally well to a savings and investment program—just do it! Start putting away some amount, no matter how small, immediately. Yes, I said it before, but have you started yet? Waiting to begin saving until you have more money or until you know everything about investments is like waiting to start jogging until you can run five miles. It isn't going to just happen. You have to begin, and usually you have to begin in a small way.

As with learning about employer and individual retirement plans, reviewing some basic investment terms helps. Then we'll move on to how to become more knowledgeable about investments, how to begin investing, and how to get good investment advice on a continuing basis. Our focus is on retirement savings, but many of the ideas apply to other financial goals you might have.

Investments: Return Linked to Risk

Saving money is not enough; you also must put those savings to work earning money. That requires investment. In any savings or investment instrument, you want to consider three basic elements:

- Safety of your invested money (your principal)—that is, are you going to get your money back?
- Rate of return—that is, how much will your money earn after the expenses of investment, if any, taxes, and inflation?
- Liquidity—that is, when can you get your hands on the money and the earnings?

As a rule, the safer and more liquid your money, the lower the rate of return, and vice versa. Investments like stocks will give you the opportunity to get a relatively high return on your money over the years, but the risk that your investment may be reduced or even lost completely is higher, too. By contrast, a savings account or a certificate of deposit will be very safe—guaranteed by the U.S. government up to $100,000 per account—but the interest you earn will be very low. In fact, after paying taxes and accounting for inflation, you may actually lose money. But within any category of investment there are individual investments that will provide more return with less risk. Learning how to find those specific investments marks you as a true investor.

Changing Asset Allocation As You Age

Generally your investments should be balanced with a few investments that are very safe, such as certificates of deposit, and most that are more risky with a greater return, such as mutual funds and income stocks. But the specific mix best for you—usually called *asset allocation*—depends partly on your age. At a younger age you can afford to put more money into slightly riskier ventures because you will have more time to correct your mistakes. This is particularly true when investing in stocks and mutual funds because the vagaries of the market often correct themselves over time. As you near retirement, you should shift a greater percentage of investment to the bottom of the risk pyramid. But even in retirement you cannot have all your capital invested in low risk/low return investments because inflation will erode it.

Debt or Equity Investments

All sorts of investments can be referred to as "securities," which in a legal sense means any sort of investment or arrangement from which you expect to receive income without working for it. There are basically two kinds of securities investments—*debt* and *equity*. If you invest in debt issues, you are a creditor for which you receive a return in the form of interest. As a creditor you are betting that the underlying entity—a corporation, the U.S. government, a municipality, or whatever—will pay its bills. Debt investments are usually called bonds or notes.

If you invest in equity, you are an owner and you receive your earnings in the form of dividends. In an equity investment you are literally buying a piece of the entity issuing the security. Equities are most frequently sold in the form of stock or limited partnerships. Remember that debtors get paid before owners, so in general bonds will be safer than stocks. But as with all rules of thumb, there are lots of exceptions.

The following outlines are some basic investment vehicles and the pros and cons of each.

Cash Equivalents

Money Market Accounts

Money market accounts are basically checking accounts that pay you interest. Your checking account should definitely be a "money market account" paying you interest and not charging you for checking. If you have your account with a federally insured institution such as a bank, savings and loan, or savings bank, your account will be insured up to $100,000 per institution.

The obvious advantage of these accounts is their safety and liquidity, but the disadvantage is that they usually pay a very low rate of return. Money market accounts are not the investment for your retirement funds, because you don't need easy access to those funds and you do need to have as high a rate of return as possible. But money market funds are very good places for your "emergency savings" and for holding funds while you are investigating long-term investments. Once you have established significant retirement savings, you should have a money market account simply to hold money between buying and selling investments.

Money Market Funds

Money market funds function like money market accounts, but they are not federally insured. They are a type of mutual fund holding several different debt instruments. (Mutual funds are discussed in detail later in this chapter.) Because money market funds usually diversify their holdings in short-term debt that have varying dates of maturity, they are considered a very safe investment. The funds are liquid. Again, their rate of return is very low, so these are not good investments for retirement funds. But money market funds may be useful as short-term holding accounts until you decide on long-term investments.

Certificates of Deposit (CDs)

Certificates of deposit—CDs—are simply deposits of cash with a bank or thrift institution. The money earns interest for the life of the CD, usually a stated period of months. The longer the period of the CD, the higher the interest rate in most cases. If you redeem the CD before its term runs, there is usually a steep penalty. If the CD is deposited in a state or federally guaranteed institution, your money is guaranteed by the government. In federal institutions the guarantee is up to $100,000. In state institutions the amount guaranteed will vary from state to state.

CDs are very safe—at least up to the guaranteed amount—but their rate of return is usually relatively small. Indeed, after taxes and inflation are factored in, you may only be breaking even. If your CDs are for a very long term and inflation is relatively high during the term, you might even lose money when you compare the amount of CD interest with the dollar's declining purchasing power. Nevertheless, CDs are easily understood and easily purchased. They are relatively liquid, depending on their term.

You can make CDs even more liquid by purchasing at one time a three-month, six-month, nine-month, and one-year CD. This is referred to as *laddering,* possibly because every three months you will have a step up in the form of a CD you can cash in without penalty if you need emergency money. Thereafter, each time one of the CDs matures, buy a one-year CD. With this system you always have a CD maturing within three months and you will have access to a major part of your savings every three months. You will also have the advantage of receiving the higher rate of return that comes with the longer-term CD.

Unless you buy CDs through a broker, who can sometimes get you higher rates than are ordinarily available, you pay no fees or commissions to buy CDs.

Given CDs' low interest rates, which in part are a trade-off for CDs' liquidity, which isn't needed for retirement accounts, CDs are not an ideal investment for your retirement savings. However, until you feel confident in investing, CDs can be a good compromise investment while you are learning about other investment opportunities. Just don't wait too long to branch out into higher-paying investments.

Bonds

Bonds are promises to repay the money you have loaned to the bond issuer at a certain time—the maturity date of the bond. Over the course of the loan, the debtor will pay you interest, often when you submit a "coupon," although for the most part the quaint exercise of actually clipping coupons to redeem this interest has gone the way of Model Ts and one-wage-earner families. Today the interest is usually paid without coupon submission. The United States government, most state and local governments, and corporations issue bonds.

Bond Values Linked to Other Interest Rates

When you invest in bonds always remember that the value of your investment is invariably linked to global interest rate changes, not just to the quality of the bond itself. The value of your underlying principal value will vary—sometimes dramatically—depending on movements of the prevailing interest rates for other debt instruments. As interest rates go up, the value of your principal investment in the bond goes down. As interest rates go down, the value of your bond goes up. The longer the term of your bond, the more the underlying value will be affected by interest-rate changes. For example, assume you bought a $10,000 bond paying a rate of 7 percent for thirty years and interest rates for similar types of debt move up to 8 percent. Even though nothing changed in the basic value of the company debt your bond represents, the underlying value of your bond on the secondary market (what another buyer would pay you for your bond) is going to be considerably reduced. Why? Because other investors can now buy newer bonds paying a higher interest rate than your bond. But if interest rates fall to 6 percent, the value of your bond in the secondary market will exceed $10,000 because there are few other investments that will pay as great an interest rate as your bond. Your bond now looks quite attractive to potential buyers.

Of course, if you keep the bond until maturity, you will receive your $10,000 back and you will have received interest on a periodic basis over the life of the bond. This is one reason why bonds can be good investments for retirement planning. If you buy a twenty-year bond, planning to hold it until retirement, the fluctuations in the bond's price in the secondary market over the two decades are immaterial to you. You have received a higher interest rate because you are willing to have your money tied up in the bond for a long time and the risk of changes in the underlying bond value before the maturity date isn't a concern for you. But be careful of buying long-term bonds in times of low inflation and low interest rates. If you buy a thirty-year bond paying 8 percent and inflation goes to 10 percent or more for a decade, you will have lost a considerable amount of money because you could not use the money tied up in the bond to seek an investment with the higher rates of return that high inflation brings.

Bond Ratings

Bonds are rated for safety by several rating agencies such as Standard & Poor's and Moody's Investors Services. The ratings range from AAA to D for Standard & Poor's and Aaa to D for Moody's. As you might expect, the closer to AAA or Aaa, the safer the bond and the lower the rate of return. This guide is helpful for the beginning investor. Ratings can change during the term of the bond, which will change the bond's secondary market value, but not its ultimate redemption price. Most bonds can be purchased through a broker for a fee.

There is a tendency to think of bonds as extremely safe with stable prices. But as illustrated in our examples, the value of bonds can fluctuate greatly—sometimes more than stocks. Investing in bonds should be a long-term proposition. Don't put money in bonds if you are going to need it before the bond's maturity date.

Treasury Bills, Notes, and Bonds

U.S. Treasury debt instruments are backed by the full faith and credit of the United States government and, more important, the United States taxpayer. *Bills* are debt instruments with maturities ranging from sixty days to one year. *Notes* have maturity dates from one year to ten years. Treasury debt instruments for more than ten years are *bonds*. Again, the longer the maturity level, the higher the interest rate usually is, but in recent years, during uncertain economic times, shorter-term maturities have occasionally had higher rates of return than the longer-term debts.

Treasuries can be purchased through brokers or a bank for a fee or from the Federal Reserve Banks. Or, after you set up an account, you can purchase Treasuries through the Internet at *www.publicdebt.treas.gov.* Alternatively you can call the Federal Reserve Bank in your region or write to Bureau of Public Debt, Department F, Department of the Treasury, Washington, D.C. 20239-1200.

Treasury debt instruments have a secondary market, meaning that they can be bought and sold through brokers after they have been issued and before they mature, so they tend to be very liquid. Treasury debt instruments are also exempt from state and local taxes, which can be quite a bonus if you live in a high-tax state such as New York, Maryland, Pennsylvania, New Jersey, or Massachusetts.

U.S. Treasury Inflation Bonds (I Bonds)

In 1998, the Treasury issued an "inflation" bond, the I Bond. I Bond interest rates are a combination of two separate rates: a fixed rate of return and a variable semiannual rate based on inflation. The fixed rate remains the same throughout the life of the I Bond, while the semiannual inflation rate can change every six months. The fixed rate of return is announced by the Treasury Department each May and November. Bonds purchased during the six-month period after the announcement will receive that fixed rate over the entire life of the I Bonds, plus a semiannual inflation rate.

The inflation rate is based on changes in the Consumer Price Index for all Urban Consumers (CPI-U), which is reported by the Bureau of Labor Statistics. I Bonds are issued in values from $50 to $10,000 and are purchased at their face value from most financial institutions. When redeemed they will pay the face value and the interest accrued over the course of the bond. I Bonds offer a relatively low basic rate of return, but their inflation-based rate of return protects your investment from erosion by inflation.

Municipal Bonds

Municipal bonds are bonds issued by state and local governments. Their interest is exempt from federal taxes and usually from tax of the jurisdiction issuing the bonds. Because of this tax advantage, the rate of return is usually lower than that of corporate bonds.

If you want to compare the tax-exempt bond rate of return to taxable rates, divide the bond's interest rate by the number that equals one minus your effective income tax rate. Include state tax in that tax rate figure, if the bonds are exempt from state tax. For example, suppose a municipal bond is offering a rate of 5 percent. Your federal tax rate is 28 percent and the state rate is 3 percent. Your overall rate is 31 percent. One minus 0.31 is 0.69; 0.69 divided into 5 is 7.25. You would need to receive at least a 7.25 percent rate of return on a taxable investment to realize a yield comparable to the tax-free investment. This formula can be used to compare any type of tax-free amount to a taxable or after-tax sum.

You should never put tax-exempt investments in your IRA or Keogh because when you begin to withdraw money from those plans, all income of the plan will be taxable at ordinary income rates, except any nondeductible contribution you may have made to your IRA. Putting tax-exempt investments in an IRA or Keogh will turn the otherwise tax-exempt income into taxable income, even though the tax will be delayed until you retire. But tax-exempt bonds may be good investments for retirement savings in addition to your IRA or Keogh account. Municipal bonds are best purchased from a broker who specializes in municipals because such brokers are more knowledgeable and have easy access to a wider variety of bonds.

Corporate Bonds

Corporate bonds are simply debt of the corporation. Corporate bonds pay interest at a fixed rate over the term of the bond, usually ten, twenty, or thirty years. With corporate bonds, the underlying value of your principal will be affected by interest rates in general, as was true with U.S. Treasury bonds. But with corporate bonds, the value of your principal will also be affected by the overall health of the company to some degree. Highly rated corporate bonds are appropriate investments for a portion of your retirement savings portfolio. As you age, their steady income becomes more important to cash flow, and the portion of your portfolio dedicated to bonds should increase.

Zero Coupon Bonds

Zero coupon bonds are offered by the U.S. Treasury, municipalities, and corporations. Zero coupon bonds are sold at a deep discount from the face value; for example, a $1,000 bond may be offered at $300. Over the life of the bond, no interest is paid. Then, at maturity, you receive the face value. The IRS treats these bonds as though interest were paid every year, so you pay taxes even though you have received no interest. Since IRAs and Keoghs do not pay tax on earnings as those earnings occur, some investment advisers urge buying zero coupon bonds for IRAs and Keoghs. They can be a good investment for those accounts, as long as you are receiving a competitive rate of return on the bond.

Junk Bonds, aka "High Yield Bonds" and "Fallen Angels"

Junk bonds may begin their lives in that status or they may descend into junkdom. Some junk bonds are natural born, issued by companies already heavily in debt or on shaky financial ground. These bonds offer a very high rate of return from the date they are issued to make up for their high risk. Highly popular in the takeover-crazed 1980s, these natural-born junk bonds are less common today.

Other high-yielding junk bonds are self-made. At initial issue, these bonds may have had an ordinary yield; however, because of financial reverses of the issuing company, the face value of the bond has fallen so low that, in comparison to the interest being paid on more secure bonds, the yield now is quite high. For example, Modern Buggy Company issues bonds at $1,000 face value, paying 5 percent. Investors come to view Modern Buggy as out of step with the current world and the face value of the bond in the secondary market now falls to $500. The 5 percent interest payments now represent a yield of 10 percent on the current value of your investment.

Unless you are very young and can allow time to even out ups and downs in value or you have the extra money to take some above-average risks, junk bonds are not an appropriate vehicle for retirement savings.

Equities

Investments in equities representing ownership are usually in shares of stock of the company. They may also be units of a partnership in which you are a *limited partner.* As an owner, you receive income only after all debts are paid. These earnings are paid as *dividends,* usually quarterly, for stocks, and *distributions* for limited partnerships. However, you also have the opportunity to share in the growth of the intrinsic value of the company. That growth should represent itself in the increase of the price of the stock or partnership units you bought. Some companies pay no dividends or distributions and your only return is from the growth of the stock price, if any.

Common Versus Preferred Stock

Common stock does not refer to ubiquitous stock. The term means you will receive dividends, if any, from a common pool of earnings. *Preferred stock* means that you will receive dividends, frequently at a stated percentage of your original investment in the stock, before any dividends are paid to the common stockholders. Preferred stock may also carry with it different voting rights than common stock. *Convertible preferred stock* is preferred stock that enables you to convert shares of your preferred stock into common stock when the common stock reaches a certain price. You make money because you paid a lower price for the preferred stock. Of course, the common stock may never reach a higher price than the preferred.

Stocks' Higher Returns – and Risks

The return on stocks can be quite high because you have the chance to receive both earnings and the growth in the value of the basic share price. But the risk is high for many stocks. Values change daily. Often the price of the stock is influenced more by rumors and the general economy than by the underlying value or management of the specific company. Much of the market is held by so-called institutional investors such as college endowments, retirement plan trust funds, other trusts, and mutual funds. These investors' funds are managed by professional asset managers, some of whom trade based on computer programs designed to respond to interest rates and other economic indicators. From an investor's perspective, it is meaningless to talk about stocks in general. Some company's shares are an extremely good value; others may be essentially worthless in a few months. Most lie somewhere in between.

Picking individual stocks for investment is a chancy business, as millions of people on Wall Street—or formerly on Wall Street—can attest. Some investment counselors even caution that the "dartboard" method of choosing stocks works about as well as the experts. Beginning in 1988, the *Wall Street Journal* has compared the results of the experts' stock choices against the overall Dow Jones industrial average and against stocks chosen by the staff's literally throwing darts at a listing of stocks. Measured from 1990 to the fall of 1998, the experts beat the dart throwers and the market about 45 percent of the time, the dart throwers won about 30 percent of the time, and the market beat both the experts and the darts about a quarter of the time. But more important, the experts achieved an average gain on their theoretical picks of almost 11 percent, compared to the average market gain of about 7 percent and the darts' gain of only 4.5 percent.[1] The experts' higher gain does suggest that knowledge helps.

Does all this risk mean you should never put your retirement savings into stocks? Absolutely not. It may be a tough game, but it's the only practical game in town to protect your savings from inflation. Some might argue that gold, diamonds, and real estate will also protect from inflation, but these are too speculative and too difficult to buy and sell for wise investors. Besides, there is a wonderful way the individual investor who does not want to spend every spare hour analyzing stocks can still play the game and use the experts—mutual funds, discussed in the following pages.

Buying Stocks

Publicly held stocks, meaning those stocks anyone can purchase, are traded on one of a number of stock exchanges. The New York Stock Exchange is the largest and trades most Fortune 500 companies. The American Stock Exchange tends to have slightly smaller, though still significant companies. Many start-up or regional companies are sold in the over-the-counter market. The over-the-counter market is a network of brokers around the country dealing in the particular stocks. This market buys and sells using the National Association of Securities Dealers' Automated Quotation system, called NASDAQ. (The American Stock Exchange and NASDAQ merged in 1998, but have not combined their listings.)

Stocks can be purchased through a stockbroker who will charge you a commission, a fee based on a percentage price of the stock you purchase. When you sell the stock through a broker there will also be a commission. Once you set up an account with a stockbroker you can call their automated telephone systems or "online" systems over the Internet to purchase stocks at a reduced commission.

Dividend Reinvestment Plans (DRIPs)

Many companies permit you to buy their stock directly and will reinvest the dividends the stock earns in more stock, through dividend reinvestment programs—DRIPs. Big-name Fortune 500 companies offering DRIPs include Anheuser-Busch, Coca-Cola, Disney, Intel, Johnson & Johnson, Kellogg, Pfizer, Sara Lee, and even stockbroker Charles Schwab.

DRIPs have several advantages. First, you save the cost of a broker's commission. Second, the automatic dividend reinvestment provides a convenient, nondiscretionary method of saving. Third, many of the programs provide an inexpensive way to let you buy small amounts of stock over the long term. (Most of the companies listed above will let you make an initial purchase without a fee and let you invest $50 or less at a time.) DRIPs also have some disadvantages. You cannot time either the purchase or sale of DRIP stock exactly. For most programs, you must request sales and nonautomatic purchases in writing. Check DRIP fees carefully; they can mount up. For example, some programs charge a five-dollar fee for purchases under a specified amount and charge an additional fee for sales of the stock.

Mutual Funds

Mutual funds are groups of stocks or bonds or a mixture of other investment assets held by an asset manager. You invest in mutual funds by buying shares of the funds. Using this technique, your small investment in the mutual fund enables you indirectly to hold at least a piece of many stocks or bonds. This diversity of ownership reduces your risk of investment. Mutual funds also offer the small investor the opportunity to enjoy the inflation protection and growth advantages of stocks, as well as the experts to choose those stocks, without spending every spare moment investigating company balance sheets.

There are literally thousands of mutual funds with a large assortment of investment goals, strategies, and pricing schemes. Some funds hold only *income stocks,* that is, shares of well-established companies such as AT&T, Coca-Cola, and Merck, which consistently pay dividends, but whose prices ordinarily do not fluctuate greatly. Other funds hold only *growth stocks* of young companies that may not even pay a dividend, but whose share price is expected to grow significantly over the years. Some funds hold combinations of these kind of stocks. So-called *sector funds* hold only stocks of a particular industry such as health companies, high-tech companies, mining companies, and so on.

Mutual funds may hold only bonds or only certain types of bonds. Some funds may hold stocks, bonds, and large sums of cash investments for so-called total investment. Others, called index funds, simply buy shares of every stock traded in a given category, such as the Standard & Poor's 500. The return and performance of these index funds have the same results as the market niche they reflect.

Closed-End or Open-End Funds

Mutual funds are either closed-end or open-end operations. Open-end funds will accept new investors and new money at any time. The price of the open-ended fund shares is determined by the value of the investments held by the fund, divided by the number of shares of the fund.

Closed-end mutual funds operate differently and are valued differently. These funds have only a limited number of shares in the fund to offer to the public. Once that number of shares is sold, the fund is closed to new investors—and usually to additional investment by current shareholders as well. Shares of these funds are traded more like stocks. The fund's shares may have a greater value than the combined value of the assets in the fund or a lesser value, depending on the market's view of the overall prospects for the fund to make money in the future.

Read the Fund Prospectus

The fund's prospectus outlines the goals, expenses, income record, investments, and managers of the fund. The prospectus will also tell you how to buy and sell shares of the fund. The prospectus will be sent to you by the fund or given to you by a broker handling the fund. Blessedly, the U.S. Securities and Exchange Commission (SEC), which regulates the sale of stocks, mutual funds, bonds, and other securities, has recently campaigned to have mutual funds draft prospectuses in plain English. Some mutual funds have actually accepted the SEC's challenge and you may now find mutual fund prospectuses that you can read and understand.

Stock mutual funds are a good investment for your retirement savings because they are equities that have the promise of keeping up with inflation. They can provide you with a diversity of ownership in assets, giving you the equivalent of stock ownership without tying up all your investments in one company's stock. Mutual funds also provide you with an expert asset manager who is responsible for analyzing the thousands of investments on the market and trading those investments at the best times.

Mutual Fund Expenses: Watch Those Fees!

Of course, this expertise and management isn't free. Part of the money you invest in a mutual fund goes to pay the fund's expenses, including paying the fund's managers. These expenses are disclosed in the prospectus and, of course, you should never invest in a fund until you have read the prospectus and done other reading on the fund's performance. Operating expenses should be less than 1 percent of total portfolio value. While a 1 or 2 percent operating fee may not sound like much, remember your time value of money tables. A monthly investment of $200 for thirty years in a mutual fund paying 13 percent would give you about $884,000 at retirement; reduce that yield each year with an extra 1 percent fee on the fund and you will have only $706,000 at retirement.

Mutual funds may charge an initial fee to purchase the fund. These so-called load funds charge fees ranging from 1 to 2 percent to as high as 8 percent of the investment. Other funds charge a fee when you sell the fund. Usually, this exit fee is reduced the longer you hold the stock. Other mutual funds have no purchase or exit fees. The funds without such fees are called no-load funds. Any list of the "best" mutual funds contains both load and no-load funds. There is no evidence to suggest that load funds as a whole perform better than no-load funds, nor do load funds on average have lower expenses than no-load funds.

Mutual Fund "Tax Efficiency"

If you are buying mutual funds for an IRA or other tax-favored account, the tax treatment will not be an issue, because the account will not generate taxable income until you make withdrawals from the account. But when you are investing in mutual funds in taxable accounts, consider the tax efficiency of the mutual fund when purchasing. The term *tax efficiency* simply means the amount and type of earnings generated by the fund. Does the mutual fund tend to grow by an increasing price of the share or by distributing earnings each year and, if earnings are distributed, do they tend to be ordinary income or capital gains? The answers to these questions will determine how much tax you may have to pay on the earnings from these funds.

As you have probably guessed, tax-efficient mutual funds are those that generate little taxable income. For example, if the fund grows primarily by increasing the face value of its shares, that growth will not be taxed until you sell the shares. If you have kept the shares more than one year when you sell, you will pay the tax at the capital gains rate, which is lower than the ordinary income tax rate. If the fund tends to issue dividends annually, those dividends will be paid as ordinary income or capital gains or a bit of both. While you will have to pay tax on those dividends, the portion of the shares that are paid as capital gains will be subject to the lower capital gains rate and the ordinary income portion will be subject to the higher tax rates that apply to that income.

The annual earnings of the fund are important, but just as important is the amount of those earnings you get to keep. So in considering the real rate of return of your mutual funds, you will want to consider their tax efficiency. Many mutual funds are designed to produce the lowest amount of taxable income possible. As your tax bracket increases, so should your concern about the tax efficiency of your mutual funds. A fund that pays 10 percent may not leave you with as much money as one that earns 9 percent if the 10 percent fund pays all its earnings in ordinary income.

Avoiding Year-End Mutual Fund Purchases

The timing of your mutual fund purchase can also be important. Generally, do not buy mutual funds near the end of the year. At that time the price of the fund reflects dividends the fund may have collected throughout the year. Once those dividends are paid out, the price of the shares will drop correspondingly. You will have the dividends, of course, but you will also have a tax bill. For example, you buy 100 shares of High Income Mutual Fund for $10 a share on December 2. On December 15, High Income pays you a dividend of $1 per share and the value of each share is reduced to $9. Your $1,000 investment is now worth $900 and you have $100 in cash on which you are going to have to pay at least $15 of tax! Not tax efficient—or smart. Wait until January, after the dividends have been paid. The share prices generally will be lower and you can buy more shares.

Buying Mutual Funds

Mutual funds can be purchased through a broker or directly from the fund itself. Simply call or write the fund and ask for the materials. They will send you a prospectus and an investment form. If you decide to invest in the fund, you fill out the form and send it back with a check. Some mutual funds also have programs permitting monthly or other periodic investing by making a withdrawal directly from your checking account. Invested amounts can be as low as $50 per month.

Mutual funds usually have a dividend reinvestment program that automatically reinvests your earnings by buying more shares of the mutual fund. Always choose this option. It will be forced automatic savings; you avoid receiving small checks that get spent without thinking; and it provides a way for you to average your investment in the funds over the years, buying sometimes when the price is high and sometimes when it is lower.

Limited Partnerships, Hedge Funds, Derivatives, and Other Temptations

Of course the investments discussed above are not the only ones available. You can buy real estate, oil wells, gold mines, and frog farms. People will be happy to sell you these directly or through limited partnerships, hedge funds, derivatives, and other exotic systems. Until you become a sophisticated investor, concentrate on more common investments. Resist the temptation to build wonderful stories for cocktail parties or the car pool about your latest venture with derivatives tied to the price of mahogany in Uzbekistan. (You're already getting more sophisticated if you just noted that mahogany doesn't grow in Uzbekistan.)

But for the record, *limited partnerships* are a fairly literal name. Your liability as a partner is "limited" to the amount of your original investment. If the partnership incurs additional debt or liability, as a limited partner you are not responsible for that debt. Your right to enjoy the profits of the partnership is also usually limited, meaning you won't begin to receive any return on your money until the general partners—that is, the ones who are on the hook for the bills—recoup their expenses and some profits for their efforts. Some limited partnerships are publicly traded, so they are bought and sold much like stocks. Most limited partnerships are not publicly traded. Consequently, once your money is invested, you will have a difficult time selling your partnership interest. Like any other investment, there are profitable limited partnerships and there are unprofitable ones. In the early stages of your investing career, if you must invest in limited partnerships, choose those that are publicly traded and investigate them very carefully.

Hedge funds basically use pools of assets that will increase sharply in value if other types of assets decrease sharply in value, hence you are hedging your bets on investments. Hedge funds are managed and traded privately and generally are only available to selected investors with very high income and net worth.

Derivatives are funds whose value is based on reference to another asset. Like hedge funds, derivatives are generally available only to selected investors with very high income and net worth.

Conclusion: There Are No Perfect Investments, Only Good Ones

No single investment vehicle is best for every person at every time in her life. Most of the investment vehicles discussed in this chapter were probably somewhat familiar to you. Now you should have a better understanding of their differences and advantages and disadvantages for retirement savings.

On balance, for those just beginning to save for retirement, a growth and income equities mutual fund is probably the best investment for several reasons.

- Such funds do not require a big investment. Many funds will open IRA accounts for as little as $250.
- These funds provide you with equities, which will tend to keep up with inflation over the long years between now and retirement.
- Because it is a fund of several stocks, you will automatically have some diversity in your investment.
- Many funds can be purchased with no investment charges so you don't lose any money to overhead with your initial purchase.
- Such funds are more likely than other investments to give you the best return on your money for the lowest risk. As your savings grow, it will then become wise to add other types of investments, perhaps at first through other mutual funds such as a bond fund.

- Highly liquid investments, such as short-term CDs, money market funds, and savings accounts, while safe, are not appropriate for retirement savings. You receive a lower rate of earnings in return for high liquidity. But you don't need liquidity for retirement savings that should be locked up for years.

13

How to Invest Wisely for Retirement

A fiduciary shall discharge his duties with respect to the plan solely in the interest of the participants . . . by diversifying the investments of the plan so as to minimize the risk of large losses.

—ERISA, Section 404, defining the legal duties of pension plan managers

Don't put all your eggs in one basket.
—your grandmother

Whether the advice is from your grandmother or the Congress—two parties expert in laying down the law—the directive is the same: diversify your investments. All investment portfolios, even those of a few thousand dollars, should be diversified to avoid big losses. Part of diversification is *asset allocation*. You also should become more educated on choosing specific investments among investment categories and on choosing effective professional help. What follows is a guide.

Principles of Investment: Diversity and Rate of Return Versus Security

Your savings should be diversified both in types of investment vehicles, or asset categories, and among different companies and bond issuers within each type of asset. Your accounts should contain several types of assets such as bonds and stocks and among those bonds and stocks several different types of companies should be represented. Most of us, at least in the early years of retirement planning, simply don't have enough money to achieve this diversity without mutual funds.

Diversity among types of investment vehicles is important because markets frequently move in opposite directions. When interest rates go up and your money funds or CDs can pay more, the stock market and existing bond values frequently go down. When interest rates go down, the stock market usually goes up. When inflation is high, stocks frequently keep pace with inflation, but bonds may be hard hit. There are always exceptions, but in general if you are diversified, one asset type such as bonds may lose value, but those losses may be offset by gains from other types of assets. Diversity within asset types is needed so that your investments are not tied to the fate of one company or industry.

Asset Allocation

This diversity is also referred to as "asset allocation" among financial planners. Generally, advisers divide the available investment options into four segments.

- cash and cash equivalents,
- fixed income (bonds, certificates of deposit),
- equities, and
- tangible assets such as gold, silver, and real estate.

How those assets are divided depends on your levels of savings, your goals, your age, and your comfort level. The division also depends on the market for various assets at the current time, but that level of analysis is generally not necessary at the beginning of your savings program.

First, the Emergency Fund

Everyone needs a minimal amount of savings that is readily available for emergencies. This fund must be in cash or cash equivalents. You don't want to sell mutual funds to meet an emergency if their price is depressed. The rule of thumb for an emergency pool of savings is six months' expenses. This cash can be in money market accounts or funds or short-term CDs. Frankly, it is difficult to have six months of expenses set aside only for emergencies. Ordinarily money set aside for retirement savings should never even be considered available for any other purpose, let alone used for any other purpose. But for beginning savers on a low budget, we have to make an exception.

Don't wait until you have saved your six-month expense reserve before you begin saving for retirement. In the early stages of your retirement savings program, hedge a little bit. For example, if your 401(k) plan permits loans, don't delay funding your 401(k) even if you don't have six months of expenses saved. The 401(k) plan may have an employer match that you will miss if you don't contribute to the plan. If the plan permits loans, you can always use that as a small part of your emergency fund for most things that are truly emergencies.

(Although you should avoid 401(k) plan loans except in the direst of emergencies, for the reasons cited in Chapter 7.)

In your early days of saving, also consider your IRA as at least some of the emergency fund. For example, if the worst befalls you and you become disabled, the IRA can be drawn on without penalty. Build toward the six months' expense emergency reserve at the same time you build toward retirement savings. Until you get the emergency reserve, some of your retirement savings may have to be in a cash-equivalent type of investment such as a money market account. Once that cash emergency reserve is established, you don't need cash assets at all for your retirement savings, at least not until you are very near retirement.

Case Study 1: Appropriate Asset Allocation for Jennifer

Let's look at Jennifer. At 30 and earning $21,000, she is just beginning to save for retirement. She has put aside $4,000 as her emergency savings in certificates of deposit with one-year maturity dates to get higher interest rates, but she has four one-year CDs each timed to mature three months apart. Each time one matures, she rolls it over for a year. She has saved $2,000 to fund an IRA account this year. Because she earns under $25,000, her IRA will be fully deductible even though she has an employer-provided retirement plan. Alternatively, Jennifer could set up a Roth IRA, which won't give her a deduction, but will allow her to take tax-free earnings at retirement. She knows CDs are safe, but interest rates are fairly low and she knows her investments should be diversified, so more CDs aren't a good idea.

Given Jennifer's age and the fact that she will not be using the money for as long as another thirty-five years, she should begin looking for mutual funds for her IRA. In addition, mutual funds enable her to have her investment supervised by the fund's professional investment manager, a good substitute for hiring a professional financial adviser of her own. She probably cannot afford a personal financial adviser at her present modest income and saving level.

She could place $1,000 in a corporate bond fund, a conservative investment that would probably earn about 8 percent per year, and $1,000 in an aggressive growth stock mutual fund. The aggressive growth mutual fund is among the riskier investments in mutual funds, but she has a long time to allow the money to grow. Even if the fund has a bad year now and again, she can wait for the price of the fund to go up again because she won't need the money for another thirty-five years.

But Jennifer has never owned stocks before and she feels she doesn't want the risk and volatility of aggressive growth stocks. She can compromise with a growth and income stock fund that invests in mature companies historically paying dividends and in companies that are still growing and have a potential for stock price increase. With all these investments, she should opt to have all dividends reinvested.

So she allocates her $6,000 of assets as follows:

Cash/cash equivalents	$4,000 (67.0%)
Bond mutual fund	$1,000 (16.5%)
Stock mutual fund	$1,000 (16.5%)

As Jennifer saves more, she will proportionately reduce her allocation in cash and cash equivalents. She is too heavily invested in cash now, because she needs the cash emergency reserve. Because Jennifer is just getting started in her savings program and has relatively little saved, in analyzing her asset allocation, she should not look at just her retirement savings assets, but should recognize her overall financial picture. Investments that may be very good for retirement savings in the future when she has more money, such as zero coupon bonds, are not appropriate for her to hold now, when it is possible that a crisis might require that she dip into retirement savings for other short-term needs.

As a younger person Jennifer could be more aggressive in her asset allocation, if she feels comfortable. As she saves more money and her portfolio grows, she should have as much as 80 percent of investments in stocks, probably through various mutual funds. The good news for Jennifer is that, because she is starting early, saving just $2,000 in her IRA each year, along with the savings she already has, will give her over $700,000 at retirement, if she averages a 10 percent annual return on her investment. The bad news: if she had started at age 22, she would have $1.3 million at retirement, using the same savings rate.

Case Study 2: Bonnie's Asset Allocation

Bonnie, now 40, faces a very different situation. First, Bonnie earns much more money and she has been in the job market longer, so she has saved her emergency reserve. She also saved $13,700 and invested it in tax-deferred IRA plans. She has twenty-two years before she wants to retire. Because she has more time than Susan or Alice to even out the ups and downs of her investment, she can more heavily invest in aggressive growth stock funds. With less than $14,000 for her portfolio, she probably should not be investing in individual stocks now, but as her portfolio grows, individual stock investments will become appropriate.

For now she might want a portfolio invested in mutual funds and stocks like this:

Aggressive growth stock fund	$5,500 (40%)
Growth stock fund	$4,100 (30%)
Growth and income stock fund	$2,050 (15%)
Midterm bond fund	$2,050 (15%)

Bonnie has most of her assets in equities at different levels of risk and only 15 percent in debt represented by the bonds. This is a riskier portfolio than someone nearer retirement should have, but given her salary level and the years to retirement, it is appropriate for her.

Case Study 3: Susan's Asset Allocation

At 50, Susan has at least fifteen years to retirement and, based on her $25,200 salary, she has saved her cash emergency reserve long ago. Like Bonnie, she can be much more aggressive with her investments, depending on her own "sleep at night" factor for risk tolerance. Some investment advisers recommend that the minimum asset allocation to stock should be a percentage equal to 100 minus your age, or in Susan's case at least 50 percent of savings in stock. But given increased life expectancies and the number of years likely to be spent in retirement, Susan wants to be more aggressive than that. Susan's $30,000 retirement saving asset allocation is:

Aggressive growth stock fund	$15,000 (50%)
Growth and income stock fund	$7,500 (25%)
Income stock fund	$4,500 (15%)
Long-term corporate bond fund	$3,000 (10%)

Susan is using the dividend reinvestment program in each fund and she has the income fund automatically deduct enough from her bank account each month to have her IRA fully funded by the end of the year. With this arrangement, the higher income this fund delivers is protected from taxes.

From the retirement estimators we ran in Chapter 11 for Susan, we know she needs to be saving between $5,000 and $6,000 a year to reach her retirement goals, assuming an average 8 percent rate of return and 5 percent inflation. Because those amounts represent such a large portion of her current income, asset allocation is critical to her. If she can increase the rate of return 12 percent, she could reduce the amount she needs to save each year to $4,200. That's still a significant sum, but it's 17 percent of income, rather than a quarter of her income.

Case Study 4: Alice's Asset Allocation

With only five years to retirement, Alice cannot afford to be as aggressive as our other retirement planners. Yet some financial experts would tell Alice that even she should have two-thirds of her retirement savings in stocks and the remainder in bonds and then reverse that proportion when she retires. Because Alice will have relatively little from her employer-provided plan, she has decided to take the more aggressive advice. She has one-third of her retirement investments in an aggressive growth mutual fund, one-third in a growth and income fund, and one-third in a fund with investment grade corporate bonds.

The Case Studies and You

Each of the retirement savers could have chosen other ways to divide her investments that might provide as good a mix of investments. The important thing is that each has allocated her assets in different investments so that no matter where the economy goes, she will have some protection from market forces. Of course, if the stock market drops significantly, because Jennifer, Bonnie, and Susan are relatively heavily weighted toward stocks, the value of their assets will plunge. But they have time to wait for the market to rise again.

Note that we did not discuss any contributory employer-provided retirement plans separately. If you have an employer-provided retirement plan that allows you to choose among investments, be sure you consider those assets in your own allocation mix as well. Some employers offer asset allocation modeling or advice in connection with their contributory retirement plans such as 401(k) or 403(b) plans. They can be useful in planning for all your retirement savings, not just the plan. Also recognize that because the investment options in the employer's plan are limited, you should start the asset allocation analysis with those options. Then determine what type of investments you should be buying on your own to balance your retirement savings—dare we say it—portfolio.

Accepting Higher Risk for a Higher Return

Women seem to have a difficult time accepting the fact of risk in their investments, although we may be overcoming the fear of investment risk.[1] Pam Harmon, a Washington, D.C., financial planner who counts many women among her clients, finds this risk aversion to be the single biggest mistake women investors make, especially in planning for retirement. To help overcome this risk aversion, Harmon resorts to charts showing the risk/reward benefits.

The effect of Jennifer's hypothetical choices for her 401(k) plan in Table 11.2 in Chapter 11 showed us how rates of return will affect her income in retirement. But of course the very safe CDs will always pay their guaranteed 6 percent. With mutual funds or other investments, some years the return will be 3 percent and some years it will be 20 percent and the only guarantee of your principal is the quality of the fund, unlike the CDs, which are guaranteed by the federal government.

We already know that the higher the risk, the higher the rate of return—usually. In choosing among individual investments, there are some ways to lessen risk and maintain a high rate of return. As we have seen, mutual funds are one way to do this. Asset allocation is another.

Investigating the Risks

Investigating investments before you consider putting in your money is the best way to manage risk. Investigate the ups and downs in the price of the investment you are considering. This volatility is charted by investment periodicals such as *Value Line* publications. There are investments that provide a higher rate of return with less volatility. Search them out to help overcome your fear of risk. Choose investments with at least a ten-year record of solid performance. Investigate before you invest; once your money is invested, be patient. Prices of stocks and mutual funds go up and down, so be prepared for that.

Don't Try to "Time the Market"

Remember the advice of millionaire financier Bernard Baruch, who made many of his millions during the Depression when financiers were jumping out windows. His guide to the stock market, "Buy low, sell high," seems rather obvious—and useless—advice. But considering how many people ignore it, apparently this advice really is a pearl of wisdom rather than ordinary common sense.

Consider the behavior of investors in two fairly recent periods. First, during the record high stock market of early 1992, investors shifted retirement assets by buying into stocks when the price was high. Then the year ended on a low note. Second, recall the stock market retreat of the late summer of 1998. When the market plunged, many individuals rushed to shift their 401(k) plans, IRAs, and other retirement savings out of the funds that held stocks and into fixed-income funds. They sold low, when they should have been buying or at least holding onto their stock investments.

There are bargains in individual stocks and mutual funds, even in high markets, but they are hard to find. Unless you consider yourself a real expert, you really should not try. Don't try to "time" the market by shifting your 401(k) plan funds or IRAs as the market moves up and down. Remember the stock market experts followed by the *Wall Street Journal*. Following the stock market for a living, this group outperforms the market less than half the time. With a full-time job, a home, and a family, what makes you think you can outperform the experts and the market?

Regular Timed Investing: Dollar Cost Averaging

Another way to reduce risk is to make small investment purchases in the same fund or stock on a periodic basis, for instance, monthly. This approach to investing, sometimes referred to as dollar cost averaging, means you will be buying some of the fund when it is relatively high priced and some when it is relatively low priced. For example, you have $3,000 you want to invest in a mutual fund that has been ranging in value from $18 to $21 a share. You could watch the fund's price every day, waiting to buy when the fund is close to $18. This will take some time and become a bit irritating. Or you could begin investing $500 monthly, recognizing that you will probably buy some shares near the $21 price and some near the $18 price and most at a price in between.

With dollar cost averaging, you avoid second-guessing yourself about whether you bought too high or should have waited another day or two. Most important, you establish a regular pattern for investing that you are more likely to maintain. When you are buying at low prices, you can congratulate yourself on getting more shares for your money, and when you are buying at higher prices, you can congratulate yourself on how well your investments are doing.

Deciding Which Investments to Choose: Read, Read, Read

Telling Alice and her colleagues to buy a bond mutual fund and an aggressive stock fund hasn't really given them much help. There are hundreds of each of these funds. Which one should they choose and whom should they consult to make their choices? Remember, the *Wall Street Journal*'s dart throwers gave the expert financial advisers a run for their money, so there don't seem to be any guarantees in investing, even when you consult an expert. Now we get to the difficult part.

Books

The bestseller lists abound with financial guidance. Several excellent books provide general investment guidance. Start with Andrew Tobias's *The Only Investment Guide You'll Ever Need* (Harcourt Brace, 1998). Tobias takes an appropriately irreverent attitude toward experts, ignores sophisticated, tax-driven schemes, and concentrates on sound advice for those of us who don't trade in thousand-share blocks of stock four times a day. He gives you practical ways to save money starting today and much of the book is laugh-out-loud funny. Jane Bryant Quinn's book, *Making the Most of Your Money* (Simon & Schuster, 1997), provides a full range of investment and money advice. For those just starting in the job market, Beth Kobliner's *Get a Financial Life* (Fireside Books, 1998) speaks directly to your status.

Magazines and Newspapers

Dozens of periodicals are devoted to investment information on specific stocks, bonds, and mutual funds. *Money, Business Week, Smart Money, Worth, Kiplinger's Personal Finance,* and *Forbes* rank mutual funds at least annually. These magazines, along with the *Wall Street Journal* and *Barron's* newspapers, provide information on stocks and other securities. *Barron's* runs a particularly interesting summary of the various stock brokerages' recommendations on which stocks to buy, sell, or hold. While you won't want to subscribe to all of these, they are easily available on the newsstand and at the library. Look at each and find one or two you want to subscribe to.

Investment Newsletters

Stock investment newsletters number in the hundreds and a subscription usually costs well over $100 a year. These newsletters provide in-depth analysis of individual stocks and probably have more information than you need on a regular basis. But some of the better-known investment newsletters, such as *Value Line Investment Survey* and *Standard & Poor's Outlook*, are available at larger public libraries. These can be useful when you are considering a specific investment or want to look up a particular stock or industry.

The Internet

There are hundreds of sites on the Internet focusing on financial planning, money, and retirement issues. You can track real-time prices of stock, use interactive software to chart retirement savings, and keep track of your stock portfolio.

But be careful. All one needs to be an expert on anything on the Internet is a web page. Stick with the known sources of financial products and information. Take all Internet information with a grain of salt.

Among some of the more comprehensive sites are: *www.stocksmart.com, www.yahoo.com, www.quicken.com, www.dailystocks.com,* and *www.stockmaster.com.* Each of these offers quotes, stock histories, current business news, and many hotlinks to other useful sites.

Seminars and Classes

Community colleges and some women's organizations have classes at all levels of financial planning. Jennifer, who is just starting her savings and investment program, may be well served by attending some community college classes on personal financial planning beginning at the basic budgeting level and then moving on to investments. Alice could find the American Association of Retired Persons–sponsored local seminars conducted through their Women's Financial Planning Program helpful. These focus on the woman nearing retirement, though much of their advice applies to younger women as well.

Stockbrokers, financial planners, and accounting firms frequently hold free seminars on investment or personal financial planning. Obviously, the seminar sponsor hopes to gain you as a client and may even be pushing a specific product at the seminar. But you will find helpful information as well, such as how to analyze a stock's potential for growth and value based on current price, asset value, and dividend history. Brokers also provide a number of useful publications such as explanations of basic investment terms, tips on how to read a balance sheet, retirement planning kits, and so on. Most of these publications you can get by simply writing. Charles Schwab, the brokerage firm, provides a quarterly guide to mutual fund performance on every fund it sells.

The American Association of Individual Investors (AAII) is dedicated to providing consumer education on investments. AAII produces a magazine, home study courses, and seminars. The address for AAII is 625 North Michigan Avenue, Chicago, Illinois 60611-3110. Its materials are designed for the investor who wants to spend a significant amount of time on investments. You may find AAII publications too technical and time-intensive if you are just starting your portfolio, but if you really want to concentrate on planning, the materials will be most educational.

Who Can Help? Financial Advisers, Accountants, Stockbrokers

There are always the professionals to fall back on. There is no magic formula for finding good advice, but there are some rules for avoiding bad advice. First, do not expect unbiased, independent advice and do not depend on financial advisers who make money by selling you a specific product such as an annuity or insurance policy. These sellers may provide you with excellent information about their products, but it will be only about their products. They are not looking out for the best investment for your portfolio of savings and investment. They are looking out for the best investment for you that they happen to sell. Or worse, they may be looking for the best investment for you that gives them the biggest commission.

Second, remember that as long as any adviser is being paid by commission, rather than directly by you, she really cannot give totally unbiased advice. Her first loyalty must be to feeding her family, not your financial well-being. This does not mean you should never deal with sellers of investments who are dependent on commissions. Stockbrokers, insurance company agents, and the like are very useful and can provide important guidance. But don't rely on them for independent advice and don't rely solely on them for financial advice.

Pick a financial adviser whose only product is her knowledge and experience and be prepared to pay for that product. After all, she's got to make a living too. All advisers are willing to talk with you initially for free for a short time, but you should not expect to call every six months for free advice. According to Pam Harmon, even women with as little as $2,000 to invest are welcomed by some financial advisers and should consider seeking professional assistance.

But you should also do your own homework before seeking a financial adviser. First decide exactly what services you want from a financial adviser. Do you want budgeting advice, credit management help, help with taxes, investment advice, or all of the above? A stockbroker can give you advice on specific investments and perhaps on asset allocation, but she won't be able to help on taxes. An accountant will take care of your taxes, but may or may not be helpful with advice on specific investments. Depending on the individual and her training and background, a financial planner may be able to provide advice at every level.

Paying for Advice

You need to consider the cost of financial advice in relation to your portfolio at any given time. Investment advisers themselves disagree about how much investment money one needs to have before you should use an investment adviser. Some financial planners will not work with you unless you have a substantial portfolio already—$200,000 or more. Others are willing to start with very small accounts of a few thousand dollars. If you have only $2,000 or $3,000, frankly, an adviser will not be very helpful simply for investment advice. Your best avenue may be educating yourself about mutual funds and buying a few different no-load funds you have researched until you reach a portfolio of $20,000 or more. Obviously, if you are paying the adviser by the hour or as information is rendered, she may be glad to advise you, regardless of the amount of your nest egg. But why spend $500 to learn how to invest $2,000? You would have to receive advice that gives you a 25 percent rate of return just to break even. Be very candid about what you have, what you can save, and how much you want to pay for advice.

Stockbrokers charge on a commission basis. Most accountants charge an hourly fee. Financial planners generally charge in two different ways, either on an hourly fee or per planning session fee or based on a percentage of your portfolio. Some advisers will allow you to choose the fee structure you want. Others will tell you how they charge and say take it or leave it. The billing method most advantageous to you depends on your approach to investing. If you want the adviser to take over managing your money with only general direction from you on goals, a percentage-of-portfolio fee approach makes sense. If you intend to take a more active role, sometimes accepting the advice and sometimes rejecting it, an hourly fee may be fairer to both of you.

Be wary of financial planners who charge you a fee directly and also earn a commission from securities you purchase. When you pay a fee to the planner, you ordinarily would assume the planner is not also receiving a commission from investment product sales, too. But this assumption may not be correct. Many financial planners do accept commissions. Be sure you know which investments will yield the planner a commission and which do not and weigh her advice accordingly.

Financial Planners

Financial advisers come in all fashions. Accountants, brokers, lawyers, and insurance agents are all financial advisers. For that matter, so is your mother. But this section limits the discussion to individuals who offer wide-ranging financial advice on budgeting, savings, and specific investment recommendations and advertise themselves as "financial planners" or "financial advisers." We will use the term financial planner here to distinguish that individual from brokers, accountants, and lawyers who may also give financial advice in their professional endeavors. Some financial planners also have credentials as accountants or lawyers, but simply concentrate on financial advice.

Anyone can call herself a financial planner. Unlike an accountant, lawyer, or broker, financial planners are not subject to licensing or training requirements in most states. There is virtually no effective regulation of financial planners or other financial advisers who are not regulated by virtue of their status as an accountant, broker, or lawyer.

To increase your chances of dealing with a qualified planner look for the following designations:

- CFP—Certified Financial Planner, awarded by the International Board of Standards and Practices for Certified Financial Planners, Denver, Colorado
- ChFC—Chartered Financial Consultant, awarded by the American College, Bryn Mawr, Pennsylvania
- APFS—Accredited Personal Financial Specialist, awarded by the American Institute of Certified Public Accountants, New York, New York

These designations mean the planner has at least gone through a training program on financial matters given by an accrediting institution. It does not necessarily mean the individual is licensed by the state or has passed any state examinations. Talk to people you know about their financial advisers. Ask a friend or business colleague who appears to be financially sophisticated. Seek someone with experience and a track record.

Depending on their size, investment advisers should be registered with the U.S. Securities and Exchange Commission or the state agency regulating securities and investment advisers. Generally, any adviser with less than $25 million under management should be registered with state securities regulators. Advisers with more than that should be registered with the SEC. But don't think adherence to state or federal investment adviser laws or registration with the SEC or the state agency is a stamp of approval. It is not.

The Securities and Exchange Commission is the federal agency that regulates stock exchanges and the registration and disclosure of "securities," usually stocks, bonds, and limited partnerships. Most states have regulatory agencies that do the same thing. The role of the SEC and most state securities regulators is to require disclosures, not to approve or disapprove of quality. The agencies do not rule on the quality or the wisdom of an investment adviser or investment.

The type of financial adviser you need depends on your own level of sophistication and how involved you wish to be in the management of your money. You can begin by getting a free listing of financial planners from two industry trade associations: International Association of Financial Planning, 2 Concourse Parkway, Suite 800, Atlanta, Georgia 30328, 404-395-1605 (free Directory of Registry of Financial Planning Practitioners) and Institute of Certified Financial Planners,

10065 East Harvard Avenue, Suite 320, Denver, Colorado 80231, 303-751-7600 (free listing of five CFPs in your zip code). You can also check membership status with the Institute on their Internet site, *www.icfp.org,* simply by typing in the name of the adviser you want to research.

The National Association of Personal Financial Advisors will also provide you with a list of their members. Members of NAPFA work only for fees and are prohibited from receiving any sales commission or other type of product-related compensation. You can write or call: National Association of Personal Financial Advisors, 1130 Lake Cook Road, Suite 105, Buffalo Grove, Illinois 60089, 800-366-2732.

Accountants

Many accountants also provide financial and investment advice beyond just completing tax returns and setting up budgets. A certified public accountant (CPA) is tested and licensed in accounting matters by the state in which she practices. An accountant may also have the AFPS designation. Accountants generally are particularly well versed in the tax and estate-planning areas of retirement planning and financial management. This may be more important as you near retirement than it is in your early retirement planning years. Accountants also are frequently savvy in the operation of employer-provided benefit plans because they or their colleagues in their firm advise employers on retirement plans. The big-five accounting firms—KPMG, Arthur Andersen, PricewaterhouseCoopers, Ernst and Young, and Deloitte-Touche—usually have personal financial planning practices in their local or regional offices. Some small accounting firms also specialize exclusively in personal financial planning.

The big five and many other firms work only on a fee-for-service basis, either on a hourly rate or on a flat fee for a project. They do not accept commissions or charge based on a percentage of your portfolio's value. Individual accountants and smaller firms may have relationships with brokers or may deal in certain investments themselves. If you rely upon an accountant as your financial adviser, you will probably also need a broker to execute trades in various stocks and bonds. Accountants will give you independent advice, but it is likely to be expensive since you will be billed on an hourly basis.

Stockbrokers

"Full-service" stockbrokers who offer investment advice work for a commission. If you don't buy or sell a stock, bond, mutual fund, or other securities, they don't get paid. For some products, however, such as new issues of stock, the issuer of the investment may pay the broker, in which case there is no commission charged to you. Because brokers are paid on a commission basis, they are under

pressure to move investment products. This pressure is tempered by the fact that they want to keep you as a customer. To do that, they realize they must help you make money. They endeavor to balance these goals by giving you the best possible investment advice consistent with shifting your investments from time to time. But because most brokers make money only when you are buying and selling securities, you must be on guard against "churning" your account with frequent sales and purchases that earn you little money—or worse, lose money—but make money for the broker.

Full-service brokers such as Morgan Stanley Dean Witter, Merrill Lynch, and Paine Webber give you investment advice, including recommendations on specific stocks, bonds, and other products, as well as overall financial planning. While there may be exceptions, generally the level of advice and assistance you can expect from a full-service broker is directly proportional to the amount you have to invest and how frequently you want to change investments. Unless you have tens of thousands to invest and intend to trade on a regular basis (at least once a month), chances are an experienced broker will be happy to execute the trades for you, but she will not be willing to provide you with in-depth, periodic advice on retirement or other financial planning.

Most of us, especially when we are in our thirties and early forties, the appropriate time to begin planning for retirement, don't have enough money to invest in individual stocks to be a desirable customer for full-service brokers. Until you have saved a large portion of the amount you need for retirement, you should not be trading in individual stocks often enough to interest the average broker.

The *discount brokers* such as Charles Schwab and Olde Company simply take orders. Their personnel are paid by salary, not by the commissions from your purchases or sales. Discount brokers do not as a rule give advice on which stocks and investments to buy. The discount brokers do provide some free information and booklets, for instance, on retirement planning and mutual funds. Discount brokers may also have affiliations with certain investment advisers or financial planners and will give a referral to them. If you are using another type of financial adviser, it makes sense to use a discount broker to execute trades based on the advice the other financial adviser has provided.

Interviewing Financial Advisers

Interview several financial advisers before choosing one. Sound out a minimum of three, though five would be better. Take some steps to prepare for these interviews.

- Outline your needs and goals. The level of advice you need will determine in part the type of adviser you want.

- Begin with a quick telephone call/interview to be sure the adviser can provide all the services you need and that she is in your price range.
- Have available a brief summary of your assets, income, obligations, salary, and other income and employee benefits.
- Be very candid about your own finances and goals.
- Demand candor from the adviser. If at any point she refuses to answer your questions or appears at all evasive, stop the interview and move on to the next potential adviser. Remember, this person will know the most intimate details about you—your earnings, financial worth, and life's goals. You are entitled to know a great deal about her in return.
- Develop a list of the same questions to ask each adviser. Photocopy the list and fill in the answers. Better yet, have the adviser fill it in as you talk.
- Keep the lists from the ones you don't reject immediately. Then after you have two or three possible candidates sit down with the list, review the answers, and make your choice.
- Do not decide in her office. Take time to reflect and make the decision only after you have reviewed your questionnaire notes.

The following sample questionnaire provides some relevant questions, and the text in italics explains some of the things you should consider when the adviser responds to those questions. If you are interviewing an accountant or broker, some of the questions listed here in the sample interview questionnaire are not applicable. But most of the questions should be posed to anyone who may be entrusted with your money.

Sample Questions You Should Ask a Potential Financial Adviser

Experience and Background of the Individual and the Firm

A. What is the background and experience of the firm?
   (Find out who the other partners or associates are. Are there experts in various areas who can share knowledge and expertise with your adviser or is everyone a generalist? How long has the firm been in business? Is it a partnership or corporation?)
B. How long have you personally been offering financial planning services? What did you do before you became a financial adviser?
   (You don't want the most junior member of the team, unless that's all you can afford. Knowing a person's background before becoming a planner will suggest some strengths and biases.)
C. What is your client base like?
   (If all the other clients are seeking aggressive growth for fast returns, the adviser probably concentrates on these types of investments and may be less

informed about the long-term growth opportunities you need. If all the other clients were millionaires when they came to the firm, you may not receive much attention. If many of the clients are women planning for retirement and putting the children through college, the adviser is likely to be very knowledgeable and current about investments that are perfectly suited to your needs.)

D. What is the size of an average portfolio you manage?

(Again, if all the other clients are interested in investing millions, your $20,000 portfolio may get short shrift.)

E. What is your basic investment strategy?

(There is no right answer, other than it should be a philosophy you are comfortable with.)

F. What are your annual results over the past ten years in terms of average return on investments managed?

(This will give you an idea of how the adviser performs in up and down markets. But be sure to get a yearly figure, too. A ten-year average return of 15 percent based on five years of losses in the 10 percent range balanced off by five years of 25 percent gains is very different for you as an investor than the same average based on returns varying between a low of 5 percent losses in some years and a high of 20 percent gains in others. The adviser's performance should have done at least a few points better than the Standard & Poor's 500 Stock Composite Index, and some experts recommend choosing only those who have done considerably better than the Standard & Poor's.)

G. What is your educational background?

College degree:

Area of study:

Graduate degree:

Area of study:

H. Which of the following financial planning education credentials and designations do you hold:

Certified Financial Planner   _____

Chartered Financial Consultant   _____

Registry of Financial Planning Practitioners _____

Other (bar member, CPA, etc.)   _____

I. How much continuing education in financial planning do you pursue each year?

1–14 hours professional education   _____

15–30 hours professional education   _____

30 or more hours professional education _____

J. Are you a member of any professional financial planning associations?

Institute of Certified Financial Planners _____

National Association of Personal Financial Advisors _____

International Association for Financial Planning _____

Registry of Financial Planning Practitioners _____

Services the Firm Will Provide

A. Does your financial planning service include:
   A review of my goals
   Retirement planning
   Cash management and planning
   Tax planning
   Investment review and planning
   Estate planning
   Insurance needs:
   Other: _____

B. Do you provide a written analysis of my specific financial situation and your recommendations for my specific goals?
   (You don't want to pay for an analysis for a typical forty-year-old earning $40,000 per year. You want an analysis for your specific financial condition.)

C. Do you offer assistance with implementing your recommendations, such as researching appropriate investments and buying and selling individual stocks and bonds, etc.?

D. Do you offer continuous, ongoing advice regarding my financial affairs, including advice on noninvestment financial issues such as purchase of a home or long-term care insurance?

E. How often will I receive reports on my financial condition and in what format? If I request an additional report will I be charged for it?
   (For long-term investments you probably don't need a report more often than quarterly. The report should contain, at a minimum, a list of all your investments, the return on each, and the overall return of your portfolio along with a breakout of any charges. An occasional request for an additional report should not be charged an extra fee, but if you regularly request more reports or development of specialized reports, you should expect to be charged a small fee.)

F. Do you take possession of, or have access to, my assets?
   (You should always have the final control over your assets, including the signoff to buy and sell any assets. All assets should be held in your name, not the name of the firm.)

G. What are the provisions for your bonding and insurance?
   (If the adviser is handling any of your money directly, even for a brief time, get evidence that the adviser and the company are bonded. While there is no way to guarantee the security of your investments once your money is invested, a company's bond can at least ensure partially against the threat of outright thievery.)

Fees and Billing Arrangements

A. Will we have a written contract?
   (Always get a written agreement and insist it be in plain English. Don't sign it until you understand it and don't rely on oral changes to it.)

B. How is your firm compensated for the financial services you provide?

_____ Fee only (flat or hourly rate)

_____ Commissions only (from securities, insurance, etc., that I might buy from your firm)

_____ Fees and commissions

_____ Fees offset by any commissions you receive

(Fee only is the best billing method to ensure the advice you receive is totally unbiased and based only on what is best for you. You do not want advice that is influenced by whether the adviser makes more money if you buy a particular investment.)

C. How is your individual compensation calculated?

Fee only based on:

_____ An hourly rate of $_____

_____ A percentage based on _____

_____ A flat fee based on _____

_____ Commission only from clients that deal with the firm you are associated with

_____ Fee and commission

_____ Fee offset—you charge a flat fee against which commissions are offset. If the commissions exceed the fee, is the balance credited to me?

D. If your firm is a "fee only" organization, is your firm affiliated with a broker/dealer?

(Broker affiliation can be an advantage. It is easier for your adviser to buy and sell investments for you, and the adviser may get a discount rate that she may pass on to you.)

E. If your firm is a "fee and commission" (or is affiliated with a broker/dealer), approximately what percentage of your firm's annual income comes from:

Fees charged to clients _____ %

Commissions on:

       Insurance products _____ %

       Annuities _____ %

       Mutual funds _____ %

       Limited partnerships _____ %

       Coins _____ %

       Stocks and bonds _____ %

       Other (explain) _____ %

F. Will you furnish me with no-load (no sales charge) product alternatives, if available?

(Some advisers who accept commissions will also offer you alternatives. You expect a "yes" answer here, so press for details about the type of "no loads" the adviser typically offers.)

G. Will you consult with other professionals such as accountants, lawyers, actuaries, and stockbrokers about my account? If so, will I be billed for that consultation? Directly or through the firm?

(You may want the answers to complicated tax or retirement planning issues that require the use of outside experts. But you should be clear on who pays for their consultation and who is choosing these experts. Additionally, if brokers' fees are included in the adviser's management fee, your overall costs will be lower than if the brokerage fees are added on to the management fees.)

H. Do you or any member of your firm act as a general partner or receive compensation from the general partner or from investments that may be recommended to me?

(This signals potential conflicts of interest. Simply be aware of this fact and make further inquiries if you are offered partnership investments.)

I. What is the average income in fees from a typical client?

$_____ (annual fee income divided by number of clients served)

J. What is the average income in commissions from a typical client?

$_____ (annual commissions income divided by number of clients served)

(The answers to these questions will give you a good idea whether the firm survives by selling its financial planning and expertise or by selling products.)

Compliance with Federal, State, and Professional Boards' Regulations

A. Is your firm registered as an Investment Adviser with the Securities and Exchange Commission?

B. If not, indicate which SEC allowable reason for nonregistration applies:

_____ Less than $25 million under management

_____ Fewer than fifteen clients

_____ Do not provide generic or specific advice on securities

_____ Do not provide financial planning advice for a fee, but only as a registered broker/dealer

C. Is your firm registered with the state securities office? If not, why not?

(Typically a firm will be registered with the SEC or with the state agency that regulates investment advisers, but firms no longer have to be registered with both. It may even be legitimate for the adviser not to be registered with either, but you should know why.)

D. Have you ever been cited by a professional or regulatory governing body for disciplinary reasons?

References

Give me three or four references, including one who is no longer a client.
(Obviously, the references given will be only those who were satisfied unless you ask for the one who is no longer a client. Even that reference may be one who was very

satisfied but moved out of the area and wanted someone close by. When you talk with the references, ask for additional references. This may get you a better picture of the adviser. Of course, don't rely just on references given. Ask around in the community as well.)

Questions the Potential Adviser Should Be Asking You

Questions from the adviser are equally important in showing her approach to helping you. Listen carefully to the questions the advisers are asking you. At a minimum, a financial adviser should be asking you the following questions.

- What are your goals? What are you saving for?
- What is your philosophy about money?
- How involved do you want to be with your investments?
- If you lost 10 percent of your investments in one year, would you be traumatized?
- If you made 20 percent on your investment in a year, would you stop saving for the next year?
- How secure is your job and what are your prospects for promotions and raises?
- Do you expect to inherit any money?
- Do you expect to support your spouse or your parents or in-laws in their later years?
- Do you intend to provide your children with financial help in their adult years?

Each of these questions goes to broad issues that won't be reflected in your statement of assets and liabilities and income. They are questions about your needs and your comfort level on money and investments. If you are losing sleep over an investment, you should not be in it. Your financial adviser must know your sleep-at-night factor and respect it.

Trust Your Instincts

Finally, consider how you feel about this person as a person. While working with a financial adviser is the ultimate business situation, it is, paradoxically, also very personal. She is not a substitute for a psychoanalyst or a best friend, but you must feel comfortable with this person and trust her. It shouldn't be a struggle to get her on the phone. Once you do, it shouldn't be a struggle to talk with her and explain your needs clearly and succinctly. When the two of you are discussing a matter unfamiliar to you, her tone should be one of a colleague instructing you on a new matter, not a teacher dealing with a dull student. If your adviser talks down to you, fails to explain issues, or evades questions, get rid of her. You are better off on your own than dealing with someone you don't trust or cannot communicate with.

Advice from the Pros

Don't Get Discouraged and Don't Be Too Conservative

Pam Harmon, the financial planner introduced earlier in the chapter, finds the second biggest mistake women make in retirement planning, after being too conservative, is getting discouraged because they feel they cannot save enough to meet their goals. Of course, the more conservative you want to be in your investments, the more you will need to save, so these two attitudes reinforce each other. She stresses the link between level of risk and rate of return, urging clients to avoid discouragement by taking a little more risk to help their investments grow more quickly.

She poses the key test for investment decisions as, "If your $2,000 investment is only worth $1,500 after one year and that will upset you so much that you cannot plan your finances any more, then don't make the investment." But if you can make yourself realize that you have decades to make back the money, then you can move toward higher-return investments with higher risk.

Start Planning and Saving for Retirement Now

Harmon also stresses that you are never too young to start planning for retirement. Starting young also reduces the discouragement factor. You have already seen how much less you need to save when you start in your twenties as opposed to in your forties. Another way to avoid getting discouraged is to save in a systematic fashion even if it is a small amount. Also start a "found money" account, preferably a mutual fund. Any windfall that you didn't expect, such as a tax refund or birthday gift of cash or money from a dress you returned, goes into the found money account. "I give an example of a woman who did this over ten years," she says, "never putting in any amount that was more than $100, yet she now has $10,000 in that mutual fund. I know it's true, because I'm the woman."

Save Realistically, According to Your Present Financial Status

The distinguishing elements between the way women and men invest are disintegrating, according to what Harmon sees in her practice. "Women are so much more knowledgeable and are taking care of themselves." But she still sees some women with the implicit feeling that "people will be there to take care of me." If a woman is single, Harmon always plans for her as though she will always be single. Of course, this may not always be true, but it is much easier and more pleasant to adjust savings requirements downward or living standards upward if the client becomes part of a two-earner household than vice versa.

Save for Long-Term Goals as Well as Short-Term Needs

William J. Goldberg, a leading partner in KPMG's personal financial planning practice, sees a problem in the tendency to focus on saving for one thing at a time, such as the house down payment, then children's education, then retirement. "It takes discipline to get past the idea of just saving for one thing. For retirement, in the early years, it may be enough just to save through your employer's plan, but know when you are going to switch over and begin serious retirement savings."

This Is Not Your Father's Retirement—and It's Certainly Not Your Mother's

Goldberg also thinks retirement saving and planning is the one area where today's workers still have the *Father Knows Best* view of family life. They envision father working at one company for a long time, mother staying home, and the children leaving home when Mom and Dad are still young enough to do a lot of retirement saving. And they see it even as they both rush out the door to work and say goodbye to 25-year-old son Bud, who is back at home. As Goldberg sees it, "Today's adults see their parents' scenarios of living very well in retirement and they assume they will, too. But they're in a totally different situation. Mom and Dad always saved; Dad stayed with the same company most of his life and has a good pension, and Social Security replaces a big portion of their income before retirement. Today's adults were single until they were in their thirties and they're almost 65 when they get the kids out of college. They didn't save much and they have been in a number of different jobs, so any employer pension is likely to be modest. And who knows what Social Security benefits will be like when they retire?"

You know your life today isn't like your parents' lives when they were your age. What makes you think it will be when you retire? Your retirement benefits from work will be different and Social Security benefits are likely to be different. And your savings pattern needs to be different, too. It should be larger—not smaller—than your parents', if you want to match their level of retirement security.

Strategy Plan for Getting Started on Savings and Investment

- If you have not started already, begin a payroll deduction plan at work or establish a savings account that automatically withdraws money from your checking account and deposits it in your IRA or other retirement savings or investment account. Better yet, consider depositing your paycheck directly into your savings account and writing yourself a check for living expenses.
- Check for local classes on investing and savings; enroll in one.
- Look for free seminars on investing and financial or retirement planning sponsored by stockbrokers, accountants, or financial planners. Attend and ask questions—but don't invest anything at that meeting.

- Calculate the real return on current investments after taxes and inflation. How much money are you really making?
- Look at your existing savings and investments for asset allocation. Do you have all your eggs in one basket or are you diversified?
- Review your investments in light of the number of years until you retire and the amount of money you are saving to decide whether your investments are too conservative. If you are on target with your retirement goals with conservative investments paying 5 percent, you probably shouldn't change, but if you are missing your goals and you have at least ten years before you retire, you may want to move into more aggressive investments.
- Decide whether you need professional advice in helping you plan for investing. If the answer is yes, begin your research process. Interview several advisers and ask around among your business colleagues and friends. Take several weeks to investigate.
- Buy—or read at the library—a copy of *Business Week, Smart Money, Money,* or one of the other business magazines or newspapers every other week for a few weeks. Try them all, then subscribe to one for a time.

PART FOUR
LIFE PHASES
AND RETIREMENT

14

How Marriage Affects Your Retirement Benefits

The old marriage vows of "'til death do us part" seem anachronistic today. In every area these vows seem more ignored than honored—except in the area of employer-provided retirement benefits. Here's the good news: your husband's pension and most other retirement benefits will be paid out as a joint and survivor annuity, providing you with an income even after he dies, unless you agree otherwise in writing. Here's the bad news: so will *your* benefits.[1]

That only seems fair, you say. And at first glance, you're right. But think a little further. Remember from Chapter 7 that, with a joint and survivor payout option, the pension benefit is smaller than it would be if payments were being made over a single lifetime. So you and your husband will receive a smaller benefit while he is alive to make up for the fact that you will continue to receive a benefit after he has died. But most women are younger than their spouses and women have a longer life expectancy even when they are the same age as their husbands. If you are in ordinary health and the same age as or younger than your husband, his chances of surviving you and receiving a benefit from your pension are practically nonexistent. But if you and he don't agree to opt out of the joint and survivor annuity payment option for your employer-provided pension, you will receive a significantly lower benefit from your pension throughout your life because he had the possibility of receiving a benefit if you died before him.

Your retirement benefits are likely to be considerably lower than his in the first place, for all the reasons discussed in Chapter 1. You may have sacrificed retirement benefits build-ups for family responsibilities. If child-rearing duties and caring for elderly parents came along, you, not he, may have left your paycheck to work for no money—and no retirement benefits build-up—at home. Finally, you

241

probably earned less money during your career, so your benefits will be based on a lower earnings record.

Laws on Spousal Rights to Benefits

In the past, laws protecting a spouse's right to a worker's retirement benefits have assumed it is always women who are being protected by various restrictions on the distribution of employer-provided benefits. But, remember, the laws are drafted to be gender-neutral. So all those protections apply to your husband as well. You may have worked as a single woman for thirty years, but a year after you marry, your husband becomes entitled to a survivor right in your pension and you become entitled to such rights, too. Once you have married, you will need his permission to choose a payment form other than the joint and survivor annuity payout method for your retirement benefits or to name a beneficiary other than him for your 401(k) plan. And he will need your permission to do the same.

ERISA, which covers most private employers' retirement plans, but not plans sponsored by government or church organization employers, always assumed the first choice for payment of retirement benefits would be a *qualified joint and survivor annuity* (QJSA). Under a QJSA, the normal form of retirement plan payment for a married retirement plan participant will be a monthly retirement benefit paid over his lifetime and the lifetime of his wife, if she survives him, which she almost always does. The monthly amount received from a QJSA payment form is smaller than the monthly amount from a single annuity form of payment, reflecting the fact that the payments are being paid over two lifetimes rather than one. But originally, under ERISA, a retiring worker was not *required* to elect the joint and survivor annuity option. He did not even have to tell his spouse what method of benefit payment he elected. And because the QJSA payment appeared smaller, the plan participant was likely not to choose the joint and survivor option, even though choosing the single annuity payment meant that his wife would be left with no benefit if he predeceased her.

The Retirement Equity Act (REA)

The 1984 Retirement Equity Act (REA) amended ERISA to preserve retirement benefits for spouses in two ways. First, REA required a worker to get the spouse's written consent if the worker elected any form of payment other than the QJSA. Second, the change required the plan to offer benefits through a *qualified preretirement survivor annuity* (QPSA) to a surviving spouse if the worker died before reaching retirement age.

As one plan administrator put it, "The enactment of REA has freed me from the most difficult conversations I have ever had to hold. I no longer have the widows calling me the first month after John's death, saying, 'Where's my pension check?' I won't have to explain to a sobbing widow that John didn't leave her any pension. He chose to take all the money himself and now that John is gone, so is the pension." With the enactment of REA, the widow will have a survivor's pension or she will at least have helped make the decision that there would be no pension for her after her husband's death.

What Plans Require Survivor Annuities

Only certain employer-provided plans are required to offer QJSAs and QPSAs. Among employer-provided plans, all defined benefit plans are required to provide spousal annuities or receive the spouse's consent not to pay out in such annuities. Most defined contribution plans, including profit-sharing plans, 401(k) plans, and employee stock ownership plans, can avoid offering QJSAs or QPSAs *if* the plans provide that, on the employee's death, the entire vested benefit is payable to the surviving spouse immediately. For example, if the employee takes the money from these plans in a lump sum and then transfers the money to an IRA, there is no requirement that the spouse receive the IRA if the employee dies.

IRAs are not required to pay out QJSAs or QPSAs or to get the spouse's consent for any sort of payout. IRA Simplified Employee Pensions, even though provided by an employer, are not covered by REA. Although state and local government and church retirement plans are not covered by REA, many of these plans do require spousal consent to waive survivor or preretirement annuities.

Qualified Joint and Survivor Annuities (QJSAs)

To calculate the benefits to be paid under a QJSA, actuaries start by looking at the total lump-sum value of the benefits that would be paid to the worker over his or her lifetime in retirement under a "single life annuity." The actuaries then adjust the monthly benefits that will be paid from that lump-sum amount to reflect the fact that those monthly payments will be paid over two expected lifetimes rather than one. With apologies to actuaries everywhere, a very simplified example follows.

The lump-sum value of Ozzie's pension plan at Acme is $200,000. Ozzie will retire at age 65 and is expected to live for another fifteen years. And his wife, Harriet, who is also 65, is expected to live for another nineteen years. If Ozzie and Harriet want the benefit paid just over his expected lifetime, the Acme pension plan could calculate payments based on fifteen years and pay Ozzie a little under $21,000 per year. But if Ozzie and Harriet want the payments paid for as long as either of them is expected to live, the benefits will have to be calculated based on the probability for two lifetimes. The expected payment period used would be closer to nineteen years of payments—Harriet's life expectancy—and will only be about $18,000.

Actual calculations are far more sophisticated. But all such QJSA payment calculations are based on general mortality tables. The calculations do not recognize individual situations. When payment is to be made over two lifetimes, the odds are payments will have to be made for a longer time. Consequently, the amount of the payments made are smaller. The calculations designed to reduce the benefit payment to cover two lives, rather than just the former employee's life, *do* take into account the age of the survivor beneficiary, but cannot legally take into account the sex of the participant or the beneficiary.

So if we were calculating payments from the same $200,000 lump-sum value in Harriet's pension in the above example, there would be no difference in the actual amount of the payments. She would receive about $21,000 if she and Ozzie elected the single annuity over life and about $18,000 if she automatically takes the QJSA option paying benefits both for her life and Ozzie's, if he survives her. The big difference is Ozzie probably won't survive her. In return for the lower benefit of $18,000, they have bought a benefit Ozzie will probably never use. If a woman worker accepts the QJSA survival rights for her husband in *her* pension plan payments, the reduction she will see in her monthly retirement benefits is likely to be too high in light of the odds her husband will outlive her and receive any payments.

Women's Pensions Should Avoid the Survivor Option

For this reason, when a married woman, who is of retirement age and is in good health, is faced with the choice of payment from a pension she has earned as a worker, she and her husband should almost always elect the option that pays the pension over her lifetime only. This will give her higher pension payments. They should reject the QJSA, because his chances of being alive to receive a survivor's benefit are very low. Conversely, because a woman is likely to survive her husband, the husband should almost always take his pension as a joint and survivor annuity. But recognize that both spouses will have to agree on each other's form of payment. They should not fall into the trap of thinking both parties should elect the QJSA form of benefit.

The Timing of Your Decision

Within a reasonable time before retirement benefits begin, usually thirty to ninety days before the scheduled retirement date, the retiring employee and the spouse must receive an explanation of the payment options and a form to choose the option they want. The form must include a waiver for the spouse to sign and have notarized if the employee wants to receive retirement benefits in any form other than the QJSA. Unless the future retiree's spouse agrees to another form of benefit payment, such as a lump sum or payment over only the retiree's life, and properly executes the form before the deadline, the payments will be in the QJSA form.

This spousal consent cannot be given more than ninety days prior to the beginning of the retirement plan payments. The consent can be changed prior to the actual beginning of the annuity payments' commencement. But once payment begins in the joint and survivor form, most plans will not let you change the form of payment. You are stuck with that form of payment forever.

No Choice or Consent if the Employer Subsidizes Survivor Benefits

These rules don't apply, and no notice or consent is required, if the employer plan does not reduce your benefit for the survivor's annuity and does not permit you to waive the survivor's annuity or choose another beneficiary other than your spouse. In these situations, the plan is subsidizing the survivor's benefit, so the spouse does not have to agree to receiving a subsidy. On balance, unless your employer does subsidize the joint and survivor benefit payment form, a highly unlikely probability since the survivor annuity is expensive to provide, you should not take the joint and survivor annuity under ordinary circumstances. Under the single annuity payment method you will have more money being paid out each month that you can both live on and that same amount will be available to you if he dies.

Of course, your and your husband's plans may have several payout options other than simply a QJSA or a single life annuity. The plans may provide for lump-sum distributions or annuity payments that are guaranteed for the longer of the plan participant's life or a guaranteed number of years, such as ten years. These payment options present other considerations we will discuss in Chapter 16.

Qualified Preretirement Survivor's Annuities (QPSAs)

The qualified preretirement survivor's annuity (QPSA) provides benefits if a vested worker dies before retirement, by requiring that the surviving spouse receive a pension benefit based on the benefit the worker had accrued at death. The catch is that the law does not require payments to begin until the date the employee would have reached retirement age. Some plans begin payments earlier. Other plans stick to the letter of the law. Another drawback is the fact that the payment is likely to be small if the employee dies young or after only a few years with the company.

Plans are permitted to reduce the retirement benefit you or your surviving spouse ultimately receive for the cost of the "insurance" provided by the possibility of survivors receiving a QPSA benefit. So your retirement benefits may be a few dollars less at retirement because you choose to have the QPSA coverage available for your spouse and children during your working years. If the plan does make such a reduction, the plan must notify the employee about the survivor benefit and the reduction as soon as she is affected by it. When you or your spouse are notified, you can choose not to receive the preretirement survivor coverage and there will be no reduction in the final retirement benefits. But to do so, you must have the permission of your spouse to waive those benefits from your pension. And, of course, he must have your consent to waive any right to a QPSA in his employer-provided plan.

Given the low probability of your actually dying and triggering the QPSA, the reduction in the benefit is quite small. Many employer plans, in fact, do "subsidize" such benefits and don't make any reduction in your retirement benefit for the preretirement survivor coverage. If the employer does subsidize the QPSA by not reducing your ultimate retirement benefit, the employer does not need to notify you about the coverage and does not need to permit you to waive the preretirement survivor coverage. Absent the employer's subsidization, the plan must notify you about the details of the QPSA by the time you are 35, become a plan participant, or leave the employer if you aren't yet 35, whichever happens last.

Special Rules for QJSA and QPSA Payments

- If a retirement plan subject to REA permits loans, the plan must obtain the spouse's consent in writing, notarized or witnessed by the plan administrator, before such a loan is made.
- Joint and survivor annuities need not be paid if the plan participant and the spouse were married less than a year before the annuity began or the plan participant died.
- If the total present value of the QPSA or QJSA payments are $5,000 or less, the plan sponsor may pay the benefit as a lump sum without the consent of either the participant or the spouse.

Prenuptial Agreements

Prenuptial or antenuptial agreements are recognized and enforced in nearly all states, unless there is evidence one of the parties was unduly pressured into the agreement or one of the parties deceived the other by hiding assets. These agreements are entered into prior to marriage. The parties agree that property owned by each prior to the marriage and obtained after marriage will not be subject to the usual state laws governing marital property. Generally, the purpose of the agreement is to continue to permit each party to the marriage to own property they have acquired individually, rather than jointly, as is usually presumed for married couples.

Prenuptial agreements are useful even if you aren't Donald and Ivana Trump or Donald and Marla Trump. With serial marriages becoming more common and women as well as men coming to the marriage with substantial assets, it is sensible for both partners to think about protecting their children by previous marriages or elderly parents or protecting themselves if the marriage breaks up. A prenuptial agreement provides that protection.

If your spouse-to-be suggests a prenuptial agreement, it can be advantageous for you both. But think ahead. If you are likely to have children together, the agreement should clearly state how the children will be supported. If the two of you are older, consider the expenses of medical care. Traditionally, wives nurse husbands through their final illnesses, often with great strain on their own health. But traditionally such wives weren't party to a prenuptial agreement. When the husband died, the wife inherited the estate. But with a prenuptial agreement, a faithful wife may find that she has used her money and health to nurse her husband through his final illness, but is left with nothing from her husband's estate. The agreement should stipulate how health care costs and caregiving services will be paid for. While this may sound crass or even cruel, not to mention unromantic, you won't feel very romantic providing twenty-four-hour-a-day nursing service and spending your money for your husband's serious illness so he can leave adult children with a large estate.

Prenuptial Agreements Do Not Affect ERISA Plans

Prenuptial agreements are creatures of state law. Because ERISA and REA are federal laws that override state law, prenuptial agreements cannot override ERISA requirements. Even if you have a prenuptial agreement in which your spouse waives all rights to your employer-provided pension, unless after the marriage he has signed a waiver for your specific retirement plans meeting the REA requirements, the prenuptial agreement will have no effect on those ERISA benefits. Of course the same is true for your agreements about his ERISA benefits. If you want to ensure that your children get your 401(k) money or the lump-sum value of your pension, get your husband to sign an ERISA waiver for the plan, acknowledging he is waiving his rights to such benefits.

Non-ERISA retirement benefits such as IRAs and Keoghs can be covered by a prenuptial agreement. Prenuptial agreements will also protect your individual savings. As we have seen, your individual savings are critical to your retirement financial security, so it is important that they be protected from your husband's creditors and any divorce proceedings.

You Can Both Agree Later to Change the Prenuptial Agreement

If the course of true love runs incredibly smoothly and after years you and your spouse feel there is no reason to have the prenuptial agreement, the two of you together may tear up the agreement and denounce such cold-blooded instruments. Send a jointly signed, notarized letter to the lawyer who drew it up stating that you both agree to repeal the agreement. Tell the children and your parents and brag about it to all your friends.

Conclusion: Strategy Plan for Coordinating with Your Spouse on Retirement Plan Payments

- Review your current employer-provided retirement plans and IRAs for beneficiary designations. Be certain the beneficiaries you want are named on all plans.
- If you want a beneficiary other than your spouse for your employer-provided retirement, have your spouse execute the appropriate spousal waiver form, which your employer or former employer, if applicable, can provide. Your spouse's signature must be witnessed by the plan administrator or notarized.
- Go through the above process even for benefits earned before you were married.
- If your own or your spouse's benefits are encumbered by a previous divorce agreement, be sure each of you recognize that fact. Each of you should know the exact details of the "qualified domestic relations order" from the divorce establishing the former spouse's rights to the benefits.
- Ask your spouse for a listing of his employer-provided benefits and the beneficiaries. Give him a list of yours.
- If he has designated or wants to designate beneficiaries other than you, and you agree, be sure to execute the necessary spousal waivers.
- Unless you are extremely wealthy, do not agree to allow your spouse to waive the "qualified preretirement survivor annuity."
- As part of the retirement savings planning, discuss with your spouse the payment form each of you will choose for your employer-provided retirement benefits. Begin explaining the value of taking his retirement benefits as a joint and survivor annuity and taking your benefits as a single annuity.

How Divorce Can Affect Your Retirement Planning

As we saw in the previous chapter, once you have married, you and your spouse have certain joint interests in each other's ERISA retirement benefits. Federal and many state and local government retirement plans also create joint rights for spouses. For many couples retirement benefits can be their largest asset, or their second largest asset after their home.

In the grief and turmoil surrounding any marriage break-up, rationally visualizing the future is hard. Retirement benefit issues are difficult and complex to deal with in the best of circumstances, demanding a clear head and calm study, two commodities frequently not available during a divorce. You may be tempted to just skip the issue of retirement benefits. Don't yield to the temptation. In a divorce, you need to be aware of your rights to your husband's retirement benefits and his rights to yours. For all the reasons we already know, your husband's retirement benefits are likely to be larger than yours, so it is in your best interest to include these benefits in the property discussions from the beginning.

This chapter outlines the protections provided by ERISA for employer plans and the importance of an appropriate court order, the *qualified domestic relations order* (QDRO). A description of the Social Security benefits for divorced spouses concludes the chapter.[1]

How the Retirement Equity Act Protects Retirement Plan Rights During Divorce

In general, ERISA forbids "alienation" of retirement benefits—that is, permitting someone other than the employee to have an interest in the employee's retirement benefits—even if the employee agrees to grant such rights. After the enactment of ERISA, state courts struggled with issues of retirement benefits in divorces. The Retirement Equity Act (REA) made it clear that retirement benefits could be subject to state law divisions in domestic relations situations, such as divorce and separation. This is one of the rare areas in which ERISA permits a future retirement benefit to become subject to the claims of someone other than the employee who is earning the benefit.

Qualified Domestic Relations Orders (QDROs)

REA strictly limits these pension domestic relations rights to state court or agency orders meeting the federal statutory requirements for qualified domestic relation orders, or QDROs. If your divorce lawyer doesn't know what a QDRO is, get another lawyer—immediately. You already know ERISA law is extremely complex. When you combine ERISA with state divorce law, the mix becomes fiendishly complex. You want a divorce lawyer who has worked through the hell before. Even then your lawyer is not likely to be as familiar with your husband's plan or your plan as you are. Don't be shy about spelling out what you believe are the important features of the retirement plans. If your lawyer isn't grateful for this, she should be.

How the Court Distributes Retirement Benefits

From the outset of property settlement discussions, you should recognize that your retirement benefits, and your other property for that matter, are just as subject to the divorce court's division as your husband's. Divorce law and property settlement procedures differ from state to state, so the following discussion can only be general in nature. But certain principles apply in almost every state.

Divorce court judges have enormous discretion to divide property based on their concept of fairness. Most state divorce laws simply instruct the court to divide property in an "equitable" fashion. Note that the law does not require that the division be "equal," so don't expect a 50-50 split of property. In today's courts women are not guaranteed continued support from their husbands. This includes even women who have spent their lives working in the home. Understand that you will need to prove your contribution to the marriage and your level of future earnings ability in very concrete terms of dollars and cents. Depending on the facts and circumstances surrounding the divorce, judges, still predominately men, are very sympathetic to the former husband's pleas of poverty and inability to support two households on his one salary.

No Settled Law on Distributions of Retirement Benefits

The state courts usually do not have definite rules on the division of retirement benefits. Courts run the gamut from awarding everything to the worker to awarding everything to the nonworking spouse, depending on other assets and the facts of the case. In the area of pensions, as with all other divisions of marital property and agreements on child support or alimony, you and your husband will be better off—and probably happier with the outcome—if you can agree to the property settlement yourselves and simply present the deal for the court's approval. While the court is not required to approve the privately negotiated property settlement, it almost invariably does unless the settlement is egregiously unfair to one of the parties.

Try to Work Out the Property Settlement

No matter how bitter you feel toward your soon-to-be-former spouse, you won't benefit financially by making lawyers wealthy with a protracted battle over finances. Depending on the emotional circumstances, if you can deal peacefully with your spouse, it will make the most sense for the two of you to work out a rough understanding of the property settlement. Then have one of your lawyers draft it for your review and the review of the other counsel. This will be the least costly method of proceeding. Of course, this level of agreement between the two parties is rarely achievable, or they wouldn't be getting divorced in the first place. But try to avoid the trap of spending $5,000 of lawyers' billable time arguing about who gets a $2,000 IRA or the dog.

If you can't talk it over face to face, think about exchanging written proposals. Just be sure you label them as "drafts" or "proposals" so your spouse doesn't end up with them in court swearing that's what you agreed to. You can leave all this to the lawyers and certainly you should not agree to a property settlement until your lawyer carefully reviews it. But if the lawyers have to start from scratch with a property settlement, it will probably cost you more in billable time. Just remember, in divorce, as in much of life, civility saves money.

Determining Your Spouse's ERISA Retirement Benefits

The first step is finding out exactly what retirement benefits your spouse is entitled to from previous and current employers.[2] Again, to save money, you may want to pursue this information yourself and then turn it over to your lawyer. You may need your husband's cooperation because retirement plans are not required to give information to anyone other than the plan participants and the government. It may increase your husband's cooperation if you remind him that property settlements are subject to change by the court even years after originally settled if one of the parties can show fraud because assets were hidden. As a last resort you might try having the judge order your husband to produce information on his retirement plans.

These plans will include defined benefit pension plans, 401(k)s, profit-sharing plans, and some employer "savings" or thrift plans. Try to get the SPDs, the original plan document, and your husband's latest employee benefit statement. Most plans provide an employee benefit statement at least annually.

Calculating the Court's Retirement Benefit Award

There is no way of knowing precisely what the court may award you from these benefits. If your husband earned most of these benefits before you and he were married, the court is unlikely to award you much, if anything, from the retirement plan. This is particularly true if you have worked outside the home and have your own retirement benefits. On the other hand, if you were married for most of the time the retirement benefits were being earned, there is a presumption (but not a certainty) that you have a valid interest in a portion of those benefits.

The uncertainty over how the benefits might be divided and awarded by the court can be a negotiating tool on your behalf. You may be able to convince your husband at the outset that the best approach might be a cash or other property settlement to you in return for your waiving all rights to his retirement benefits.

What Is the Value of His Benefits?

Even if you take the cash-settlement approach, you will need to know what benefits he has. Once you have found all the various possible sources of retirement benefits, determine your husband's vested benefits. Then look at the value of those benefits likely to be vested within a short time. You may consider nonvested benefits as well, but the court will probably not consider them. Nevertheless, they can be part of your negotiations with your spouse.

Determining the present value of the defined contribution plans, such as 401(k) plans, will be relatively easy. That will be the value of his "individual account" in the plan. If the account is invested in nonpublicly traded stocks or guaranteed income contracts, there may be an issue of valuing those assets. But that valuation problem will be no more difficult than valuing the assets if they were outside the plan.

Defined benefit plans will be more difficult to value. Remember, these plans are based on a number of variables, including your husband's length of service with the plan sponsor, his age, and usually his salary. Actuarial calculations will be required, too, if you want to know the present value of the benefits accrued to the time of the divorce or to his possible retirement date. Depending on the potential dollar value of the benefits involved, you may need to hire your own actuary to calculate the defined benefit values. While the calculations should be based on the interest and mortality factors contained in the plan, there may be a choice of variables for calculating the value to you. Your lawyer should have a pension actuary she has worked with before. Be certain the actuary has the latest plan document and all relevant information regarding your husband's accrued benefits such as his earnings history, length of service, and so on.

Negotiating Your Fair Share of the Benefits

Once you have calculated the value of all the retirement benefits, you can then begin negotiating your share. There are a number of approaches you—or the court, if you and your spouse cannot agree—can take in calculating your share. Some courts might give you half of a fraction of the retirement benefit under the so-called time rule. The fraction is based on the number of years during the marriage when benefits were earned, divided by the number of total years the benefits were earned. For example, assume that you were married for fifteen years and your husband earned benefits all those years and had been earning benefits for five years prior to your marriage. His benefit has a present value of $60,000. Under the time rule, you would be awarded one-half of an amount equal to $60,000 times the fraction 15/20, for a value of $22,500.

The time rule usually calculates the award based on the current value of the benefit at the time of the divorce, not when your husband could retire. This means you will miss the bigger build-up in the value of a defined benefit plan especially in those last years of work. Remember that in defined benefit plans the value really grows in the last years of working. (Refer to Chapter 7 for the discussion on how benefits accrue under defined benefit plans.)

You might ask for a fixed percentage of the pension when your husband retires. Using the above example you could avoid the loss of the last years' build-up by asking for three-eighths of his monthly retirement benefit, assuming payment based on a single life annuity, at normal retirement age.

Don't be surprised if your husband's attorney suggests adding in the value of your retirement benefits during the marriage and dividing the value of the two benefits equally between the parties. Since your benefit is likely to be lower, you will still be a net recipient.

Choosing the Payment Method for Retirement Benefits in Divorce

The dollar figures being equal, far and away the best form of receiving the value of the retirement benefits is cash at the settlement of the divorce. If your husband's retirement plan will release the money pursuant to a QDRO, you may then take the sum represented by the retirement benefits and roll it into your own IRA, where it can grow on a tax-deferred basis until you retire. If you do not place the money in an IRA, you will not be subject to the 10 percent early withdrawal penalty, but you will pay ordinary income tax on the amount. You also will miss the advantage of having the money grow on a tax-deferred basis for several years until you retire or reach age 70½. If your husband gives you a cash equivalent amount from funds outside the retirement plan, the amount probably will not be eligible for a tax-free rollover into an IRA.

The Advantages of a Cash-Out

In addition to the rollover advantages, this cash value approach has several other advantages.

- You avoid waiting for years to receive the award granted by the QDRO.
- You don't have to deal with the plan administrator of your husband's plan for possibly decades until your spouse's retirement eligibility date.
- You don't have to worry about the plan's being terminated and the possible loss of a portion of your benefits.
- There will be no issue about the proper interpretation of the QDRO years after the court issued the order and a different plan administrator now has questions about it.

In short, the money is in your hands and not in a plan with payments scheduled to start years from now. But the reality is that qualified retirement plans probably will not be willing to issue the benefit in cash and, depending on your husband's age, may not be able to by law. Further, cash is often in short supply when couples divorce. Your spouse simply may not be able to come up with the cash to pay the full value of the retirement benefits to you directly if the plan cannot or will not pay the amount.

As an alternative, your spouse may suggest purchasing an annuity for you in an amount equal to the retirement benefit you would receive. This could be a reasonable compromise, but be careful. It could be difficult to force him to continue making the payments for the annuity or the company issuing the annuity may permit him to change the annuity beneficiary or cash in the annuity. Finally, if you and he do elect the annuity purchase option, be certain the annuity is held in your name, by you. Choose a highly rated company. (Refer to Chapter 9 for a discussion on purchasing individual annuities.) Also be alert to changes in the law on the income tax treatment of annuities. Congress has consistently shaved away at the tax-favored status of annuities and you could find yourself paying taxes on the income from the annuity even though you haven't received the income yet.

If neither of these options is suitable, you will have to rely on the QDRO to spell out your rights for the plans holding those benefits.

Get It Right the First Time: What Should the QDRO Contain?

By law a QDRO must contain certain information listed in the statute. But the QDRO should also very clearly define the benefit that you—the "alternate payee" in QDRO-speak—are to receive under all the contingencies you can imagine. The

QDRO must be a court or state agency order pursuant to state domestic relations law involving marital property rights, child support, or alimony to a spouse, former spouse, or dependent of a plan participant. The QDRO must create or recognize:

- the right of an alternate payee (that's you)
- to receive benefits from a qualified plan
- that would otherwise not be required to honor such an order
- because ERISA's antialienation provisions prevent the plan from paying benefits to anyone but the plan participant (that's him).

A QDRO will take precedence over any other required payment except an earlier filed QDRO, regardless of the dates of the marriage. If your spouse has been married before and has an existing QDRO applying to his retirement plan, that earlier QDRO must be paid and any benefits you receive from your QDRO are based only on the benefits left after the first QDRO is satisfied.

By law the QDRO must contain:

- the name and last known mailing address of the plan participant (your former spouse)
- the name and address of all alternate payees (that's you, but if the decree gives the children rights in the retirement plan, be sure they are included as well)
- the amount or percentage of the participant's benefit to be paid to each alternate payee or the method to be used by the plan administrator to determine the amount to be paid to the alternate payees
- the number of payments or the period of time the QDRO covers
- the name of each plan covered by the QDRO.[3]

Model Language May Be Available

The IRS has developed pieces of model language for QDROs, which may be useful. The Department of Labor, the federal agency with authority to interpret the law regarding QDROs, has produced a booklet of questions and answers on QDROs[4] available from their Internet site, *www.dol.gov/dol/pwba*. If your spouse's plan is being administered by the Pension Benefit Guaranty Corporation, that agency has a model QDRO your lawyer can use. Call PBGC's Customer Service Center at 1-800-400-PBGC or use their Internet site, *www.pbgc.gov*.

Some plan sponsors will provide a model QDRO that they will accept. Contact your husband's plan to see whether it will supply such a model. If so, get the form, but use it only as a guide. The model was developed by the plan administrator and reflects the procedures and payment forms that are in the best interests of the plan and the most efficient for the administrator. These procedures are not necessarily in your best interests. The model will still be a useful guide for your attorney to follow, but you are not required by law to follow it slavishly.

Common Problems Causing Plans to Reject the QDRO

Before drafting the QDRO, your attorney should talk with the plan administrator about any unusual provisions in the plan or the most common errors the plan administrator finds in QDROs. This discussion may avoid having the QDRO rejected by the plan's administrator, which would then require redrafting, resubmission to the court for its approval, and then resubmission to the plan administrator. According to surveys, over 70 percent of plan administrators find handling QDROs difficult and time-consuming and over 80 percent find the language spelling out the amount to be paid to the spouse to be unclear or uncertain.[5] A phone call may save costly and embarrassing delays.

The QDRO should first of all get the name of the plan correct. This seems obvious enough, but many plan administrators complain that the QDRO arrives with an incorrect name. Most plan sponsors have several plans all with similar names, so the plan administrator may not know which plan you have the claim against. If your QDRO seeks payment from the Acme Retirement Security Plan, but the real name of the plan is the Acme Retirement Income Security Plan, the plan administrator would be violating ERISA and her fiduciary duties to honor the QDRO.

The QDRO should spell out exactly the benefit you are getting in a dollar sum, a percentage of the benefit, or a combination of both. Give the date on which the benefit value is to be fixed, if the award is a percentage of his benefit. For example, is the percentage based on the accrued benefit as of the date of the divorce, the spouse's benefit at his earliest retirement date, or his benefit at his normal retirement age? If your benefit is defined in terms of a percentage of your former spouse's benefit, be sure you describe the benefit payment form used in your calculation. For example, a single life annuity form of benefit will give him the largest monthly annuity sum. Even though he might not take his benefit in that fashion, you should specify that your percentage is to be based on a single life annuity payment, if you are taking your benefits in annuity form. That way if your husband remarries and takes his benefit in the lower-paying form of a joint and survivor annuity for his new spouse, your benefit won't be reduced.

The QDRO should also specifically state that your benefit is based on the gross value of his benefit, exclusive of deductions for taxes, health insurance, union dues, and so on. This stipulation will have no effect on the taxes you must pay. But it will mean the difference between your receiving 50 percent of the pretax pension of, say, $1,000 per month as opposed to 50 percent of the after-tax pension amount of $720 per month, for example.

The QDRO cannot require the plan to give you any form of benefit or use any type of payment option that is ordinarily not available to any participant under the plan. For example, if the plan does not provide for lump-sum payments, the QDRO cannot compel a lump-sum payment. However, a QDRO can require that you begin to receive payments before your former spouse leaves the company or reaches normal retirement age. Such payments can begin at the *earliest* of the following dates:

- your husband's potential early retirement date under the plan
- his fiftieth birthday, if he would also be entitled to take the benefit, if he left the employer then
- the earliest age over 50 when he could begin receiving the benefit, if he has already left the employer.

For example, assume that under your husband's plan, early retirement is age 60; payout could be received any time he left the company regardless of his age; and he is 50 years old. Your QDRO could ask for payments to begin immediately because he is 50 and he would be able to begin payment now under the plan if he left. Supposing the same facts, but your husband is only 49, your QDRO cannot get a payout until he becomes 50.

Or let's assume another plan that sets early retirement at age 62, but does not permit any other payout if you leave the employer until you reach 59½. Your husband is 50. The earliest date your QDRO can demand payment is age 59½, because that is the earliest date on which he could get the money. It doesn't matter that your husband is 50 now. Because he could not receive a payout under the plan if he left now, you can't either.

The QDRO Should Name You as the Surviving Spouse

Be sure the QDRO spells out what happens if your husband dies before he is eligible to receive his retirement benefit and what happens when he dies after retirement. You should be designated in specific terms in the QDRO as the surviving spouse. Otherwise you may not receive the benefits of a survivor under the plan. For example, under the Retirement Equity Act, most plans must provide for a benefit for the surviving spouse, but once you divorce, unless the QDRO names you as the surviving spouse, the plan may decide there is no surviving spouse. Hence, no benefit is payable even though you have a QDRO stating you are entitled to half of your spouse's benefit at retirement. If he dies before retirement, he didn't retire, so there is no benefit. If the QDRO names you as the surviving spouse, you receive the benefits of a surviving spouse under REA.

You need to decide whether you want your benefit paid over your lifetime or in some other form. You are entitled to use any payment form offered under the plan, except the joint and survivor option. For example, if the plan permits a lump-sum payment, you may want to take your QDRO benefit in a lump sum as soon as you could receive it under the plan. Even if you are not retired at that time or don't want the money then, you may roll the sum into an IRA on a tax-deferred basis.

If you elect a periodic form of benefit payments, be sure the QDRO requires that the plan send you a check directly. If your husband receives the full amount of the benefit and then writes you a check, you will have a needless delay in receiving your benefit. And if he is short of money one month, he may be tempted to "borrow" from you. If creditors begin to pursue him or he should declare bankruptcy, they will go after your benefits in his bank account.

Submitting the QDRO to the Plan Administrator

Once the divorce judge authorizes the QDRO, you or your lawyer—*not* your former husband—should submit the QDRO to the plan administrator. Be sure you do this promptly and be sure you have evidence, such as a signed return receipt, that the plan administrator in fact received the QDRO. The QDRO is not effective until it is in the plan administrator's hands.

The plan administrator then has a "reasonable period" to decide whether the QDRO is, in effect, qualified. The law does not define what "reasonable" means, but your attorney or you should call the plan administrator about a month after sending the QDRO to ask whether there are any problems. You should count on giving the plan administrator about ninety days to fully review and rule on the QDRO.

Earlier care by you and your lawyer should avoid these common QDRO problems that slow down approval by the plan administrator.

- The order demands payment in a form the plan does not permit.
- The exact amount of the benefit the alternate payee is entitled to cannot be determined from the order.
- The order is not clear as to when the benefit is to be paid to the alternate payee.
- The name of the plan is incorrect on the order (61 percent of the problem cases involve this mistake).
- The form of the payment (i.e., lump sum, annuity, etc.) is not clear from the order.[6]

The plan can withhold your benefits up to eighteen months while it decides on the validity of the order. This delay is only an issue if you are entitled to benefits immediately. Once a valid order is issued, if you are entitled to receive the benefits immediately, you must receive the withheld benefits immediately.

If the Plan Administrator Refuses to Honor the QDRO

If the plan administrator refuses to honor the QDRO on the grounds that it is not qualified, you have two courses of action. If the mistake is clearly an error due to your or your lawyer's lack of knowledge about the plan, try to get a written explanation of the problem. Redraft the QDRO and take it back to the judge for reissuance. The difficulty with this approach will depend on the law of the state issuing the QDRO and, sometimes, on the judge's mood.

If you or your lawyer feel the plan administrator is incorrectly interpreting the plan or simply being overly persnickety, you may appeal the decision pursuant to the plan's ERISA appeal procedures. Unless there is a clear error on your part, you should use the claims appeal procedure first, then return to the court if the appeal under the plan is denied. Once the court reviews the QDRO and determines it is, in fact, correct, the plan administrator must honor it.

If the plan administrator feels the court's QDRO is incorrect, resulting in a violation of ERISA or the Internal Revenue Code, the plan administrator may intervene in your divorce on behalf of the plan. Again, trying to involve the plan administrator from the outset may avoid this kind of misunderstanding and delay.

Dividing IRAs in a Divorce Property Settlement

IRAs are also subject to division in divorces, although no QDRO is required because IRAs are not qualified retirement plans. A transfer from an IRA under a divorce decree is not a taxable event to the former IRA holder. At the time of the transfer of assets, the assets will be treated as though a new IRA was created for the benefit of the receiving spouse.

You should immediately set up an IRA with any money you receive from your former husband's IRAs. That money will continue to grow in your new IRA on a tax-deferred basis. As with any other IRA, if you take the money out before you reach age 59½, you will pay immediate tax on it and a 10 percent early withdrawal penalty, absent one of the exemptions for IRA withdrawals such as disability.

Social Security for Divorced Wives

As a divorced spouse, if you were married for at least ten years, you are eligible to receive Social Security benefits based on your husband's earnings when you reach age 62, even if he is not yet receiving such benefits and even if he is remarried. Your spouse also must be at least age 62. If he is not retired then, the divorce must have occurred at least two years before you can receive benefits. Benefits based on your former spouse's earnings will cease if you remarry, unless your new spouse is receiving Social Security as a widower, parent, or disabled child. Chapter 8 gives more detail on the rights of divorced spouses under Social Security.

Conclusion: Know Your Rights to Retirement Plan Benefits at Divorce

- Recognize that accrued retirement benefits of both you and your spouse are subject to division by the courts during a divorce.
- Be sure your divorce lawyer is fully familiar with ERISA law governing the treatment of qualified retirement plans.
- Find and value all your husband's accrued retirement benefits from current and former employers. These include 401(k) plans, profit-sharing plans, thrift plans, and ESOPs, as well as traditional pension plans.
- If your retirement benefits are being considered part of the property settlement, be sure your husband's lawyer has properly valued those benefits.
- Talk to each plan administrator about their plan's requirements for QDROs and common problems to avoid. Ask if a model QDRO for the plan exists.
- If the potential amounts from a defined benefit plan are very large, consider hiring an actuary to produce precise figures for the court to use in determining the value of the benefit.
- Be sure the QDRO specifically spells out the benefit you are to receive and the benefit payment form to be used for calculating the benefit, and includes the time at which the accrued benefit will be fixed—that is, date of divorce, date of retirement, and so on.
- Be sure you are listed as a surviving spouse for plan purposes. Otherwise, if your former spouse dies before he retires, you may not receive a benefit.

..

If You Are Near Retirement

16

This chapter is for readers who feel that they are two to three years away from retiring, not necessarily for those who are 62 to 65. Remember that when you retire depends on when *you* want to retire. You cannot be forced to retire at 65 or any other age, unless you are a police officer, firefighter, or other type of public safety officer or a partner in an enterprise. If you think you must retire only because you are near 65—forget it.

What Makes You Think You're Ready to Retire?

Under the Age Discrimination in Employment Act (ADEA) you cannot be forced to retire or be demoted because of your age unless you're working in one of the age-critical professions mentioned. Of course, ADEA does not and should not protect you against dismissal, if you really are not capable of doing your job and your performance on the job is showing that. But age alone cannot justify your dismissal. Unlike other discrimination in employment laws, such as those protecting you from sex and race discrimination, ADEA permits you to bring your case before a jury (lots of older people serve on juries). And if the employer acted willfully to deny your rights, you can receive attorney's fees, costs, and damages, in addition to back pay.

You probably won't be surprised that employers take ADEA complaints seriously. Once an employer is gently reminded about ADEA and its remedies, the employer's hints to older employees about slowing down, enjoying time away from work, and so on magically cease in most cases.

Ask yourself why you feel you are near retirement or ready to retire. The only appropriate answer is because you want to—and because you have enough money to live comfortably for the next twenty-five years. If you did not give those answers, save this chapter for a few more years.

Once you really do want to leave the work force, begin a set of planned steps for leaving your job. Start at least a year before you intend to leave.

Set Up Your Retirement Budget

If you are within a year or two of retiring, you can now refine the budget estimating we did in Chapter 11. Set up the budget that you think you can live with. Hypothetical budgeting is always an annoying task because it involves lots of speculation and pondering on the unpredictable. But start with last year's checkbook and credit card receipts to see how you spent your money for a year. Once you have done that, modify the unusual and nonrecurring expenses, but add in expenses that might come up in the first year of retirement. If you have decided to move, add in those expenses. If you plan to take an art course, tuition needs to be added into your budget.

Depending on how realistic your budget is, the next step might be even more annoying, or it may be intensely gratifying. Try living for six months now on the retirement budget you set up. Granted there may be some significant differences between your cost of living while working and after retirement. But trying to live now with your retirement budget will give you some valuable insight, before you approach your boss with your advice about your replacement on the job and what he might do with the job. It may also change your ideas about when you want to retire.

How Much Will You Have?

Part of your budget must encompass the income side of your plan. Begin looking at your three-legged stool of retirement income with a precise measuring stick for its legs and a sharp pencil. Review your personal savings, find out what your Social Security benefits will be, and calculate the total of your employer-provided retirement benefits. The next sections of this chapter describe the calculations in detail.

Review Your Own Savings

Begin calculating how much money you will need for retirement by reviewing your own personal savings, which are the easiest to determine. If you want to know what sort of a monthly income you could expect from personal savings, consult the Appendix. Choose the number of years you think you will live and the average rate of return you think your savings and investments can realistically receive over those years. From that you can derive a rough idea of the amount of monthly withdrawal you can make until your money runs out.

For example, let's assume the following scenario:

- you have saved $100,000;
- you are retiring at age 65;

- you will live until age 90 (another 25 years); and
- you believe you can earn 10 percent per year during your retirement on your savings.

In this case you know the present value of your "annuity." It is $100,000. So you divide that amount by the factor for 10 percent interest over twenty-five years, which from the Appendix Table A.4 is 9.077. You may withdraw $11,000 annually from your savings until you are 90, when your savings will be exhausted. Try several calculations to see how the amount can vary based on the assumed interest rate and number of years of assumed life. For example, under the same situation, if you assume you can only earn 7 percent annually, you could only withdraw about $8,600 annually. And don't forget the effects of inflation on the buying power of that annual amount in the later years of your retirement. (See Chapter 11 to review the effects of inflation.)

Ask the Social Security Administration About Your Benefits

Social Security will provide an important part of your retirement income once you reach the age of eligibility. There are several variables involved in determining exactly how much your benefit will be. It is important to look at all the options before you elect to begin benefits. Once you begin receiving benefits under your earnings history, you are usually locked in. For example, when will you start receiving the benefit? You can start as young as 62. Will you receive the benefit based on your own earnings history or as a spouse based on your husband's or former husband's earnings history? Remember, Social Security benefits are based on your highest earnings for thirty-five years of your working life. If you have less than thirty-five working years, the nonearning years will be averaged in as zeros. You may find that you could substantially increase your benefit by working a few more years, especially if your current salary is considerably larger than earlier salaries, as is usually the case, or if you have not yet been in the work force for thirty-five years.

Submit another Form SSA-7004, Request for Earnings and Benefit Estimate Statement, to the Social Security Administration to get an updated estimate of your Social Security wage history and potential benefits. (Get the form from Chapter 8, order it by calling 1-800-772-1213, or print the SSA-7004 from the Social Security Internet site, *www.ssa.gov*). Four to six weeks after you submit the SSA-7004, you will receive the Personal Earnings and Benefit Estimate Statement. This statement will contain both your Social Security earnings history and your estimated benefits.

If you have been submitting the form and getting your estimated benefits statement every three years or so, you can be fairly certain that you have kept the wage history accurate. Regardless, check the estimated benefits statement carefully. If you find mistakes, call the number on the form and then follow up in writing to Social Security. In most cases the Social Security Administration can only correct errors occurring within the past three years or so. The statement will also tell you how many quarters of coverage you have earned. You must have forty quarters to be eligible to receive benefits based on your own earnings history. That is about ten years of work.

Most important, the statement will show your expected benefit payment if you retire at age 62 and your expected benefit if you retire at your normal retirement age, the date at which you will receive your full Social Security benefit. Remember, if you were born after 1937, your normal retirement age is higher than age 65. See Table 8.2 in Chapter 8 for your exact age for normal retirement.

Call the Social Security Administration at 1-800-772-1213 and ask for their informational booklets. Also ask your employer's human resources or personnel department if they have information on Social Security. Many employers do provide excellent information on Social Security; others supply nothing. A useful guide for all types of government assistance, including Social Security, Medicare, and help from the federal government with private pension problems can be found in Ellen Hoffman's *Bankroll Your Future: How to Get the Most from Uncle Sam for Your Retirement Years—Social Security, Medicare, and Much More* (Newmarket Press, 1998).

Early Benefits Equal Lower Benefits

Once you know approximately what your retirement benefit from Social Security will be, you can plan more realistically. From your statement, you will readily see the difference between benefits received at different ages. It will also show you your normal retirement age, which will be past 65 if you were born after 1937. (Because of the differences in normal retirement age under Social Security based on when you were born, we will refer to "normal retirement age" as the time you receive your highest ordinary Social Security benefit, rather than age 65.)

If you elect to retire before your normal retirement age, remember that your benefit will be reduced and will always remain reduced. You will not receive the higher benefit when you reach normal retirement age, although you will receive the cost-of-living adjustments applied to all Social Security benefits in future years. You are not required to begin receiving Social Security benefits when you retire, even if you begin to receive employer-provided retirement benefits.

Good Reasons to Delay Benefits

If you are retiring before your normal retirement age and you can live without the Social Security payments for a few years or even a few months, there are three good reasons to think about delaying the receipt of Social Security benefits.

- Your Social Security benefits will be higher the longer you wait to enroll.
- If you intend to work part-time, your earnings could reduce the amount of benefits you receive and could trigger income tax on the Social Security benefits you do receive. If you are under age 65 and earn more than $9,600 a year (in 1999), your Social Security benefits will be reduced by one dollar for every two dollars over the limit. If you are age 65 to 70 and earn more than $15,500 (in 1999), your Social Security benefits will be reduced by one dollar for every three dollars over the limit. These limits are scheduled to increase rapidly, up to $30,000 in 2003 for those age 65 to 70. (See Chapter 8 for the increases for those 65 and older.) There is no limit on the amount of wages you can earn once you reach age 70.
- Your Social Security wages become subject to federal income tax once your income exceeds $25,000 for singles and $32,000 for couples. Unlike the Social Security earnings limitation, this includes all income, not just wages.

Delaying Benefits Past Normal Retirement Age Further Increases the Payments

From your Social Security benefits statement, you will also see the significant benefit you receive from delaying benefits past normal retirement age. Of course, you are delaying the time value of having the money early and you are reducing the number of years you will receive payments. You can roughly calculate the number of years it would take you to break even in terms of receiving the same total amount of benefit by making three columns headed "Age 62 or current age benefit," "Normal Retirement Age Benefit," and "Age 70 Benefit."

Delaying Social Security payments past your normal retirement age will increase your final benefits by between 3 percent and 8 percent for each year past the normal retirement age you delay the benefits up to age 70. See Table 16.1.

Let's look at Alice. Suppose she decides to delay retirement to age 68. Alice was born in 1932, so her normal retirement age is 65 and her increase in benefits is 5 percent per year of delayed retirement. She is delaying retirement for exactly three years, so her ultimate Social Security benefit will be increased permanently by 15 percent.

Calculating whether to delay your Social Security benefit payments past the earliest available age is a complicated task. You have to consider several factors, including:

- what your other income will be
- whether you will work part-time and exceed the earnings limitation
- whether that income will trigger federal income tax on your Social Security benefits
- the earnings you have lost on the money you might have received if you had started payments earlier.

Table 16.1
Late Retirement Social Security Benefit
Increase Factors

| Birth Year | Percentage Increase in Benefit | |
	Per Year of Delay	Per Month of Delay
Before 1924	3	$1/24$
1925–1926	3.5	$7/24$
1927–1928	4	$1/3$
1929–1930	4.5	$9/24$
1931–1932	5	$5/12$
1933–1934	5.5	$11/24$
1935–1936	6	$1/2$
1937–1938	6.5	$13/24$
1939–1940	7	$7/12$
1941–1942	7.5	$15/24$
After 1942	8	$2/3$

Should You Receive Benefits as a Spouse or on Your Own?

If you are married or were married for ten years and are now divorced, check to see whether you could receive a higher benefit as a spouse based on your husband's earnings record. In most cases when you apply for Social Security, the Social Security Administration will tell you which benefit is larger and automatically give you the larger benefit. Because women earn so much less than men and work fewer years, even a woman who has worked steadily over the years may receive a lower Social Security benefit based on her own earnings record than she can receive as a spouse under her husband's record.

When you order your own Personal Earnings and Benefit Estimate Statement, ask your spouse to order his as well. Each of you must order your own statement because in ordinary cases the federal privacy laws prohibit giving Social Security information to anyone other than the individual. Each statement will show both the benefit estimate for the wage earner and an estimated benefit for the spouse based on the wage earner's earnings. In rare cases, it is possible your husband could earn a higher benefit filing under your earnings history.

Unlike most employer-provided retirement benefits, the wage earner's Social Security retirement benefit is not reduced if a spouse also claims benefits based on that wage earner's history. Because there is no penalty for using the spouse's earnings history rather than your own, if the spouse's history gives you a bigger benefit, file under his benefit.

If you are married, your husband must be receiving his Social Security benefits before you can receive benefits based on his earnings record. However, if you were married ten years and now divorced, you do not need to wait for your former spouse to begin receiving benefits. You may apply if he is at least 62 even though he may still be working. The catch here is that you must have been divorced at least two years or he must have been entitled to benefits when you divorced. For example, assume you and John were married for twenty-three years and divorced when he was 61 and you were 62. John is still working. You must wait two years until you can file for benefits as a spouse based on his earnings. If he had been 63 when you divorced, you could file immediately.

Applying for Social Security Benefits

Once you have decided you want to begin receiving your Social Security benefits, you must begin the application process. You must apply for Social Security. The checks don't just start coming when you reach normal retirement age. Start by calling the Social Security Administration's number for applications, 1-800-772-1213. Most if not all the work for your application can be done by phone.

Documents Needed

You will need a certified copy of your birth certificate, not just a photocopy. If you don't have an extra certified copy you can give Social Security, start to work on this today. It may be as easy as writing the records division of the state in which you were born or it may be a long process. It all depends on the jurisdiction. If you do not have a copy of your birth certificate, other documentation will be accepted, such as the birth certificates of your children showing your age. If you are relying on your spouse's wage history, you will need a certified copy of your marriage certificate and, if you are divorced, a certified copy of the divorce decree.

If you don't have these documents, it can take time to get them together, so start early. Do not delay beginning the application process just because you do not have these documents. Begin the application process and keep working on the documentation search. The Social Security Administration will give you tips on ways to find documents or, if you don't have documentation, they will tell you what sort of alternative documentation is acceptable.

When to File

File your application at least three months before you want to begin receiving benefits. It's even better to file your application the January before you want benefits to begin. If you are retiring at normal retirement age, Medicare Part A (hospitalization) and Part B (doctors and other medical services) will be covered automatically, unless you tell the Social Security Administration you do not want Medicare Part B coverage. You will pay for Part B coverage; there is no premium for Part A. If you file for Social Security benefits as soon as you become eligible, you can continue working that year until you reach the earnings limitation and then retire. That will avoid the possibility of Social Security benefits reductions because of earnings, but depending on other income for the year, some of your Social Security benefits may be subject to income tax.

If There Is a Problem

Chances are you will have no trouble receiving your appropriate benefit once you have provided the needed data. However, if you do have problems, be sure you document your case in writing. Get names of the people you are dealing with and persevere. If after a few months you continue to have problems, contact the staff of your member of Congress, not the representative directly. Your representative will know little or nothing about the details of applying for Social Security. But there will be a person on the staff who does little else but deal with Social Security benefits issues for constituents. It's best to make this contact in writing, but you might start with a phone call to the representative's local office for the name of the staff person.

If all else fails, you may want to consult a lawyer for assistance, but be sure you choose one who specializes or is highly experienced in Social Security issues. Avoid a generalist. She will spend too much time learning about the Social Security system at your expense.

Calculate Your Employer-Provided Retirement Benefits

Hopefully, your employer-provided retirement benefits will supply a significant portion of your retirement income. This is when your knowledge of retirement benefits learned in Chapters 5 and 7 will serve you well. Begin by reading your retirement plan summary plan description and your most recent employee benefits statement. The SPD will outline the payment options, if any, you can choose for the receipt of your retirement benefits. Your most recent employee benefits statement should show you the monthly payment you could expect from your pension or the balance in your defined contribution account.

Schedule a Meeting with a Human Resources Representative

Once you have refreshed your memory about the payment options and your estimated benefits, schedule an appointment with a member of the human resources department. Reconfirm your understandings about payment options and your benefit amount. Ask about any recent changes not reflected in your SPD. Be sure both you and the human resources representative are working from the most recent SPD or plan provisions. Do not rely on anything you do not get in writing. Only the actual plan language controls. While oral promises might be enforced after a long and expensive court case, you don't want to be the one spending tons of money to get your employer to live up to the oral promise made by the human resources clerk.

As you already know, retirement benefits administration is complex and difficult. The employers who provide their employees with retirement benefits act in good faith. The person dealing with retirement benefits wants to do it right and give you your full benefit, but sometimes the knowledge does not match the good intentions. This is the time to ask lots of questions. The knowledge of the human resources person giving you information will vary widely. Some personnel have in-depth knowledge and know more about retirement planning with your employer's plan than expert financial planners and ERISA attorneys. Others may not know as much as you do about the plan. They may be new to the job, or they may have been administering the plan for the last fifteen years—and doing it wrong every time.

If Retirement Plan Problems Occur

If what you are being told doesn't match your understanding of your options or the amount you think you should be receiving, say so. In a polite but persistent manner, ask the plan administrator to look at the provisions again or re-do the calculations. Point out where you think there are problems. Acknowledge that benefits calculations are complex. If you still feel that your payment options or benefits are not being properly calculated or offered, you have the right under ERISA to appeal the decisions, and you must receive a reply to your appeal within a reasonable time. If your plan is not covered by ERISA, chances are it also has an appeals procedure. Inquire about it or ask for the plan document and look it up yourself.

Contact Former Employers Too

Don't limit your benefits inquiries to just your current employer. Contact all your former employers and any unions you may have joined. For some of the employers, you may *know* you are entitled to a benefit. It is your responsibility to notify the employer of your whereabouts and to ask to begin receiving your benefits. Ask for the current SPD and an estimate of your benefits. Once you receive these materials, do some digging around in your records to try to match the benefit estimate with what you think you are entitled to. But recognize that the current SPD may not reflect the benefits you earned when you were with the company.

Contact former employers even if you do not think you are entitled to a benefit from them. Things do change. You may have forgotten a benefit program or you may be unaware of benefits changes or new benefits that were adopted. Send a letter to your former employers including your Social Security number, the approximate dates you worked there, and the name and location of the division where you worked. Again, it is your responsibility to keep in contact with your former employers who may hold benefits for you. Contacting them all may not

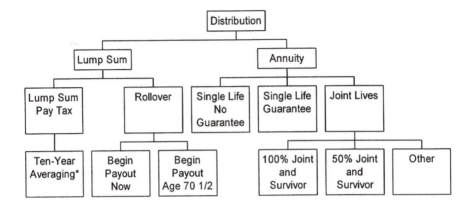

*Available only if you were age 50 or over in 1986.
The 1986 tax rates apply.

Figure 16.1 Decisions on Retirement Plan Payouts with Lump-Sum Payment Options

turn up any forgotten benefits, but you are only investing a little time. Finally, check the Pension Benefit Guaranty Corporation's Internet site (*www.pbgc.gov*) for their list of individuals who are owed benefit payments.

Choosing Among Payment Options

Your retirement security for the rest of your life will likely depend on your choosing the retirement plan payment option best for you and ensuring you get the most favorable tax treatment for that option. Unless you have won a lottery, you are about to have the opportunity to manage more money than you have probably ever had at one time in your life. Even if you have never been in a tax bracket higher than 15 percent and got a tax refund check every year you filed, you need to know about taxes now. The next section talks about whether to hire a professional to help, but before we get there, keep one thing in mind: The most critical single decision you will make about retirement will be the payment form and treatment of any employer-provided retirement plan you have. Let's see why.

Payment options basically fall into annuity payments—the periodic payments, usually every month for life—or a lump-sum payment—you receive the full value of your benefit immediately when you retire. There are variations on both of these approaches. The decision-tree chart in Figure 16.1 provides a visual picture of most of the options available and their tax consequences. Which is best for you depends on your family situation and on your ability to manage large sums of money. Generally, defined benefit plans will pay benefits in the annuity form and defined contribution plans will pay benefits as a lump sum. But both types of plans may offer other options.

Some plans have no payment options. You simply receive an annuity of monthly payments as long as you live, and, if you are married, as long as your husband lives, if he survives you. Other plans have a number of options. In most cases the tax treatment of the benefit distribution does not have to be a controlling factor because lump sums can be rolled over into an IRA on a tax-free basis. You then pay taxes only on the money you withdraw from the IRA. You must begin receiving periodic payments from your traditional IRA by April 1 of the year after you reach age 70½, just as you must begin receiving benefits from an employer plan at that age, if you have stopped working for that employer. And if you don't take these minimum distributions, you will pay both income tax and an excise tax of 50 percent of the amount you should have taken out. (You don't have to take these minimum benefits from a Roth IRA.)

Annuity Form of Payment

If you are married, the ordinary method of payment of your ERISA defined benefit retirement plan (and many non-ERISA defined benefit plans as well) will be a joint and survivor annuity, that is, payment in monthly installments to you for your lifetime and to your surviving spouse. In most cases this is not the form of payment you want.

Under the qualified joint and survivor annuity, or QJSA, payment option (see Chapters 7 and 14 for details), your benefit will be reduced because it is being paid over two lifetimes rather than one. It may be reduced again for your survivor when you die. But as a woman you are likely to outlive your husband and there will be no survivor. You will have received a reduced benefit for nothing in return. Of course, if you are in very poor health and your husband is very healthy or your husband is much younger, a QJSA option may make sense. You will need your husband's written, notarized consent to avoid taking this payout option. Also there are a few plans that "subsidize" the survivor annuity by not reducing the amount paid originally if a survivor annuity option is taken. If yours is one of these rare plans, then there is no penalty for taking the QJSA and you should take it.

If you are not married, the ordinary way your defined benefit pension would be paid is through a single life annuity in monthly installments as long as you live. Your plan may give you the option of choosing a QJSA and naming a survivor. As with a married couple, your initial benefit will be reduced to compensate for the expected payments to the survivor.

Other options for annuity payments include "life and with a guaranteed minimum period of payments," such as "five years certain" or "ten years certain," or some other number of years. Under these payout options, for example, if you retire at age 65, begin receiving benefits, and live to 100, you receive your benefits until you die and nothing is paid to your beneficiary. But if you were killed in a sky-diving accident at age 67, your named beneficiary would continue receiving a benefit for the eight remaining years of the guaranteed ten-year-certain time span.

The Lump-Sum Payment Option

Lump-sum payment options are the normal form of payment for most defined contribution plans such as profit-sharing plans and 401(k) plans. Many defined benefit plans also provide for a lump-sum payment option. Lump-sum distributions require careful thought and treatment. You can roll over the lump sum into a traditional IRA, deferring the tax until you withdraw the money, or you can pay taxes immediately. If you were age 50 or more in 1986, you may also be able to use a ten-year income tax averaging technique.

Usually because of the mortality factor reduction taken in converting lump sums (discussed in Chapters 7 and 14), the annuity form of benefit will be the best option. But there are exceptions. If the retiree is in poor health, she may not reach her life expectancy. In that case the lump sum may provide the largest sum of money. If the retiree believes she can invest the lump sum and generate a greater return than the pension plan, she should also take a lump sum. This ability to generate a greater return on the lump sum may not be as difficult as it seems in times of very high inflation. For example, in the double-digit inflation of the 1970s, the buying power of pension payments begun in 1970 eroded to less than half by 1979. Because interest rates were equally high during much of that period, a retiree might have been able to protect her income much more effectively by taking the lump-sum payment and investing it, rather than taking a life stream. But such market timing is extremely difficult.

Your overriding consideration is to remember that this money must last you a lifetime—and it may be a far longer lifetime than you expect. Other considerations are your comfort level with managing large sums of money, the immediate need for large cash sums (for example, if you are considering relocating), and estate and tax considerations. With the annuity form of payment, you will receive retirement plan benefits over your lifetime, no matter how long you live. You cannot outlive your capital. But with a lump sum that you are managing, once all the money is gone, it's gone.

A word of caution on lump sums: if your plan has a cost-of-living adjustment (COLA) factor, which is very rare for private-sector pension plans, but more common in government plans, the lump-sum option is almost always a poor choice. In such cases, once you receive a lump-sum payment, you will not receive any future cost-of-living adjustments. If your plan has a cost-of-living adjustment, it is almost never wise to elect a lump-sum option, unless you are terminally ill and expect to die within the next few years.

How Long Can You Live on the Lump Sum?

To get an idea of how long you can live on periodic payments from your lump sum, use the same analysis we used for your individual savings. Look at the lump-sum value of your benefit. Suppose you have a 401(k) plan worth $150,000. You are 65 and you think you will live to be age 90. You conservatively estimate you can invest the money at 6 percent. Referring to Table A.4 in the Appendix, we find the value factor for an annuity at 6 percent for twenty-five years and divide that into the present value of our "annuity" of $150,000. You can "pay" yourself a little over $11,700 per year under these facts. You have used conservative estimates for a low rate of return and a long life.

If you have a defined benefit with payout options of an annuity or a lump sum, it is easier to compare annuity payments from your management of the money with your employer's management. Let's look at Alice. When she retires she will receive annual annuity payments of $4,633 or she can take a lump sum of $39,191. Using the same assumptions, rolling over the lump sum and earning 6 percent on it while paying herself an annual payment for twenty-five years, Alice could give herself benefits of only $3,065 annually. Receiving the annual benefit is the better value under these assumptions. But if Alice thought she could make 10 percent on the money and would only live another fifteen years, until she is 80, she could pay herself $5,150 annually, clearly a better payout than the employer's annuity. But these high rates of return and early mortality assumptions would be far too optimistic to really rely on. Alice should stick with her employer's annuities.

Be very careful with this lump sum versus employer's annuity analysis if you begin to use more optimistic figures on rates of return you could earn on your management of a lump-sum distribution. Using the table you can see what a dramatic difference changing the assumptions makes. For example, if you assume you could earn 10 percent on your lump sum, you could pay yourself over $16,500 annually until you were 90. But those returns would take very aggressive money management.

Beware the Changing Interest Rate

Changing interest rates also can have a dramatic effect on the size of your defined benefit lump sum, if you choose to take a lump sum rather than the annuity. Be sure you base your decision on the interest rate that will actually be used to calculate your lump sum, not on an estimate you received several months before. By law, when distributing lump sums, the employer must use a Pension Benefit Guaranty Corporation interest rate assumption.

In times of very low interest rates, the lump-sum value of your accrued benefit in a defined benefit plan will be much larger than in times of higher interest rates. This is because the interest rate is used to estimate how much the lump sum will earn over the course of your remaining life to give you the equivalent of the monthly benefit you would have received under the annuity payout. If interest rates and, hence, earning assumptions are low, you will need a larger lump-sum amount to pay the same annual benefit each year than you would need to pay the same benefit when interest rates are high and the lump sum was earning more money.

Depending on the sum involved and your age and length of service, the difference in amounts can be tens of thousands of dollars. At times of very low interest rates, taking a lump-sum payout from a defined benefit plan may result in a significantly larger benefit than you might have received in annuity form. The disadvantage is that you probably will earn less on your money. You will need to be very confident of your money-managing and investment abilities.

Always Transfer Lump Sums into an IRA

If you elect the lump-sum payment option, except in extraordinary cases, you should have your employer transfer the money directly into an IRA or give you a check payable, not to you, but to your IRA. This avoids having 20 percent withheld for taxes on the money at that time and your having to pay perhaps even more tax on the payout. The importance of getting a lump-sum payment into an IRA to protect it from current taxation cannot be overstated. Look at what happens to Alice if she doesn't use the IRA.

Alice retires from her $37,650 a year job at the end of the year. Her taxable income would be about $32,000, on which she pays federal income taxes of approximately $5,700. She decides to take all her pensions as a lump sum, which totals $39,000. She doesn't move the money into an IRA. She will owe tax of approximately $11,200 on the lump-sum payment. That reduces her lump-sum amount from retirement to $27,800. That $39,000 invested at 8 percent would have given her annual income of about $4,000 for twenty years. The $27,800 will give her less than $3,000 per year.

And the tax hit will continue, because she will pay tax every year on the earnings on the remaining lump-sum amounts, further reducing her income. If she had placed the lump sum in an IRA, not only would she have avoided $11,200 of extra taxes in the first year, but she would only be paying income taxes on the amounts she withdrew from the IRA each year, not on the entire remaining amount.

Alice's retirement life style will be dramatically lower for the rest of her life if she fails to move her retirement plan lump-sum distribution into an IRA.

IRAs can be invested in almost any traditional securities. Also, you may change your IRA investments at any time, so don't worry about being locked in once you put the money in an IRA. Even if you want to buy a retirement home with your lump sum, you should hold the money in an IRA. You will be earning tax-deferred money and you will pay taxes only on the amounts you withdraw from the IRA.

Lump-Sum Averaging

Prior to the year 2000, the law permitted a "lump-sum averaging" technique to reduce taxes on lump-sum pension plan distributions that were not transferred to an IRA. This could help Alice somewhat. However, beginning in the year 2000, this technique will only be available if you were age 50 or over in 1986. If you were, you can use an averaging period of ten years and the old pre-1986 tax rates and you may be able to apply the old capital gains tax rate to certain assets in the plan acquired prior to 1974.

For the 1999 tax year, any individual (including those 50 and over in 1986) can use an averaging period of five years, applying ordinary income tax rates. You pay tax on all the money in the year in which you receive it, but at a tax rate applied as though you received the money over five (or ten years, if applicable). It is possible, but highly unlikely, that Congress could extend five-year averaging, but even if the law were extended to 2000 and beyond, lump-sum averaging is complicated and saves far less tax than putting your money in an IRA.

Tax treatment for distributions from retirement plans is an area where you really need expert advice. If you elect to receive a lump sum and not roll it into an IRA, find an experienced tax accountant or financial adviser before you take any distribution. Work with her to determine whether your lump sum will qualify for averaging and, if so, that it is done correctly. In seeking such a person ask them how many IRS Form 4972s (the form for reporting tax on lump-sum averaging) they complete each year. Unless the answer is several, keep looking for your tax adviser.

Maybe It's Time to Call in a Pro?

Even if you are not using something so complicated as lump-sum averaging, clearly you must consider a great many financial issues and options for your employer plans and savings as you retire. The decisions you make now on the payment options from your employer-provided plans and on the timing of applying for Social Security are literally once-in-a-lifetime decisions. You will have to live with the consequences for the rest of your life and those decisions will largely govern your life style.

Although you may not have used a financial adviser in the past, this may be the time to consider one who specializes in financial planning at retirement to help you in calculating the dollar value of the options. You should always make the final decisions, but experts to check plan calculations and the latest tax treatment of retirement plan income can be invaluable. If your employer plans provide you with a number of payment options or if you have a plan that only makes lump-sum distributions, you should seriously consider seeking some professional advice, if you do not already have an adviser. The tax savings alone may more than pay for the advice.

Consult the checklist in Chapter 13 for qualities to look for in a financial adviser. As always, experience and up-to-date knowledge are the key qualities, followed by listening skills and responsiveness. Also be sure the adviser is expert in interpreting retirement plan provisions and has either actuarial skills or access to an experienced pension actuary who can provide advice at a reasonable fee. Make clear from the outset that your primary goal is a set of reports showing the payout options available to you and the tax consequences of each one. Any investment advice should come only after you have decided on the payout and tax options.

With investment advice, the sleep-at-night factor is the primary guide. After all, the whole reason for retirement planning is to create security. You're not secure if you are worrying about investments. But unlike the decisions on benefits payments, your investment decisions can, and definitely should, be revised from time to time. There is no great urgency in *how* you invest your retirement savings, but there *is* some urgency in making the right decisions on *the form of payment from your employer plans* and *the tax consequence of those decisions.*

What If It's Not Enough?

Like Alice you may find that once you have totaled your potential Social Security benefits, your employer-provided retirement benefits, and your savings, it simply isn't enough to live on. "Keep working" is the first and obvious response. That option has advantages in addition to the income it will provide. By delaying retirement, you will increase the benefits you receive from Social Security, from your employer's plan, and from your own savings. You will likely receive at least a cost-of-living raise during the years you work and that, along with the additional years of service you will have put in, will increase your other retirement benefits.

Change Partners, but Keep Dancing: Part-Time Work or a Different Job

There are also other options. It may be possible to find another, less demanding full-time job. Or part-time work can provide necessary income as well as ease the transition from full-time, heavily scheduled work days to seemingly endless unstructured time in retirement. About 25 percent of women over 50 are working at "bridge jobs" such as part-time work or self-employment, after having worked a "career job."[1] More than 16 percent of those over age 65 derive income from earnings and those earnings supply, on average, 18 percent of the income for those over age 65, suggesting that work for older workers is both available and desired by those workers.[2]

Your employer might be eager to arrange a part-time position to keep your expertise available while reducing her payroll. The bias against older employees is eroding. Many employers are recognizing the value of older employees. Studies show that older employees have better attendance records and lower turnover and learn tasks just as rapidly as their younger colleagues.

Perhaps you cannot, or do not want to, remain with your present employer. You have a lifetime of contacts both in the work place and in the community. Use them in seeking new part-time or full-time employment. Update that resume and don't leave off volunteer work and community service. Stress computer skills and any recent job-related training you have had.

If you have been volunteering, find out if the organization can use some part-time paid help. You have already proved your usefulness, now ask to be paid for it. If there is no money, but a clear task to be performed or service to be given through the nonprofit program, offer to seek a grant for the money with the understanding that if your proposal results in a grant, you will be hired to do the work. Make that clear in the proposal, too.

Unless *you* feel the work is beneath you, don't be deterred by discussions about your being overqualified from either your friends and family or the potential employer. You aren't looking for a career track, you are looking for income and ways to employ your skills. Remind the person interviewing you that one way to meet the constant mandates from her boss to "do more with less" is hiring you, especially if you are "overqualified." It is an opportunity for her to "do more with more" in your case. Be aggressive in your job search and do not be modest about your accomplishments. You have years of talent and skill to offer. You're not bragging about it. You're just stating the facts.

Put Your Home to Work: Home Equity Conversions

The biggest areas of expense are likely to be taxes and housing expenses and a move can reduce both of these. Other ways to reduce housing expenses and perhaps take some equity out of your house are through a sale and leaseback, a reverse mortgage, or other types of home equity conversion loans. These options are designed to enable you to remain in your own home while "spending" some of the equity you have in it. "Home-Made Money: Consumer's Guide to Home Equity Conversion," published by the American Association of Retired Persons and updated periodically, provides an excellent and highly detailed guide to the various home equity conversion programs along with the names, addresses, and telephone numbers of lenders. AARP's Internet site, *www.aarp.org/hecc,* also has extensive information on using home equity conversion. You can receive updates on available home equity conversions by emailing *rmroundup@aarp.org.* More information is available by writing AARP Home Equity Information Center, 601 E Street, N.W., Washington, D.C. 20049. On the subject of reverse mortgages, *Your New Retirement Nest Egg: A Consumer Guide to the New Reverse Mortgages* is available from the National Center for Home Equity Conversion, 7373 147th Street West, Suite 115, Apple Valley, MN 55124.

Reverse Mortgages

With a reverse mortgage, also called a reverse annuity mortgage, or RAM, you receive a stream of monthly payments from the mortgage company. The mortgage is then repaid from the proceeds of the house after your death. You retain title to the house and full responsibility for its upkeep. Should you wish to sell the house at some point, you can do so and repay the "mortgage" under most arrangements.

Reverse mortgages are now permitted in almost every state. Before you enter into any agreement you should seek expert advice and get all your questions answered in writing. For example, what happens if you live beyond the mortgage payments? Who owns the appreciation in the house? Also, reverse mortgages tend to be an expensive way to borrow money. When fees are included, the overall interest rate charged is relatively high. If your house appreciates in value over the years after you have acquired the reverse mortgage, there may still be some value left for your heirs or estate when you die. But if values hold steady, there may be little or nothing left at the end of the mortgage term.

Also, some RAMs are gender-biased. Because of women's longer life expectancy, these RAMs will give you a lower monthly payment than a man would receive based on the same home value. Federal Housing Authority (FHA)–guaranteed RAMs cannot use this gender bias. The FHA can provide you with a list of lenders in your area who provide FHA-guaranteed RAMs. Call the local U.S. Housing and Urban Development office for the information.

Sale and Leaseback

Under a sale and leaseback, you convey title to your home to the buyer. You continue to live there paying a monthly "rental." Appreciation and upkeep of the home belong to the buyer, not you. The advantage of a sale and leaseback arrangement is that it permits you to use the homeowner's tax break of an exclusion from federal income taxes for up to $250,000 of gain or up to $500,000 for a married couple. You must have used the house as your principal residence for at least two of the five years prior to the sale. You may only use this exclusion every two years.

You should undertake any of these approaches only with independent expert advice from a lawyer or real estate expert whom you have hired and whom you know has experience in these transactions and in your community. If you are retiring at 65 today, neither of these should be your first choice in financing retirement. In most cases, you will be too young to receive a significant monthly income from the RAM and you may run the risk of outliving your "payments" from the mortgage company. But you should be aware of these options for consideration later in your retirement.

Change Your Life Style

As a last resort, think about changing your life style to reduce expenses. Maybe you *can* live on less. Early in your retirement, selling your home and buying a less expensive, lower-maintenance house might be a much better approach than the home equity conversion plans. It will not only give you extra cash now to invest for income; it will also reduce expenses.

But be very realistic in examining the life style change alternative. Moving to a state with lower taxes and a lower cost of living will save you money, but if you don't know anyone there and miss your former community, the trade-off isn't worth it. (More about moving in the next chapter.) Selling your house might give you a huge nest egg, but if you hate apartments, you will be miserable and feel trapped. You may be happier continuing to work and maintaining your current life style than making dramatic changes. On the other hand, if you have dreaded yard work for years and longed to move back to the small town where you went to college, you may find that you can get along financially and emotionally very well with that change in life style.

Conclusion: Strategy Plan If You Are Near Retirement

- File Form SSA-7004 with the Social Security Administration to receive your most recent estimated earnings and benefits statement.
- Read your most recent employee benefits statements from your employer-provided retirement plans. Check these statements for accuracy.
- Review your employer plans' summary plan descriptions.
- Review your own retirement savings. Using the Appendix, calculate how much you can pay yourself from those savings each month, using different assumed earning rates and life expectancies.
- Construct a "retirement budget" and try to live within it for six months.
- Consider hiring a financial adviser to calculate various payout methods under your employer-provided plans and under other retirement savings.
- Begin the application process with the Social Security Administration at least three months before you expect to receive benefits. You can do this by phone.
- Contact all former employers about retirement benefits. Include your Social Security number and your approximate dates of employment.
- Schedule an appointment with your employer's human resources department to discuss retirement plan options and confirm benefits levels.
- Think about beginning to change some of your investments in light of your impending retirement.

Life in Retirement

You've made your decisions about retirement, done your planning, and are now ready to take the plunge and leave your career job. What are the resources available to you and what new challenges will you face?

Resources for Retiring Women

The Older Women's League (OWL), a grassroots organization with seventy-three chapters across the country, is consistently involved in public education campaigns on issues involving midlife and retired women. Contact OWL at 666 Eleventh Street, N.W., Suite 700, Washington, D.C. 20001. The National Center for Women and Retirement Research, located at Long Island University, New York, provides a Pre-Retirement Education Planning program involving seminars and handbooks for women nearing or in retirement. Contact them through their Internet site, *www.southampton.liunet.edu*. Women's professional organizations are also beginning to focus on the needs of their retiring members. Check with organizations you belong to for special "alumni" treatment and programs.

Guard Your Health

At any age your ability to enjoy life is directly linked to your health. Evidence suggests that health issues drive retirement decisions and can have more effects on retirement satisfaction than income.[1] Of course, poor health can also quickly deplete income. Retirement is no time to let down your guard on your health. With more time, it should be easier to exercise and to cook and eat nutritiously.

With medical science learning more and more about aging, the link between good health, both physical and mental, and exercise is well established. More important, exercise trainers are focusing on the different training needs for mature adults. If you have been exercising all along, don't let your new routine diminish your activity. If you haven't been exercising, now is a great time to start. Find a program geared to your age group and begin.

Now also would be a good time to take a cooking class focusing on healthy, low-fat ways to cook. You'll probably find new recipes you like and new preparation methods for your old favorites, as well.

To Move or Not to Move?

For many retirees moving seems to be part of the package. The first step after signing up for Social Security is selling the house and hitting the road. But moving seems like very poor timing for a number of reasons. While moving can help to reduce expenses if you move to a state and locality with lower taxes, lower housing costs, and lower general living costs, you need to be comfortable there too. After all, states and localities have been known to raise taxes and living costs change.

Radical changes in life such as changing jobs, getting married, or moving are significant stresses, although they may be pleasurable stresses. Retirement is likely to be such a stress, even though you may be looking forward to it immensely. Why add the stress of moving? You are already saying good-bye to a number of colleagues at work, probably with a mixture of relief and regret, depending on the colleague. Why compound that with leaving your friends from your congregation, exercise class, and volunteer activities?

What's Your Hurry?

If you are determined to relocate, why not take the first year of retirement and explore at your leisure—finally—instead of during pressured two-week vacations? Visit during several seasons. Attend church or synagogue. Take a tour of the hospital. Consult *Fifty Fabulous Places to Raise Your Family* (2nd ed.) by Melissa Giovagnoli, Lee Rosenberg, and Saralee H. Rosenberg (Career Press, 1997). They recommend subscribing to the local newspaper for a picture of the housing market, crime problems, and local economy. They also recommend talking with the local sheriff or police about crime and with other recent retirees about their overall satisfaction.

Even if you have never been sick a day in your life, check out the quality and cost of medical facilities in any potential new hometown. Medical costs can vary dramatically across the country. Reality will tell you that medical facilities are likely to be more important as you age. Think about new hobbies you would like to try. Are there support facilities for them? You will have more time for reading and exercise, but less money to spend. Are there good libraries and places to exercise? If you think you need or want to work part-time, are there likely to be jobs that can use your skills?

Why not rent a place and live in some of your potential new hometowns for awhile? Unless there is some compelling reason to move, take a lot of time. And get used to the New Retired You before changing venue. The sleepy little town that seemed so attractive when you were working fifty hours a week and commuting ten hours a week in the big city may be hopelessly dull when you no longer have a brutal schedule.

Adult Communities

Several builders are focusing on "adult only" communities designed for those fifty years and older. These usually involve lots of recreational facilities—a golf course is a must—and various types of homes, including town homes and single-family dwellings. Houses are designed with the mature adult in mind, right down to a preference for faucets with lever handles that are easier to use than knobs for those with arthritis.

You may find these to be wonderful neighborhoods with lots of like-minded new friends—or you may miss the stimulation of people of all ages. Many of these communities are well established, so talk with people who live there—and who lived there and moved. Their experiences should help you weigh your own reaction.

Continuing Care Retirement Communities

Early in your retirement your health will probably be good and the idea of needing help with daily living tasks or medical facilities is not an issue. But you may find yourself in the traditional role of the daughter or spousal caregiver to an elderly parent or ill partner. When faced with deteriorating health of you or your spouse or even your parent, a continuing care retirement community could be an option. These communities are designed as a campus, combining apartments, town houses, detached houses, and a nursing home and/or hospital in one location. Such communities provide aspects of housing, health care, social interaction, and health insurance. These facilities are usually populated with those who are 75 and older, but the ages are dropping. They enable older persons to have the minimal level of assistance they need.

The arrangement is particularly helpful for married couples where one spouse needs more medical attention than the otherwise healthy spouse can provide. The couple can remain together, but medical services can be provided in the home. If the condition worsens, the ill spouse can be moved to the nursing facility, which is within walking distance or perhaps in the building. The disruption in day-to-day life is mitigated.

Financial arrangements for such facilities vary widely. Most require a large up-front payment and monthly fees. Depending on the contract, if nursing care is required, an extra fee may be charged. In other situations, joining the continuing care community carries with it an element of insurance, so there are no other fees whether you use the nursing or medical facilities or not. There have been long waiting lists for most such facilities. Some "young" retired couples sign up for these communities years in advance of when they think they will need them so that when they are ready to enter the community, they are near the top of the list. But to date, continuing care communities have been run by nonprofit organizations such as religious groups. As the age wave of baby boomers progresses, for-profit continuing care communities are growing and that has reduced the waiting times. These facilities may be an option for you. But only consider a continuing care community after long-range investigation and planning, backed up by your own independently hired lawyer to review the contracts. Consult *www. retirement-living.com* for more information on various types of adult communities.

What to Do with All That Spare Time: You Don't Have Any

Some people fear the psychological effects of retirement may be more troublesome than the financial ones, or at least as troublesome. There is very little in the literature about women's reactions to their own retirement. One pioneer in this field is Dr. Eileen Johnstone Feuerbach, who, near what some would consider to be retirement age, got her doctorate in psychology after studying women's attitudes toward their own retirement.[2] She surveyed 149 women between the ages of 55 and 62 on their work and retirement attitudes, in part based on their years in the work force. Dr. Feuerbach found in her study that being in and out of the work force or entering the work force later in life did not appear to affect significantly career satisfaction or attitudes toward retirement. She found all the women in the study had generally positive attitudes toward retirement. But she also noted that adequate income and good health go hand in hand with satisfaction in retirement, and most of her subjects had both.[3]

In fact most retirees find they love it and they are busier than ever before. For the first time in your life—or at least since you were five—you will have blocks of unstructured time. You will have the asset that most Americans yearn for but cannot buy, time. And, if you wish, you can become the philanthropist to many among your friends, your family, and your community with that asset.

Instead of shopping and agonizing over the red sweater or the blue one at holidays and for birthdays, you can wrap an elaborate box and give the recipient a chit worth one day of your time. You can wait for their repairman, run errands, or take the children to and from soccer practice or an elderly parent to and from the doctor. Remember how much you would have appreciated that gift when you were working? You know such a gift is the thing most of your friends would find more valuable than diamonds.

More than one-fifth of the children in this country grow up in poverty. Estimates are 25 percent of our citizens are functionally illiterate. In five minutes, you can count at least a dozen things in your community that ought to be done. Do a few of them. Or organize others to do them. Surely, you have little free time with an agenda like that to address. You now have what it takes to help deal with these problems. Whether it is tutoring, lobbying for more services, or calling on a home-bound elderly person, you can be a part of the solution. And if you really miss the nine-to-five routine, you can perform your new activities on a nine-to-five basis. You will be paid more than you ever dreamed you would earn.

Enjoy your retirement with new experiences and thanksgiving. And revel in how much your wage-slave sisters envy you.

Strategy Plan in Retirement

- Explore volunteer activities worthy of your commitment.
- Now make a commitment to those activities.
- Guard your health. Find an appropriate exercise routine and follow it. Learn new ways of cooking and eating to help maintain your health.
- Enjoy yourself. You've earned it.

Epilogue

Retirement planning for women requires the same elements as for men. Social Security will provide a subsistence, retirement benefits earned while working will add no more than a third of necessary retirement income, and the remaining 40 percent to 70 percent needed for retirement must come from individual savings. Indeed many retirees, especially women, may need as much as 80 percent of their retirement income coming from their own savings because they may not have employer benefits.

The percentage of retirement income needed from personal savings is likely to increase, not decrease. Social Security cannot politically or economically justify the high taxes needed to continue today's relatively generous benefits for the retired baby boomers. Employers are moving away from generous pensions. More employers are simply helping employees save for their own retirement through defined contribution plans like 401(k) plans that require a contribution from the employee before the employer adds its contribution.

Retirement planning for women will remain more challenging than for men until women receive equal wages throughout their careers. Because women earn less, they have a more difficult time saving, and because almost all employer and government benefits are based on wages while working, women also receive disproportionately smaller retirement benefits, when they receive them at all.

So we end where we started: save and invest. If you don't want to join millions of your sisters in poverty in your retirement years, you really can rely only on your own savings.

Focus on eight basic principles.

1. The sooner you start saving, the less you will need to save, because money doesn't grow on trees, but it does grow in investment accounts. A dollar saved in your twenties is worth about ten times as much as a dollar saved in your forties.

2. Even small amounts of saving are important. Remember the magic of compounding.

3. Know what employer plans are available to you and take full advantage of them. Remember, any money you contribute to a retirement plan is always fully vested. Missing an employer matching contribution to a retirement plan is like turning down a raise. No, it's worse. You pay taxes on a raise immediately; you don't pay tax on the employer contribution for decades.

4. Never, never spend retirement plan distributions when you leave a job. This is your retirement security. It must be preserved in an IRA or other retirement account.

5. A bad tax-favored investment is still a bad investment. Consider the tax treatment of investments, but don't let taxes drive investment decisions.

6. Don't get discouraged with the size of your savings and investments. Always keep saving something.

7. Learn to accept greater risks for more return, especially when you are younger.

8. Be an investor, not a gambler. Don't try to "time" the market. Stay in for the long haul.

Appendix: Tables for Calculating the Time Value of Money

Table A.1
The Future Value of a Dollar

Period	1%	2%	4%	6%	7%	8%	9%	10%	11%	12%	14%	16%	20%
1	1.010	1.020	1.040	1.060	1.070	1.080	1.090	1.100	1.110	1.120	1.139	1.160	1.200
2	1.020	1.040	1.082	1.124	1.145	1.166	1.188	1.210	1.232	1.254	1.297	1.346	1.440
3	1.030	1.061	1.125	1.191	1.225	1.260	1.295	1.331	1.368	1.405	1.478	1.561	1.728
4	1.041	1.082	1.170	1.262	1.311	1.360	1.412	1.464	1.518	1.574	1.683	1.811	2.074
5	1.051	1.104	1.217	1.338	1.403	1.469	1.539	1.611	1.685	1.762	1.917	2.100	2.488
6	1.062	1.126	1.265	1.419	1.501	1.587	1.677	1.772	1.870	1.974	2.183	2.436	2.986
7	1.072	1.149	1.316	1.504	1.606	1.714	1.828	1.949	2.076	2.211	2.487	2.826	3.583
8	1.083	1.172	1.369	1.594	1.718	1.851	1.993	2.144	2.305	2.476	2.833	3.278	4.300
9	1.094	1.195	1.423	1.689	1.838	1.999	2.172	2.358	2.558	2.773	3.226	3.803	5.160
10	1.105	1.219	1.480	1.791	1.967	2.159	2.367	2.594	2.839	3.106	3.675	4.411	6.192
11	1.116	1.243	1.539	1.898	2.105	2.332	2.580	2.853	3.152	3.479	4.186	5.117	7.430
12	1.127	1.268	1.601	2.012	2.252	2.518	2.813	3.138	3.498	3.896	4.767	5.936	8.916
13	1.138	1.294	1.665	2.133	2.410	2.720	3.066	3.452	3.883	4.363	5.430	6.886	10.699
14	1.149	1.319	1.732	2.261	2.579	2.937	3.342	3.797	4.310	4.887	6.185	7.988	12.839
15	1.161	1.346	1.801	2.397	2.759	3.172	3.642	4.177	4.785	5.474	7.045	9.266	15.407
16	1.173	1.373	1.873	2.540	2.952	3.426	3.970	4.595	5.311	6.130	8.024	10.748	18.488
17	1.184	1.400	1.948	2.693	3.159	3.700	4.328	5.054	5.895	6.866	9.139	12.468	22.186
18	1.196	1.428	2.026	2.854	3.380	3.996	4.717	5.560	6.544	7.690	10.409	14.463	26.623
19	1.208	1.457	2.107	3.026	3.617	4.316	5.142	6.116	7.263	8.613	11.856	16.777	31.948
20	1.220	1.486	2.191	3.207	3.870	4.661	5.604	6.727	8.062	9.646	13.504	19.461	38.338
25	1.282	1.641	2.666	4.292	5.427	6.848	8.623	10.835	13.585	17.000	25.888	40.874	95.396
30	1.348	1.811	3.243	5.743	7.612	10.063	13.268	17.449	22.892	29.960	49.626	85.850	237.376

Table A.2
The Present Value of a Dollar

Period	1%	2%	4%	6%	7%	8%	9%	10%	11%	12%	14%	16%	20%
1	.990	.980	.962	.943	.935	.926	.917	.909	.901	.893	.878	.862	.833
2	.980	.961	.925	.890	.873	.857	.842	.826	.812	.797	.771	.743	.694
3	.971	.942	.889	.840	.816	.794	.772	.751	.731	.712	.677	.641	.579
4	.961	.924	.855	.792	.763	.735	.708	.683	.659	.636	.594	.552	.482
5	.951	.906	.822	.747	.713	.681	.650	.621	.593	.567	.522	.476	.402
6	.942	.888	.790	.705	.666	.630	.596	.564	.535	.507	.458	.410	.335
7	.933	.871	.760	.665	.623	.583	.547	.513	.482	.452	.402	.354	.279
8	.923	.853	.731	.627	.582	.540	.502	.467	.434	.404	.353	.305	.233
9	.914	.837	.703	.592	.544	.500	.460	.424	.391	.361	.310	.263	.194
10	.905	.820	.676	.558	.508	.463	.422	.386	.352	.322	.272	.227	.162
11	.896	.804	.650	.527	.475	.429	.388	.350	.317	.287	.239	.195	.135
12	.887	.788	.625	.497	.444	.397	.356	.319	.286	.257	.210	.168	.112
13	.879	.773	.601	.469	.415	.368	.326	.290	.258	.229	.184	.145	.093
14	.870	.758	.577	.442	.388	.340	.299	.263	.232	.205	.162	.125	.078
15	.861	.743	.555	.417	.362	.315	.275	.239	.209	.183	.142	.108	.065
16	.853	.728	.534	.394	.339	.292	.252	.218	.188	.163	.125	.093	.054
17	.844	.714	.513	.371	.317	.270	.231	.198	.170	.146	.109	.080	.045
18	.836	.700	.494	.350	.296	.250	.212	.180	.153	.130	.096	.069	.038
19	.828	.686	.475	.331	.277	.232	.194	.164	.138	.116	.084	.060	.031
20	.820	.673	.456	.312	.258	.215	.178	.149	.124	.104	.074	.051	.026
25	.780	.610	.375	.233	.184	.146	.116	.092	.074	.059	.039	.024	.010
30	.742	.552	.308	.174	.131	.099	.075	.057	.044	.033	.020	.012	.004

Table A.3
The Future Value of an Annuity of One Dollar per Year

Period	1%	2%	4%	6%	7%	8%	9%	10%	11%	12%	14%	16%	20%
1	1.000	1.000	1.000	1.000	1.000	1.000	1.000	1.000	1.000	1.000	1.000	1.000	1.000
2	2.010	2.020	2.040	2.060	2.070	2.080	2.090	2.100	2.110	2.120	2.139	2.160	2.200
3	3.030	3.060	3.122	3.184	3.215	3.246	3.278	3.310	3.342	3.374	3.436	3.506	3.640
4	4.060	4.122	4.246	4.375	4.440	4.506	4.573	4.641	4.710	4.779	4.914	5.066	5.368
5	5.101	5.204	5.416	5.637	5.751	5.867	5.985	6.105	6.228	6.353	6.597	6.877	7.442
6	6.152	6.308	6.633	6.975	7.153	7.336	7.523	7.716	7.913	8.115	8.514	8.977	9.930
7	7.214	7.434	7.898	8.394	8.654	8.923	9.200	9.487	9.783	10.089	10.697	11.414	12.916
8	8.286	8.583	9.214	9.897	10.260	10.637	11.028	11.436	11.859	12.300	13.184	14.240	16.499
9	9.369	9.755	10.583	11.491	11.978	12.488	13.021	13.579	14.164	14.776	16.017	17.519	20.799
10	10.462	10.950	12.006	13.181	13.816	14.487	15.193	15.937	16.722	17.549	19.243	21.321	25.959
11	11.567	12.169	13.486	14.972	15.784	16.645	17.560	18.531	19.561	20.655	22.918	25.733	32.150
12	12.683	13.412	15.026	16.870	17.888	18.977	20.141	21.384	22.713	24.133	27.104	30.850	39.581
13	13.809	14.680	16.627	18.882	20.141	21.495	22.953	24.523	26.212	28.029	31.871	36.786	48.497
14	14.947	15.974	18.292	21.015	22.550	24.215	26.019	27.975	30.095	32.393	37.301	43.672	59.196
15	16.097	17.293	20.024	23.276	25.129	27.152	29.361	31.772	34.405	37.280	43.486	51.660	72.035
16	17.258	18.639	21.825	25.673	27.888	30.324	33.003	35.950	39.190	42.753	50.531	60.925	87.442
17	18.430	20.012	23.698	28.213	30.840	33.750	36.974	40.545	44.501	48.884	58.555	71.673	105.931
18	19.615	21.412	25.645	30.906	33.999	37.450	41.301	45.599	50.396	55.750	67.694	84.141	128.117
19	20.811	22.841	27.671	33.760	37.379	41.446	46.018	51.159	56.939	63.440	78.103	98.603	154.740
20	22.019	24.297	29.778	36.786	40.995	45.762	51.160	57.275	64.203	72.052	89.960	115.380	186.688
25	28.243	32.030	41.646	54.865	63.249	73.106	84.701	98.347	114.413	133.334	179.048	249.214	471.981
30	34.785	40.568	56.085	79.058	94.461	113.283	136.308	164.494	199.021	241.333	349.829	530.312	1181.882

Table A.4
The Present Value of an Annuity of One Dollar per Year

Period	1%	2%	4%	6%	7%	8%	9%	10%	11%	12%	14%	16%	20%
1	.990	.980	.962	.943	.935	.926	.917	.909	.901	.893	.878	.862	.833
2	1.970	1.942	1.866	1.833	1.808	1.783	1.759	1.736	1.713	1.690	1.649	1.605	1.528
3	2.941	2.884	2.775	2.673	2.624	2.577	2.531	2.487	2.444	2.402	2.326	2.246	2.106
4	3.902	3.808	3.630	3.465	3.387	3.312	3.240	3.170	3.102	3.037	2.920	2.798	2.589
5	4.853	4.713	4.452	4.212	4.100	3.993	3.890	3.791	3.696	3.605	3.441	3.274	2.991
6	5.795	5.601	5.242	4.917	4.767	4.623	4.486	4.355	4.231	4.111	3.899	3.685	3.326
7	6.728	6.472	6.002	5.582	5.389	5.206	5.033	4.868	4.712	4.564	4.301	4.039	3.605
8	7.652	7.325	6.733	6.210	5.971	5.747	5.535	5.335	5.146	4.968	4.654	4.344	3.837
9	8.566	8.162	7.435	6.802	6.515	6.247	5.995	5.759	5.537	5.328	4.964	4.607	4.031
10	9.471	8.983	8.111	7.360	7.024	6.710	6.418	6.145	5.889	5.650	5.237	4.833	4.192
11	10.368	9.787	8.760	7.887	7.499	7.139	6.805	6.495	6.207	5.938	5.475	5.029	4.327
12	11.255	10.575	9.385	8.384	7.943	7.536	7.161	6.814	6.492	6.194	5.685	5.197	4.439
13	12.134	11.048	9.986	8.853	8.358	7.904	7.487	7.103	6.750	6.424	5.869	5.342	4.533
14	13.004	12.106	10.563	9.295	8.745	8.244	7.786	7.367	6.982	6.628	6.031	5.468	4.611
15	13.865	12.849	11.118	9.712	9.108	8.559	8.061	7.606	7.191	6.811	6.173	5.575	4.675
16	14.718	13.578	11.652	10.106	9.447	8.851	8.313	7.824	7.379	6.974	6.298	5.668	4.730
17	15.562	14.292	12.166	10.477	9.763	9.122	8.544	8.022	7.549	7.120	6.407	5.749	4.775
18	16.398	14.992	12.659	10.828	10.059	9.372	8.756	8.201	7.702	7.250	6.503	5.818	4.812
19	17.226	15.678	13.134	11.158	10.336	9.604	8.950	8.365	7.839	7.366	6.587	5.877	4.843
20	18.046	16.351	13.590	11.470	10.594	9.818	9.129	8.514	7.963	7.469	6.662	5.929	4.870
25	22.023	19.523	15.622	12.783	11.654	10.675	9.823	9.077	8.422	7.843	6.916	6.097	4.948
30	25.808	22.396	17.292	13.765	12.409	11.258	10.274	9.427	8.694	8.055	7.049	6.177	4.979

Notes

Chapter 1. Why Retirement Planning Is Different for Women

1. U.S. Department of Labor, Bureau of Labor Statistics, *Current Population Survey, 1993: Median Weekly Earnings of Workers Who Usually Work Full-Time, 1993 Annual Averages* (Washington, D.C.: The Bureau, 1994).

2. U.S. Bureau of the Census, *Statistical Abstract of the United States: 1998* (118th ed.; Washington, D.C.: The Bureau, 1998), table 129. (Hereafter *1998 Statistical Abstract.*)

3. U.S. Bureau of the Census, *Statistical Abstract of the United States: 1991* (111th ed.; Washington, D.C.: The Bureau, 1991), table 736.

4. U.S. Bureau of the Census, *Measuring Fifty Years of Economic Change: Current Population Report* (Washington, D.C.: U.S. Department of Commerce Economic and Statistics Administration, 1998), p. 15.

5. *1998 Statistical Abstract*, table 754.

6. U.S. Department of Labor et al., *Pension and Health Benefits of American Workers: New Findings from the April 1993 Current Population Survey* (Washington, D.C.: U.S. GPO, 1994), table B11, pp. B16–17.

7. Bureau of Labor Statistics, "Employee Tenure in the Mid-1990s," News Release USDL 97-25 (Washington, D.C.: U.S. Department of Labor, 1997), table 1.

8. *1998 Statistical Abstract*, table 645.

9. U.S. Department of Labor, Pension and Welfare Benefits Administration, *Retirement Benefits of American Workers: New Findings from the September 1994 Current Population Survey* (Washington, D.C.: U.S. GPO, 1995), table B-2, pp. 47–48. (Hereafter *Retirement Benefits of American Workers: 1994.*)

10. *1998 Statistical Abstract*, tables 672 and 702.

11. Emily S. Andrews, *The Changing Profile of Pensions in America* (Washington, D.C.: Employee Benefits Research Institute, 1985), p. 65.

12. Employee Benefit Research Institute, "New Findings from the March 1991 CPS on Pension Coverage and Participation," *EBRI Employee Benefit Notes*, March 1992, table 2.

13. U.S. Department of Labor, *Current Population Survey, March 1998*, unpublished data, cited in "Women and Retirement Security," published by the White House National Economic Council Interagency Working Group on Social Security, Oct. 27, 1998.

14. *Retirement Benefits of American Workers: 1994*, table D-6, p. 95.

15. Employee Benefits Research Institute, American Savings Education Council, Mathew Greenwald & Associates, *Not Your Mother's Retirement: Women and Saving in 1998: Results of the 1998 Women's Retirement Confidence Survey* (Washington, D.C.: EBRI, ASEC, Mathew Greenwald & Associates, 1998), p. 8.

16. Ibid.

17. Ibid.

18. Richard P. Hinz, David D. McCarthy, and John A. Turner, "Are Women Conservative Investors? Gender Differences in Participant-Directed Pension Investments," p. 99, and Vickie L. Bajtelsmit and Jack L. VanDerhei, "Risk Aversion and Pension Investment Choices," pp. 56 and 60, both in Michael S. Gordon, Olivia S. Mitchell, and Marc M.

Twinney, eds., *Positioning Pensions for the Twenty-First Century* (Philadelphia: Pension Research Council and University of Pennsylvania Press, 1997), p. 99. Note that Bajtelsmit and VanDerhei qualify their findings because they could not control for other economic factors. They also cite studies with conflicting findings. At least one study, prepared for the Pension Research Council of the Wharton School but not yet released, suggests that this risk aversion is moderating and in large employer retirement plans does not exist at all.

19. Of all elderly women, 60 percent are unmarried: 45 percent are widowed, 9 percent are divorced or separated, and 6 percent have never married. "Women and Retirement Security," citing the Social Security Administration Office of Policy, Oct. 1998.

Chapter 2. Retirement Benefit Growth

1. The scenarios involved here have the following assumptions unless otherwise stated. The retirement plan provisions are as follows. Defined benefit plan formula: 1.25 percent of final five-year average earnings times years of service to a maximum of thirty years. Integrated defined benefit plan: 1 percent of final five-year average earnings for wages subject to FICA tax and 1.65 percent for wages above that base. Defined contribution formula: 5 percent of earnings each year. The economic assumptions are: rate of inflation, 5 percent; salary increase rate, 6 percent; defined contribution plan interest rate, 7.5 percent; and rollover interest rate, 7.5 percent. The annual and lump-sum figures are usually rounded to the nearest hundred dollars. Note that all figures are in constant 1999 dollars, so the nominal dollars at retirement will be much larger. Comparisons remain the same in percentage terms.

2. U.S. Department of Labor, Pension and Welfare Benefit Administration, *Retirement Benefits of American Workers: New Findings from the September 1994 Current Population Survey* (Washington, D.C.: U.S. GPO, Sept. 1995), table B-2, p. 48.

3. U.S. Department of Labor, *Current Population Survey, March 1998,* as reported in "Women and Retirement Security," published by the White House National Economic Council Interagency Working Group on Social Security, Oct. 27, 1998, p. 16.

4. Employee Benefits Research Institute, *EBRI Databook on Employee Benefits* (4th ed.; Washington, D.C.: EBRI, 1997), tables 17.1–17.3, pp. 137–139.

5. Ibid., table 17.3.

Chapter 3. Basics of Retirement Savings and Planning

1. Employee Benefits Research Institute, *EBRI Databook on Employee Benefits* (4th ed.; Washington, D.C.: EBRI, 1997), table 24.7, p. 200. (Hereinafter *EBRI Databook on Employee Benefits,* 4th ed.)

2. Summary of the *1998 Report of the Board of Trustees of the Federal Old-Age and Survivors Insurance Trust Funds* (Washington, D.C.: U.S. GPO, 1998).

3. *1998 Report of the Board of Trustees of the Federal Old-Age and Survivors Insurance Trust Funds.*

4. "Women and Retirement Security," published by the White House National Economic Council Interagency Working Group on Social Security, Oct. 27, 1998.

5. *EBRI Databook on Employee Benefits,* 4th ed., pp. 12 and 190.

6. *EBRI Databook on Employee Benefits,* 4th ed., table 7.2, p. 58, based on the March 1996 Current Population Survey.

7. *EBRI Databook on Employee Benefits,* 4th ed., table 10.4, p. 86, and Emily S. Andrews,

The Changing Profile of Pensions in America (Washington, D.C.: Employee Benefits Research Institute, 1985), p. 13.

8. *1998 Statistical Abstract,* table 702.

9. U.S. Department of Labor, *Current Population Survey, March 1998,* unpublished data, cited in "Women and Retirement Security."

10. Ibid.

Chapter 5. The Employee Retirement Income Security Act

1. U.S. Department of Labor, Pension and Welfare Benefits Administration, *Private Pension Plan Bulletin: Abstract of 1995 Form 5500 Annual Reports* (Washington, D.C.: U.S. GPO, 1999), p. 4, table A-1.

Chapter 6. How Taxes Affect Retirement Planning and Retirement Income

1. Congressional Budget Office, *Tax Policy for Pensions and Other Retirement Saving* (Washington, D.C.: U.S. GPO), p. 4, table 1, April, 1987.

2. Ibid.

3. Joint Committee on Taxation, "Estimates of Federal Tax Expenditures for Fiscal Years 1999–2003," JCS Rept. 7-98, Dec. 14, 1998.

Chapter 7. Employer-Provided Retirement Plans

1. U.S. Department of Labor, Pension and Welfare Benefits Administration, *Private Pension Plan Bulletin: Abstract of 1995 Form 5500 Annual Reports* (Washington, D.C.: U.S. GPO, 1999), table A2, p. 5.

2. *EBRI Databook on Employee Benefits,* 4th ed., table 10.4, p. 86.

3. Employee Benefit Research Institute, *Pension Investment Report, Fourth Quarter 1997* (Washington, D.C.: Employee Benefit Research Institute, 1997).

4. Joint Committee on Taxation, "Estimates of Federal Tax Expenditures for Fiscal Years 1999–2003," JCS Rept. 7-98, Dec. 14, 1998.

5. Olivia S. Mitchell, "Trends in Pension Benefit Formulas and Retirement Provisions," in John A. Turner and Daniel J. Beller, eds., *Trends in Pensions, 1992* (Washington, D.C.: U.S. Department of Labor, Pension and Welfare Benefits Administration, U.S. Government Printing Office, 1992), table 9.13, p. 206.

6. U.S. Department of Labor, Pension and Welfare Benefits Administration, *Private Pension Plan Bulletin: Abstract of 1994 Form 5500 Annual Reports,* table A-1, p. 5.

7. KPMG, *Retirement Benefits in the 1990s: 1998 Survey Data* (Washington, D.C.: KPMG LLP, 1998), p. 23.

8. U.S. Department of Labor, Pension and Welfare Benefits Administration, *Private Pension Plan Bulletin: Abstract of 1994 Form 5500 Annual Reports,* table E23, p. 85.

9. KPMG, *Retirement Benefits in the 1990s: 1998 Survey Data,* p. 32.

Chapter 8: Government-Supplied Retirement Benefits

1. *1998 Report of the Board of Trustees, Federal Old-Age and Survivors Insurance Trust Fund,* (Washington, D.C.: U.S. GPO, 1998).

2. See Table 16.1 for the precise percentage increases for delaying Social Security Benefits.

3. U.S. Bureau of the Census, *Statistical Abstract of the United States: 1998* (118th ed.) (Washington, D.C.: The Bureau, 1998), table 180 (hereinafter *Statistical Abstract of the United States: 1998*).

4. *Statistical Abstract of the United States: 1998,* table 171.

5. National Association of Insurance Commissioners and U.S. Department of Health and Human Services Health Care Financing Administration, *1998 Guide to Health Insurance for People with Medicare* (Washington, D.C.: U.S. GPO, 1998). Also available at *www.medicare.gov/publications.html.*

6. *Statistical Abstract of the United States: 1998,* table 166.

7. KPMG LLP, *Health Benefits in 1998,* a survey of more than 1,500 randomly chosen employers; 86 percent were enrolled in some form of managed care plan. (Washington, D.C.: KPMG LLP, 1998).

Chapter 9: Your Individual Savings for Retirement

1. Employee Benefits Research Institute, American Savings Education Council, and Mathew Greenwald & Associates, Inc., *Not Your Mother's Retirement: Women and Saving in 1998: Results of the 1998 Women's Retirement Confidence Survey* (Washington, D.C.: EBRI/ASEC/MGA, 1998), p. 20.

2. IRS Publication 560, "Retirement Plans for the Self-Employed." This booklet is available from IRS for free by calling 1-800-TAX-FORM or by downloading from the IRS's Internet page, *www.irs.gov.*

3. Albert B. Crenshaw, "Policyholders, Beware: Insurers May Sell Contracts to Other, Less Sound Firms," *Washington Post,* May 10, 1992, p. H-3.

4. U.S. Department of Labor, Bureau of Labor Statistics, *Employee Benefits in Medium and Large Private Establishments, 1995* (Washington, D.C.: U.S. GPO, 1998), p. 7, table 1.

5. A copy can be obtained from the National Association of Insurance Commissioners, 120 W. 12th Street, Suite 1100, Kansas City, MO 64105. You may also order through their Internet site: *www.naic.org.*

Chapter 10. The Role of Benefits in Taking or Leaving a Job

1. The formula to use to compare the values of pretax and after-tax dollars is: after-tax amount needed ÷ (1 − effective tax rate) = pretax amount you must earn. So in Jennifer's case the calculation to see how much she would need to earn before taxes to replace her previous tax-favored $2,700 worth of benefits is as follows: $2,700 ÷ (1 − 0.22) = $3,462.

2. KPMG, *Retirement Benefits in the 1990s: 1998 Survey Data* (Washington, D.C.: KPMG LLP, 1998), pp. 23–24.

Chapter 11. How Much Do You Need for Retirement?

1. U.S. Bureau of the Census, *Statistical Abstract of the United States: 1998* (118th ed.; Washington, D.C.: U.S. GPO, 1998), table 180.

2. Ibid., table 118.

3. Pension and Welfare Benefits Administration, U.S. Department of Labor, *Retirement Benefits of American Workers: New Findings from the September 1994 Current Population Survey* (Washington, D.C.: U.S. GPO, 1995), table D8, p. 99.

Chapter 12. Becoming Familiar with Investment Vehicles

1. "A Brief History of Our Contest," *Wall Street Journal*, Oct. 7, 1998, p. C1.

Chapter 13. How to Invest Wisely for Retirement

1. See the studies cited in Richard P. Hinz, David D. McCarthy, and John A. Turner, "Are Women Conservative Investors? Gender Differences in Participant-Directed Pension Investments," p. 99, and Vickie L. Bajtelsmit and Jack L. VanDerhei, "Risk Aversion and Pension Investment Choices," pp. 56 and 60, both in Michael S. Gordon, Olivia S. Mitchell, and Marc M. Twinney, eds., *Positioning Pensions for the Twenty-First Century* (Philadelphia: Pension Research Council and University of Pennsylvania Press, 1997). Note that Bajtelsmit and VanDerhei qualify their findings because they could not control for other economic factors. They also cite studies with conflicting findings. At least one study, prepared but not yet released for the Pension Research Council of the Wharton School, suggests this risk aversion is moderating and, indeed, in large employer retirement plans does not exist at all.

Chapter 14. How Marriage Affects Your Retirement Benefits

1. Domestic partners who are not spouses are not discussed here for two reasons. First, a main theme of this book is to plan for retirement as an individual, without relying on another's benefits or income. Second, it has been my experience from many years in the retirement benefit field that most employers are not extending retirement or survivor benefits to domestic partners.

Chapter 15. How Divorce Can Affect Your Retirement Planning

1. For an excellent guide to all aspects of financial planning at divorce or the death of a spouse, see Kerry Hannon, *Suddenly Single* (New York: John Wiley & Sons, 1998).
2. For an extensive discussion of divorce rights including specific discussions of rights under the Federal Civil Service Retirement, the Military Retirement, the Railroad Retirement, and the Foreign Service Retirement systems, see *Your Pension Rights at Divorce: What Women Need to Know,* written by Anne E. Moss for the Pension Rights Center. This book can be ordered through the Pension Rights Center, 918 Sixteenth St., N.W., Suite 704, Washington, D.C. 20006.
3. See Internal Revenue Code, sec. 414(p).
4. *QDROs: The Division of Pensions Through Qualified Domestic Relation Orders* (Washington, D.C.: U.S. Department of Labor, Pension and Welfare Benefit Administration, 1997). This is available from their Internet site at *www.dol.gov/dol/pwba.*
5. Buck Consultants, "QDROs: A Survey of Employer Practices," May 1991.
6. Ibid., p. 6.

Chapter 16. If You Are Near Retirement

1. Joseph F. Quinn, "New Paths to Retirement," paper presented to the Pension Research Council 1998 Symposium "Forecasting Retirement Needs and Retirement Wealth," Wharton School, Philadelphia, April 27–28, 1998.

2. Employee Benefits Research Institute, *EBRI Databook on Employee Benefits* (4th ed.; Washington, D.C.: Employee Benefits Research Institute, 1997), table 7.5.

Chapter 17. Life in Retirement

1. Evidence from the Health and Retirement Survey, a national longitudinal survey, is just beginning to yield data that experts are mining. See D. S. Dwyer, and O. S. Mitchell, "Health Shocks as Determinants of Retirement," *Journal of Health Economics* (1997).

2. Eileen Johnstone Feuerbach, "Women's Retirement: The Influence of Work History on Retirement Attitudes and the Retirement Decision," Ph.D. diss., George Mason University, Fairfax, Virginia, spring 1990.

3. Ibid., p. 81.

Acknowledgments

Thanks are in order to a number of people. Anna Rappaport, an actuary who specializes in work force demographics, first interested me in the subject of women's retirement planning many years ago. Susan Korn and Drew Douglas at the Bureau of National Affairs first gave me a forum to discuss the issue.

Without Olivia Mitchell, executive director of the Pension Research Council and professor at the Wharton School, this new edition would not have been possible. Cindy Hounsell, executive director of Women's Institute for a Secure Retirement and a tireless advocate for women's pension equity, has provided particularly helpful advice and examples of women's pension problems from real life. Paul Yakoboski of the Employee Benefits Research Institute and Don M. Blandin, president of the American Savings Education Council, have been generous with data and assistance for the book—as they always are to benefits researchers. Sondra Nelson of KPMG read the book's first edition and put it to work. Now she tells me she is well on the road to retirement security. She now offers her coworkers some of the most effective retirement planning seminars I have ever heard.

And saving the best for last, Laurence I. Barrett, whose writing and reporting skills impressed me long before I knew him, helped me put complex ideas in simple sentences. Larry is an indefatigable editor. Each of these individuals and many others provided invaluable assistance.

Index